The Modern
Jewish Experience

The Modern
Jewish Experience

Advisory Editor

Moses Rischin

Editorial Board

Arthur A. Goren

Irving Howe

Epstein

An Autobiography

Jacob Epstein

ARNO PRESS

A New York Times Company

New York / 1975

Reprint Edition 1975 by Arno Press Inc.

Reprinted from a copy in
  The Newark Public Library

THE MODERN JEWISH EXPERIENCE
ISBN for complete set: 0-405-06690-2
See last pages of this volume for titles.

Manufactured in the United States of America

——◦◦◦——

Library of Congress Cataloging in Publication Data

Epstein, Sir Jacob, 1880-1959.
  Epstein, an autobiography.

    (The Modern Jewish experience)
    Published in 1940 under title: Let there be sculp-
ture.
    Reprint of the 1955 ed. published by Dutton, New York.
    1. Epstein, Sir Jacob, 1880-1959. 2. Sculptors--
Great Britain--Correspondence, reminiscences, etc.
I. Series.
NB497.E6A2 1975   730'.92'4 [B]   74-27978
ISBN 0-405-06707-0

EPSTEIN

AN AUTOBIOGRAPHY

The Sculptor, aged 27, with one of the Strand Statues, 1907

Epstein

An Autobiography

E. P. DUTTON AND COMPANY, INC.

PUBLISHERS   NEW YORK

First published by E. P. Dutton and Company, Inc., 1955

This is a revised and extended edition of the work by
Sir Jacob Epstein first published in 1940 under the title
Let there be Sculpture

Printed in Great Britain by William Clowes and Sons Ltd.

CONTENTS

v

Contents

ILLUSTRATIONS

List of Illustrations

facing page

ix

List of Illustrations

I

NEW YORK: 1880

My earliest recollections are of the teeming East Side where
I was born.

This Hester Street and its surrounding streets were the
most densely populated of any city on earth, and looking back at it,
I realise what I owe to its unique and crowded humanity. Its swarms
of Russians, Poles, Italians, Greeks, and Chinese lived as much in
the streets as in the crowded tenements, and the sights, sounds, and
smells had the vividness and sharp impact of an Oriental city.

Hester Street was from one end to the other an open-air market,
and the streets were lined with push-carts and pedlars, and the
crowd that packed the side-walk and roadway compelled one to
move slowly.

As a child I had a serious illness that lasted for two years or more.
I have vague recollections of this illness and of my being carried
about a great deal. I was known as the "sick one". Whether this illness gave me a twist away from ordinary paths, I don't know, but it
is possible. Sometimes my parents wondered at my being different
from the other children, and would twit me about my lack of interest
in a great many matters that perhaps I should have been interested
in, but just wasn't. I have never found out that there was in my
family an artist or anyone interested in the arts or Sciences, and I
have never been sufficiently interested in my "family tree" to bother.
My father and mother had come to America on one of those great
waves of immigration that followed persecution and pogroms in
Czarist Russia and Poland. They had prospered, and I can recall
that we had Polish Christian servants who still retained peasant
habits, speaking no English, wearing kerchiefs and going about on

I

bare feet. These servants remained with us until my brother Louis, my older brother, began to grow up; and then with the sudden dismissal of the Polish girls, I began to have an inkling of sexual complications. My elder sister, Ida, was a handsome, full-bosomed girl, a brunette, and I can recall a constant coming and going of relatives and their numerous children. This family life I did not share. My reading and drawing drew me away from the ordinary interests, and I lived a great deal in the world of imagination, feeding upon any book that fell into my hands. When I had got hold of a really thick book like Hugo's *Les Misérables* I was happy, and would go off into a corner to devour it.

I cannot recall a period when I did not draw, and at school the studies that were distasteful to me, Mathematics and Grammar, were retarded by the indulgence of teachers who were proud of my drawing faculties, and passed over my neglect of uncongenial subjects. Literature and History interested me immensely and whatever was graphic attracted my attention. Later, I went to the Art Students' League up town and drew from models and painted a little, but my main studies remained in this quarter where I was born and brought up. When my parents moved to a more respectable and duller part of the city, it held no interest for me whatever and I hired a room in Hester Street in a wooden, ramshackle building that seemed to date back at least a hundred years and, from my window overlooking the market, made drawings daily. I could look down upon the moving mass below and watch them making purchases, bartering, and gossiping. Opposite stood carpenters, washerwomen, and day-workers, gathered with their tools in readiness to be hired. Every type could be found here, and for the purpose of drawing, I would follow a character until his appearance was sufficiently impressed on my mind for me to make a drawing. A character who interested me particularly was a tall, lean, and bearded young man, with the ascetic face of a religious fanatic, who wandered through the streets lost in a profound melancholy. His hair grew to his shoulders, and upon this was perched an old bowler hat. He carried a box in one hand, and as he passed the push-carts, the vendors would put food into his box, here an apple, there a herring. He was a holy man and I followed him into synagogues, where he brooded and spent his nights and days.

On one occasion I was taken to see the Chief Rabbi, a man of great piety, who had been brought from Poland to act as the Chief Rabbi; but as New York Jews do not acknowledge a central authority, he never attained this position. An attempt to use him to monopolise the Kosher meat industry was indignantly rejected. This sage and holy man lived exactly as he would in a Polish city, with young disciples, in ringlets (payism), who attended him as he was very infirm, lifting him into his chair, and out of it, and solicitous of his every movement. The patriarchal simplicity of this house much impressed me. The New York Ghetto was a city at that time transplanted from Poland. Parallel with all this was the world of the "intelligentsia", the students, journalists, scholars, advanced people, socialists, anarchists, free-thinkers, and even "free lovers". Newspapers in Yiddish, Yiddish theatres, literary societies, clubs of all kinds for educational purposes, night-classes abounded, and I helped to organise an exhibition of paintings and drawings by young men of the quarter. There existed a sort of industry in enlarging and colouring photographs, working them up in crayon, and there were shops that did a thriving trade in this. I had student friends who, to earn money, put their hands to this hateful work, and by industry could earn enough to go on with more serious studies. I never had to do this, as I could always sell my drawings.

I kept the room on Hester Street until on returning to it one morning I found it burnt to the ground, and my charred drawings (hundreds of them) floating about in water with dead cats. I had to find another room, this time in a tenement with clothing workers, where I restarted my studies. I never remember giving up this second room, and perhaps because of that it has returned to me in dreams with a strange persistence; even in Paris and in London, in my dreams I find myself in the room as I left it, filled with drawings of the people of the East Side.

The many races in this quarter were prolific, children by hundreds played upon the hot pavements and in the alleys. Upon the fire-escapes and the roofs the tenement dwellers slept for coolness in summer. I knew well the roof life in New York, where all East Side boys flew kites; I knew the dock life on the East and West Sides, and I swam in the East River and the Hudson. To reach the river the boys from the Jewish quarter would have to pass through the Irish quarter, and that meant danger and fights with the gangs of that quarter: the children of Irish immigrants.

The Jewish quarter was on one side bounded by the Bowery, and this street at that time was one long line of saloons, crowded at night by visitors to the city, sailors, and prostitutes. As a boy I could watch through the doors at night the strange garish performers, singers and dancers; and the whole turbulent night-life was, to my growing and eager mind, of never-ending interest. I recall Steve Brodie's saloon with its windows filled with photographs of famous boxers, and the floor inlaid with silver dollars. A tour along the Bowery, for a boy, was full of excitement, and when you reached Chinatown, crooked Mott Street, leading to Pell Street, you could buy a stick of sugar-cane for one cent and, chewing it, look into the Chinese shop windows, and even go into the temple, all scarlet and gilding, with gilded images. The Chinamen had a curious way of slipping into their houses, suddenly, as into holes, and I used to wonder at the young men with smooth faces like girls. Chinese children were delightful when you saw them, although no Chinese women were to be seen. Along the West Front, on the Hudson side, you saw wagons being loaded with large bunches of bananas, and great piles of melons. Bananas would drop off the overloaded wagons; you picked them up, and continued until you came to the open-air swimming baths with delightful sea water. I was a great frequenter of these swimming places, and went there until they shut down in November for the winter.

New York was at this period the city of ships of which Whitman wrote. I haunted the docks and watched the ships from all over the world being loaded and unloaded. Sailors were aloft in the rigging, and along the docks horses and mules drew heavy drays; oyster boats were bringing their loads of oysters and clams, and the shrieks and yells of sirens and the loud cries of overseers made a terrific din. At the Battery, newly arrived immigrants, their shoulders laden with packs, hurried forward, and it must have been with much misgiving that they found their first steps in the New World greeted with the hoots and jeers of hooligans. I can still see them hurrying to gain the Jewish quarter, and finding refuge amongst friends and relatives. I often travelled the great stretch of Brooklyn Bridge, which I crossed hundreds of times on foot, and watched the wonderful bay with its

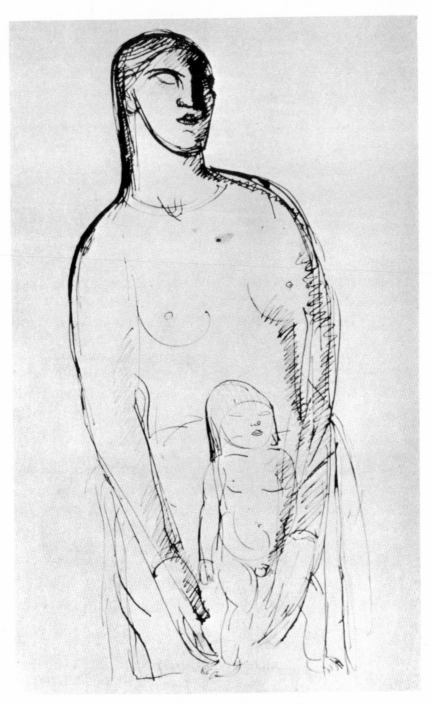

MOTHER AND CHILD, 1908

CHILD STUDIES, 1909

steamers and ferry-boats. The New York of the pre-skyscraper period was my formation ground. I knew all its streets and the water-side, I made excursions into the suburbs; Harlem, Yonkers, Long Island, and Coney Island I knew well, and Rockaway where I bathed in the surf. I explored Staten Island, then unbuilt on, and the palisades with their wild rocks leading down to the Hudson river.

Early on I saw the plastic quality in coloured people, and had friends amongst them, and later was to work from coloured models and friends, including Paul Robeson, whose splendid head I worked from in New York. I tried to draw Chinamen in their quarter, but the Chinese did not like being drawn and would immediately disappear when they spotted me. The Italian Mulberry Street was like Naples, concentrated in one swarming district. Within easy reach of each other, one could see the most diverse life from many lands, and I absorbed material which was invaluable.

At this time I was a tremendous reader, and there were periods when I would go off to Central Park, find a secluded place far away from crowds and noise, and there give myself up to solitary reading for the day, coming back home burnt by the sun and filled with ideas from Dostoyevsky's *Brothers Karamazov*, or Tolstoy's novels. Also I absorbed the New Testament and Whitman's *Leaves of Grass*, all read out of doors, amongst the rocks and lakes of the Park. It was only later I read the English poets, Coleridge, Blake, and Shelley, and still later Shakespeare. During my student days at the League, I would drop into Durand Ruel's gallery on Fifth Avenue, and there see the works of many of the Impressionist painters, which were not so sought after in those days. I saw splendid Manets, Renoirs, and Pissarros, and Durand Ruel himself, noticing my interest, gave me special opportunities to see pictures which went back to Europe and are now in the Louvre and National Gallery. I was very well acquainted at this time with the work not only of the American artists who were influenced by the Impressionists, but also with the works of the older men who now constitute the "Old Masters" of America —Winslow Homer, George Innes, Homer Martin, Albert Ryder, and Thomas Eakins. The sincerity of these men impressed me, and my boyhood enthusiasms have been justified by time.

I began to feel at this period that I could more profoundly express myself, and give greater reality to my drawings by studying sculpture.

I had been drawing and reading to excess, sometimes in dim light, and my eyes had suffered from the strain, so that sculpture gave me relief, and the actual handling of clay was a pleasure.

Naturally my family did not approve of all that I did, although they saw that I had what might be called a special bent. My turning to sculpture was to them mysterious. Later they could not understand why I did certain things, any more than do the critics who profess to see in me a dual nature, one the man of talent, and the other the wayward eccentric, the artist who desires to *épater*. What chiefly concerned my family was why I did things which could not possibly bring me in any money, and they deplored this mad or foolish streak in me.

They put it down to the perversity that made me a lonely boy, going off on my own to the woods with a book, and not turning up to meals, and later making friends with negroes and anarchists.

My grandmother on my father's side was a cantankerous old creature who swore that we children were going to the dogs, and were *goyim*, and she continued travelling between Poland and New York, as she declared she would not die in a pagan land; but—alas! for her wish—it was in New York she died.

My grandparents on my mother's side were a dear old couple, whose kindness and patriarchal simplicity I remember well. Every Friday evening the children would go to them to get their blessing. Before the Sabbath candles they would take our heads in their hands and pronounce a blessing on each one of us in turn. Then followed gifts of fruit and sweets. I was one of a large family, a third child, and my elder brother Louis was at all times sympathetic and helpful. Of my brothers, Hyam was an exceptionally powerful youth, a giant of strength, headstrong and with a personality that got him into scrapes. My sister, Chana, a beautiful, fair-haired girl, with a candid, sweet nature, was a great favourite of mine, and we often went out together. My father and mother in the evenings would lie in bed reading novels in Yiddish; my father would read aloud, and I often stayed awake listening to these extravagant romances. Saturday in the synagogue was a place of ennui for me, and the wailing prayers would get on my nerves, and my one desire would be to make excuses to get away. The picturesque shawls with the strange faces underneath only held my attention for a short while; then the tedium of the interminable services would drown every other emotion. Certainly I had no devotional feelings, and later, with my reading and free-thinking ideas, I dropped all practice of ceremonial forms, and as my parents were only conventionally interested in religion, they did not insist. I was confirmed at the age of thirteen in the usual manner, but how I ever got through this trying ordeal I cannot now imagine. The Passover Holidays always interested me for the picturesque meal ceremonies, and I remember my father, who was "somebody" in the synagogue, bringing home with him one of the poor men, who waited outside to be chosen to share the Passover meal. These patriarchal manners I remember well, although there was about them an air of bourgeois benevolence which was somewhat comic. The earnestness and simplicity of the old Polish Jewish manner of living has much beauty in it, and an artist could make it the theme of very fine works. This life is fast disappearing on contact with American habits, and it is a pity that there is no Rembrandt of to-day to draw his inspiration from it before it is too late.

My parents did not discourage me, but could not understand how I could make a living by Art. Their idea of an artist was that of a person who was condemned to starvation. Sculpture became to me an absorbing interest. When I started seriously to work I felt the inadequacies of the opportunity to study. For one thing, only a night class existed in New York, and also there was very little antique sculpture to be seen; modern sculpture hardly existed. I longed to go to Paris, and my opportunity came when I met Hutchins Hapgood, the writer, who was very interested in the East Side, and asked me to illustrate a book which he had written about it. I drew for him the poets, scholars, actors, and playwrights, and also made some drawings of the people.

I remember well the great actor Jacob Adler, at whose flat I called to make a drawing of him. He was surrounded by a houseful of dependants of all kinds, apart from his numerous family, and the confusion and excitement were immense. Finding a clean collar out of bags that contained hundreds of collars took up most of the time. Adler had a head like those you see in Japanese prints, long and white, and with heavy, chameleon-like eyelids. This Jewish actor had a court, and when you saw him in the streets he was preceded and followed by his fans. He lived in public. I also drew Jacob Gordon,

2

who wrote plays about Jewish life which had a strong Ibsenish flavour. He was a heavy, bearded man, whom I recall reading to an audience one of his plays, sitting informally at a table, smoking a cigar.

In their dressing-rooms, I drew Kessler the actor, also Moscowitch, and the poets Lessin and Moritz Rosenfeld, who had spent his early life in tailors' shops.

I was known in the market, and wherever I took up a position to draw I was looked upon sympathetically, and had no difficulty in finding models. Jewish people look upon the work of an artist as something miraculous, and love watching him, even though they may be extremely critical. I sometimes think I should have remained in New York, the material was so abundant. Wherever one looked there was something interesting, a novel composition, wonderful effects of lighting at night, and picturesque and handsome people. Rembrandt would have delighted in the East Side, and I am surprised that nothing has come out of it, for there is material in New York far beyond anything that American painters hunt for abroad.

I took this East Side drawing work very seriously, and my drawings were not just sketches. With Gussow, my Russian artist friend, I drew the life of the East Side, and one or two other artists joined us, so that we might have developed a School had we kept on. Since then I know of no one except John Sloan and George Luks who were inspired by New York life.

I should like to recover some of these drawings I made of East Side life, but I understand they were dispersed in sales, and perhaps destroyed. I also drew for periodicals, and the Century Company purchased drawings from me. I could have remained in America and become one of the band, already too numerous, of illustrators, but that was not my ambition, and at the school I felt something of a fish out of water. The art students' life was distasteful to me. I could not join in their rags and their beer; and their bad jokes got on my nerves. Nevertheless, there were students who purchased my studies from the model for a dollar or two, and I was especially friendly with James Carrol Beckwith, an American painter who was the drawing teacher at the League. He was sympathetic to me, and very interested in what I told him and showed him of the East Side life, which to the up-towner was like the life of the jungle for strangeness.

A great friend was James Kirk Paulding, a man of fine literary discernment, and a friend of Abraham Kahan, the editor of *Vorwarts*. Paulding was in the habit of reading to four or five of us boys on a Sunday morning, and this was my first introduction to Conrad's work. In this way I heard *The Nigger of the Narcissus* and *Typhoon*, also most of Turgeniev. I attended concerts of symphonic music, and went to the Metropolitan Opera House and heard Wagner's *Ring*, naturally from the gallery, miles away from the stage. Also I went to political meetings where I heard Prince Kropotkin and Eugene Debs, also Henry George, the Single Taxer. I observed, drew a great deal, and dreamed a great deal more. In connection with political meetings and what would now be called "left wing" sympathies and friends, I was an observer only, and never a participator, as my loyalties were all for the practice of art, and I have always grudged the time that is given to anything but that. This is not to say that I am a believer in the "ivory tower" theory. On the contrary, a wide knowledge of men and events seems to me necessary to the artist, but participation and action in political events and movements must remain a matter of personal predilection. In this connection I think of Courbet, whose life was embittered and whose work suffered because of the part he took in the Commune.

My people were not, as has been stated, poor. On the contrary, they were fairly well off, and as the family was large I saw a great deal of Jewish orthodox life, traditional and narrow. As my thoughts were elsewhere, this did not greatly influence me, but I imagine that the feeling I have for expressing a human point of view, giving human rather than abstract implications to my work, comes from these early formation years. I saw so much that called for expression that I can draw upon it now if I wish to.

As we are living in a world that is changing rapidly, I may be compelled to modify this attitude and plump for direct participation and action.

I was not altogether a city boy, and my excursions to the country outside New York bred in me a delight in outdoors. In this connection I well remember that one winter my friend Gussow and I hired a small cabin on the shores of Greenwood Lake, in the State of New Jersey. In this mountain country I spent a winter doing little but tramping through snow-clad forests, cutting firewood, cooking meals and reading. To earn a little money we both helped to cut the ice on the lake, this work lasting about two weeks. This was very hard but congenial work, as we were taken to the ice-fields by sledges drawn by a team of horses in the early morning over the hard-frozen lake, and returned in the evening on the sledges, when we saw wonderful snow views of mountain sides ablaze with sunset colours. It was a physical life full of exhilaration and interest. At this place lived a couple with whom I became very friendly, a Mr. and Mrs. Wells. This Mr. Wells made photographs of visitors for a living during the summer, and in the winter he painted. His wife, a little Welsh woman, had psychic powers, and she prophesied a great future for me, so Wells informed me. This couple were looked upon by the villagers as queer. They were the only persons in the place who took an interest in art or in anything but village life. It was rather a degenerate place altogether, where there had been a great deal of inbreeding, as only three family names existed.

After this winter at Greenwood Lake I determined to work at sculpture. I entered a foundry for bronze casting and attended a modelling class at night at the League. George Grey Barnard was the teacher. The class was mostly made up of sculptors' assistants, and we had to have some ardour to put in an evening's modelling after a hard day's work in ateliers and workshops. Barnard would come one evening of the week to give us criticisms, but he rarely got through a full class of students. He would look at the study and give you a penetrating glance (he had a cast in his eye), and then start his talk, in which he would usually lose himself for the rest of the evening. The students would gather round him, and as he was a man of great earnestness, he was very impressive. Barnard was ascetic in his habits, and hated the notion that his students drank or were at all Bohemian: later when I was to meet him in London and lunch with him, he thought it was a concession, as he was on holiday, to let me have wine. I knew his early work, and at that time he was the only American sculptor one could have any respect for.

I met Tom Eakins, but as a sculptor he impressed me as being too dry and scientific, and I looked forward to the day when I would be able to see the Ancients and Rodin. I longed to see originals of Michelangelo and Donatello, and Europe meant the Louvre and Florence.

There has been a tremendous impetus given to American sculpture since I was a boy in New York, and numerous commissions are given to sculptors, but of the lasting value of this renaissance of sculpture I am unable to judge from here. Mountains have been carved, and on reading of these tremendous-sounding events, I imagined that I might have played a part in all this, but it was another destiny that called me, and I have had to create heroic works from time to time in my studio, without commissions and with little or no encouragement from official bodies.

Native American sculptors did not give one much inspiration, and at that time no one thought of Mexican or pre-Columbian Indian work. The fact was, the interest in early American Continental sculpture came from Europe. By a sort of reaction American artists now try hard to be American.

My desire now was to get to Paris. With the money from my drawings for Hapgood's book I bought a passage for France. I can recall, with the unthinking heedlessness of youth, climbing the gangway to the vessel that was to take me away from America for a period of twenty-five years. When I reached the top of the gangway, my mother ran after me and embraced me for the last time.

One night, in March, 1913, in Paris, I dreamed of my mother, and immediately received news of her early death.

2

ON my first walk out in Paris to see Notre Dame and the Seine, I passed over a bridge, where right in the centre was a small building, the morgue, and I had to regret the morbid curiosity that took me into that tragic building. On the second day I went with a great procession to Emile Zola's funeral at the Cimetière Montmartre, and witnessed the clashes between the gendarmes and anti-Semites. Visits to the Louvre opened my eyes. The great storehouse of painting and sculpture held me for days on end. The thrill of crossing the Pont des Arts to the Louvre! Probably a student of to-day would be admonished by his abstractionist master to jump into the Seine rather than do that. In my prowlings through the Louvre, I discovered works which were not at all famous then, but have since come into their own—early Greek work, Cyclades sculpture, the bust known as the Lady of Elche, and the limestone bust of Akenaton. And at the Trocadero was a mass of primitive sculpture none too well assembled (as our British Museum collection is still). There was also the Musée Cernusci with its Chinese collection. What a wonderful city for a young student to wander about in, with something interesting in every part, except the quarter round the Arc de Triomphe, the Elysées; that was always and still is a desert of boring streets. At that time I never went to cafés. I neither had the money to spend there, nor had I the inclination. I concentrated with a fanatical zeal entirely on my studies. I worked at the school with a sort of frenzy. I hurled myself at the clay. For relaxation I went to the lovely Luxembourg Gardens, with its statues of the Queens of France, to listen on Sunday afternoons to the band. I shared a studio with my New York friend, Bernard Gussow, in the

rue Belloni, in a rambling block of buildings behind the Gare Montparnasse. Our food we bought in a near-by cook-shop in the rue de
la Gaîté in the popular working quarter, and for a change in the
evenings we walked to a Russian students' restaurant near the Jardin
des Plantes. Here for about one franc and a half you could get a meal,
mostly *kasha*. Bread was free. Russian tea was the only drink. The
Russian students who frequented this place ran it without waiters in
the cafeteria style of to-day. The light frequently failed, and candles
were brought in. Russian refugees from the Czardom ate the bread
of exile here, and as Gussow and I were the only "foreigners", we
were sometimes regarded with suspicion, and on one occasion a
Russian suddenly started denouncing us as spies. He seemed to be
drunk. Not much notice was taken of him, and he eventually calmed
down. In the rue Belloni studios, only the Frenchmen had mistresses,
and they naturally laughed at us Americans and English who seemed
able to do without. For one thing, the mistress was also the model,
and we "foreigners" had to pose for each other and mark up the
hours on the walls. Strange proceedings! I had only been three or
four days in Paris, and was eager to enter the Beaux Arts School.
With hardly any French at my command I applied for admission,
and was placed with other students in an amphitheatre, to construct
a figure from the living model.

I had practice in modelling, and set to work with confidence. I
passed the test and entered one of the three modelling ateliers, one
under an old man, Thomas by name. The usual ragging of students
took place, and a deaf and dumb Frenchman was put up to have a
boxing match with me. He was short and very powerful, and I saw
that I had a very formidable customer to deal with. He came at me
grunting as an animal might. Luckily I hit him first and, with the
French students howling that I was taking the affair too seriously,
the combat finished.

The "foreigners" were few and unpopular, and it was not unusual
for a French student to turn on a foreigner and ask him why he
didn't stay in his own country. On Monday the *massier* of the class
would appear with a girl. She would strip and the students would
vote to have her. Every week the *massier*, a genuine apache type from
the Butte, appeared with a new girl, who would be accepted and
generally traded during the morning to the students. After Monday

the *massier* would disappear, only making a pretence of working. The week would commence with numbers of students present, and as new students had to take back places, one was so far away from the model that it was a case of running long distances, back and forth, to get anything; but by about Wednesday, most of the students had dropped out, and one could get quite close and see very well.

My mornings were spent in modelling from life, and I ate a hasty lunch which I brought with me, and then went into the carving class, and also drew from the Michelangelo casts, of which there was a room full. In carving there was practically no instruction, and we were left alone to do pretty well what we pleased. Advantage was taken of this by two or three French professional marble carvers, who came in and got what was a studio and material free of charge, made small copies of Italian Renaissance heads (such as you see in shops on the Boulevard des Italiens), and then smuggled these carvings out under their overcoats.

One morning I decided to attend the anatomy lecture and, with a crowd of other students of all classes, listened to a lecture, with a corpse as model; when a green arm was handed around for inspection I nearly fainted, and left the class, never to return. I always felt ashamed of this episode, as I knew that Michelangelo and all great Renaissance artists had made intensive research from *cadavres*, until years later I read, in an account of the Ingres' atelier, that Ingres himself could never stand dissection, and even objected to a skeleton being in his classroom, and would not enter it until the skeleton had been removed. There are infinite modes of expression in the world of art, and to insist that only by one road can the artist attain his ends is to limit him. The academic mind violates this freedom of the artist to express himself as he knows best. Personally I have always been for freedom of expression, and I am amused at the intolerance of some of our later abstractionists, who, claiming the utmost freedom of expression for themselves, yet look with disdain upon all who diverge from them. I daresay that to the dancing dervish the monotonous twirlings have their ecstasy, but not to the onlookers.

I had worked for a spell of about six months at the Beaux Arts, when one Monday morning the period of the Prix de Rome Concours commenced, and the new students were supposed to fag for the men who entered Concours, and carry clay and stands to the *loges*, and wait upon these immured geniuses. This would have completely cut my morning's work, so I refused point-blank. The French students were astonished, and could hardly believe their ears. I was all the more determined as there were plenty of *gardiens* (uniformed assistants) to fetch and carry.

On returning to the atelier next morning, the study I had begun lay in a ruined mass on the ground. I built up a new study, but the following morning it was again on the ground. The Frenchmen stood silently around, watching me, I said nothing and, picking up and shouldering my modelling stand, went over to the Julian Academy.

My stay at the Beaux Arts, though it ended so badly, had given me training in modelling for six months, and besides this I spent the afternoons drawing from the Michelangelo casts, and in carving in marble in the marble atelier. It was good training, although one learnt more from capable students than from the masters, who seemed just men with sinecure jobs.

At Julian's, things went better. One paid a fee for the term, but there were fewer students and no routine academy habits. I worked hard, in a sustained explosion of energy, and I remember a Czech student who deplored my ardour and prophesied that I would wear myself out early.

I thought one week of going into the life class and drawing from the model. This particular atelier was under the great Jean Paul Laurens, and his habit was to go from drawing to drawing, with the students following him, and give criticisms. When Jean Paul sat down on my stool he looked at my drawing, then at the model, looked up at me and then got up and passed on. A silent criticism! It is interesting to recall here that this Jean Paul Laurens was on Le Comité d'Esthétique de la Préfecture de la Seine which condemned my Oscar Wilde monument in 1912.

One day a German student pulled the model about brutally, a timid girl too frightened to protest. When I asked him why he behaved like that he was astonished. "Why, in Germany," he said, "we give them *den Fuss*," accompanying the words with an appropriate gesture.

On one occasion I watched (as it was more of a spectacle than anything instructive) the great Bougereau criticism in drawing. The old man, very feeble, would be assisted by two students into his chair

15

and out, and an awed assemblage of French students would follow him. It must be remembered that his pictures sold for many thousands of dollars in America, and it is an ironical fact that Henri Rousseau declared that it was his ambition to paint like him. After one or two criticisms from the master at Julian's, I gave up taking criticism, and in my impatience always covered my figure when the master came in. He noticed me doing this one day and referred in an audible tone to "ce sauvage Américain". I can recall that at the end of the session, in fact long before the session ended, almost all of the students got busy on their preparations for the Bal des Quatres Arts, and they dropped all work for the floats and scenic effects of that great occasion. I went to this uproarious and blasting saturnalia and turned out with the rest in the daylight, with nude girls astride the cab horses; and I remember the amused greetings of the Parisian workpeople who hailed this strange company of revellers, debouching through Paris *en route* for the Place St. Michel, where we dispersed.

This whole student period in Paris that I look back upon now, I passed in a rage of work; I was aflame with ardour and worked in a frenzied, almost mad manner, achieving study after study, week after week, always destroying it at the end of the week, to begin a new one the following Monday. Little outside sculpture interested me. I heard music sometimes of a Sunday afternoon at Symphony Concerts, listened to Paderewski, and heard Richard Strauss conduct, and also heard the new opera, *Pelléas and Mélisande*. I saw Isadora Duncan dance to the Seventh Symphony. She looked puny at the Trocadero with a full-sized orchestra on a vast stage. After a Sunday passed in the woods of Chaville, I would return to the modelling class and no one outstripped me in ardour. The *massier* of the class, a certain Cladel, would sit perched upon a high stool, yards away from the model, tinkering with the clay. He would watch me darting in and out of the stands to get different, almost simultaneous views of the model, and remarked facetiously about such unorthodox behaviour. I would throw back at him my contempt for a fellow who thought he could do sculpture sitting on a high stool. One very Assyrian-bearded student asked me to see his work at home. When I arrived I saw a study hardly begun. He then said: "Would you do a study for me so that I can show it to my family?" and he explained that when he had a model in his room it was impossible for him to

work. He saw nothing wrong in palming off on his family in the provinces a work done by someone else.

Another student, an American, was a champion boxer, but a very poor sculptor. He was wealthy, and French girls would come into the atelier and wait for him to get through his morning's work, and go off with him. This man visited me later in London, coming over with a polo team. He was still a hopelessly amateur sculptor, and his athletic vigour had tragically diminished.

During all this period I was sustained by a wonderful health and strength. When I left the school and attempted working on my own I was not at all clear in my mind as to how to work out my ideas for sculpture. I started two large works, one of which I remember was a group of "sun-worshippers" which I should have kept. I have since seen early Egyptian figures which bear a remarkable resemblance to this early group of mine. This and another heroic-sized group I destroyed. I was completely at a loss as to how to work out my ideas. I had, so it seemed to me, come to a dead end in Paris. I felt that if I went somewhere else and got into new surroundings, I would make a new start. It was in this mood that I debated in my mind whether to return to America or go elsewhere, perhaps to London.

3

LONDON: 1905

WHILE I was at work at the École des Beaux Arts, I was asked to dinner by a Belgian, Victor Dave by name, a publisher and anarchist who had suffered imprisonment for two years for activity in anarchist propaganda. He had been associated with Michael Bakunin. I was very cordially received by Victor Dave and his wife in their Passy flat, and there I met the Scottish lady whom I later married. I was invited to London and met friends, with whom I went on a boating trip up the Thames, and also on what would now be called "a hike" up Snowdon. I recall this walking trip up the wild Welsh mountains, and how the mountain grandeur and loneliness impressed me.

When thinking of leaving Paris, I determined to go to London, and see if I could settle down and work there. First impressions of the English were of a people with easy and natural manners, and great courtesy, and a visit to the British Museum settled the matter for me, as I felt that I would like to have a very good look round at leisure.

From Paris I arrived in London and found a studio in the Camden Town quarter. After a day in the studio I would go to Hyde Park of an evening and listen to the orators at the Marble Arch. London of that period was, as I recall it, more racy, and the types in the park, peculiar to the Cockney, interested and amused me, and one saw scenes that often were of a Hogarthian nature. This has disappeared like the old-time music-halls.

I met at this period John Fothergill, of whom I did a portrait in crayon, and he bought, and made his friends buy, some of my drawings. I felt extremely discouraged at this time, and started destroying all that was in the studio. By a sudden impulse I took a passage to

New York, going steerage. This was in no way disagreeable, in fact, very interesting. The food was bad, but I found that many passengers, knowing this, had provided themselves with a store of sausages and other edibles, very good food, which they asked me to share with them. Middle Europeans and refugees from Russia and Poland, where they were persecuted as Jews, made up the third class. The steerage passengers were quartered altogether, and we slept in tiers of bunks, and near where I slept four Chinamen played a game of chance with chips, throughout the voyage. I never saw them on deck and at night, were I to wake, they were still there with their chips, and monotonous chanting.

Arrived in New York, I did not stay long. A friend whom I had met in London wrote to me, and in a fortnight I had made up my mind to return to London and work there. This time I took a studio in Fulham. I worked hard and seriously for two years, making studies. In these tumble-down studios in Fulham I was first made aware of the ludicrous snobbishness that artists are supposed to be free of. The other occupants of the studios were artists who were beginning their careers. One was a young Australian sculptor, who, I was given to understand, "bid fair to be Australia's premier sculptor". He was at the time doing a portrait of the Australian Prime Minister's daughter, and this romantic affair, through the smarter setting it obviously clamoured for, might possibly have had unpleasant consequences for me. One day I heard that the landlady, who lived on the premises, had been requested by the artists to have me removed from the studios, as my clothes were somewhat too Bohemian for the place, not, in fact, respectable enough. The promising Australian sculptor and a now well-known caricaturist were the prime movers against me in this, and had it not been for the women artists in this beehive, who were all in my favour, I would have been given notice to quit "The Railway Accident", as it was called.

At that time I made the acquaintance of Muirhead Bone, Francis Dodd, Augustus John, and other New English Art Club members. These were still the days of struggle, and I was far from satisfied with what I was doing. My aim was to perfect myself in modelling, drawing and carving, and it was at this period I visited the British Museum, and whenever I had done a new piece of work I compared it mentally with what I had seen at the Museum. These rich collections are rarely visited by sculptors. You could pass whole days there and never come across a sculptor. It would be considered a lack of originality to be discovered there. Fancy a dramatist or poet willingly eschewing Shakespeare and the Elizabethans, or a composer of music deliberately avoiding Bach and Beethoven! Early on, about 1910, I was tremendously interested in the Elgin Marbles and Greek sculpture, and later in the Egyptian rooms and the vast and wonderful collections from Polynesia and Africa.

4

ONE day in the spring of 1907 Mr. Francis Dodd asked me if I could accept a commission from an architect he knew, and decorate a building. This led to my meeting Mr. Charles Holden, the architect, and to the decorating of the new British Medical Association building in the Strand.

I set to work and made models of eighteen figures, which were accepted by the architect. I moved into a large studio in Cheyne Walk, and began the work. It was a tremendous change for me to move away from "The Railway Accident" to a fine studio, and to receive an advance payment on the commission. I thought I was wealthy, and the future looked bright. I could now pay for models, and get to work on large figures. With experience I learned how quickly one's funds could be depleted. Sculpture, I should say, is about the most expensive mode of making a living. I cannot think of any other occupation into which you must put so much. When you come to reckon up your out-of-pocket expenses against your remuneration, the balance is invariably all on the wrong side. So it was with the Strand Statues, unfortunately. The decoration was important—large figures on which I could let myself go. I had been like a hound on leash, and now I was suddenly set free, and I never reckoned the cost. I worked with ardour, feverishly, and within the space of fourteen months the eighteen over-life-size figures were finished. At first I was somewhat held back by the admonitions of the architects, who, although they had given me a big commission, yet felt that I might do something rash. I already had a reputation for wildness; why, I don't know. It is quite possible my appearance at this time was that of the traditional anarchist. However, later gathering strength, as the architects gathered faith, I managed to impose my own ideas upon the decoration, and had only one bad halt, when they totally rejected one of the figures, and would not have it included. I considered it one of the best.

However, I went on, not anticipating any other kind of trouble. All was quiet, until after the scaffolding was removed from the first four figures, then a storm of vituperation burst out suddenly in *The Evening Standard and St. James's Gazette* that was totally unexpected and unprecedented in its fury.

One would have imagined that my work was in some manner outrageous. It consisted, for the most part, of nudes in such narrow niches that I was forced to give simple movements to all the figures. In symbolism I tried to represent man and woman, in their various stages from birth to old age—a primitive, but in no way a bizarre programme.

Perhaps this was the first time in London that a decoration was not purely "decorative"; the figures had some fundamentally human meaning, instead of being merely adjuncts to an architect's mouldings and cornices.

When the commission was first given me, a member of the British Medical Association suggested that the decoration should consist of their historically famous medical men, but I was determined to do a series of nude figures, and surgeons with side-whiskers, no matter how eminent, could hardly have served my purpose as models.

The whole effect of the façade was extremely rich and handsome, despite the mutilations the figures underwent later.

At the time of the dispute, the scaffolding at one side still being up, as the decorations were not quite finished, some "experts" (including a policeman sent by Scotland Yard, who took notes in his little book), wanted to view them closer. In one of the notes in the policeman's book which I happened to catch sight of "rude" was the word applied to one of the figures—a Cockneyism meaning obscene. On the other hand, the Bishop of Stepney, Dr. Cosmo Gordon Lang, later Archbishop of Canterbury, asked me to show him the sculpture. He mounted the ladders to the scaffolding and made a close inspection of the figures. He declared that he saw nothing indecent or shocking about them.

Strand Statues: 1908

There came sculptors, artists, and directors of galleries. From below, as the open buses passed by, the passengers would stand up in a mass and try to view the now famous Strand Statues. A meeting was called of the Council of the British Medical Association to consider what to do. I was a witness, and this tribunal, resembling an ancient ecclesiastical court to consider a heresy case, was most impressive. The art of the cartoonist was brought into play, and music-halls and comedians incorporated the Strand Statues in their songs. London had become sculpture-conscious.

There were letters to *The Times*, petitions and counter-petitions, and questions in Parliament were asked. Bishops gave their views, newspaper boys, dustmen, business men, policemen, all aired their opinions on the subject.

The Evening Standard and St. James's Gazette started hostilities on June 19th, 1908, with an article on its front page, entitled BOLD SCULPTURE; it went as follows:

We draw attention with some reluctance to five amazing statuary figures which are meant to adorn the fine new building of the British Medical Association in course of erection at the corner of the Strand and Agar Street. From the point of view of the sculptor, they will doubtless be regarded as work of an excellent kind, but outside the studio, and one or two galleries, they represent a development of art to which the British public, at any rate, are not accustomed. With regard to their appearance, it is unnecessary to say any more than that they are a form of statuary which no careful father would wish his daughter, or no discriminating young man, his fiancée, to see. Nude statuary figures in an art gallery are seen, for the most part, by those who know how to appreciate the art they represent, and it is in only the most exceptional cases that they afford subjects for the vulgar comment of the inartistic, who visit art galleries out of purposeless curiosity, or with the object of whiling away an idle hour—people for whom art galleries are never intended. To have art of the kind indicated, laid bare to the gaze of all classes, young and old, in perhaps the busiest thoroughfare of the Metropolis of the world, and portrayed in the form it is on the new building of the British Medical Association, is another matter. The degree of nudity which has been chosen for the figures to which we particularly refer, is not calculated to enhance the artistic effect of the Statuary: Art would not have suffered by more discriminating treatment. For a certain type of mind, on the other hand, it cannot but have a demoralizing tendency, and it is surely unnecessary, having regard to the

3 23

condition of some of our West End streets, to give further opportunities for vulgarity.

We are concerned most of all, however, with the effect which the figures will produce on the minds of the young people. They cannot be expected to exercise a full discrimination, and in any case the sight is not one which it is desirable in the interests of public morality to present to their impressionable minds. The same view unfortunately, we think, seems not to be taken by the British Medical Association.

The difference between a nude figure in sculpture in a gallery, and one exposed to the public gaze in a busy thoroughfare is too obvious to need emphasising. If the statues had been erected inside the building, no objection could or would have been offered. But in their present position, they are certainly objectionable.

The question arises as to how they were permitted to be erected. So far as we can ascertain, they are not sanctioned by any public authority, and inquiries go to show that no authorisation is needed to put figures in sculpture on a building. The London County Council, who passed the general plan with the figures indicated but not outlined in detail, had no jurisdiction. The Police, if photographs of the statues were exposed for sale, could intervene. Their statements, however, with regard to sculpture on a private building, notwithstanding that it may be seen by the public, if they care to look at it, appear to raise a doubt as to whether they are entitled to interfere. The absence of any supervising authority as such in this case calls for revision of the building laws.

It is to be hoped in the case to which we refer, that the British Medical Association will see the wisdom of modifying their plans. At present only one of the figures to which we have taken exception is exposed to full public view, the other being partially obscured by the hoarding which still surrounds the figures in Agar Street. The appearance of the building will not suffer if the features alluded to are eliminated.

The paper further stated:

The Scotland Yard authorities, we are informed, have the question of the Strand statues under consideration. In an informal way, an Inspector of police has already called upon a representative of the British Medical Association and indicated that objection is taken to the figures, and particularly to one of the female representations which is still obscured by the hoarding in Agar Street.

The National Vigilance Society has also taken action.*

* For Further *Evening Standard* articles see Appendix, Strand Statues, 1908.

Strand Statues: 1908

My statues were defended in *The Times* by C. J. Holmes, Slade Professor of Fine Arts, Charles Ricketts, Charles Shannon, Laurence Binyon, and by *The Times* itself; I reproduce their letters and *The Times* Leader, June 24th, 1908:

DEAR SIR,

May I ask the protection of your columns for the sculpture decorating the new building of the British Medical Association in the Strand, which seems in some danger from an ill-informed, but none the less violent attack?

The impression left by the anonymous critic's words is one of meretricious audacity: "On a Strand frontage such figures would constitute a gross offence," and it was suggested that the figures still concealed by the hoarding were even more objectionable than those as yet on view. What was my surprise on seeing the building to find it a structure on which austerity was carried to an extreme and the sparse figures recessed some 40 feet above the street frontage, to be conceived in the grave heroic mood of pre-Pheidian Greece. By the courtesy of a friend, I was enabled to see photographs of some of the work behind the now notorious hoarding.

It was evident at a glance that we were once more face to face with a situation exactly like that of 1850 when Millais exhibited "Christ in the House of His Parents". We smile nowadays at the accusations of indecency, blasphemy, and incompetence, which that painting aroused.

May we not derive from them also the lesson of caution in dealing with a new phase of sculpture? The pre-Raphaelites, it will be remembered, turned back from an over-ripe tradition of painting to the example of an earlier age. Is not Mr. Epstein doing exactly the same in turning back from our tired and sweetened adaptations of late Greek ideals to the stern vigour of the pre-Pheidian epoch? I believe he is a young man, and as with most sculptors of keen perception, there are some traces of the influence of Rodin here and there in his work, but its main impulse is derived entirely from nature, as its technical treatment is derived from pre-Pheidian Greece, and of all the work done in England of recent years I know none that is more truly living, scholarly and monumental.

In dealing with the æsthetic side of the work, I trust I have also dealt with the question of decency. I can imagine a super-sensitive conscience hesitating before some of the sculpture which passes current in the Salon, at the Royal Academy, in the Tate Gallery, or at Shepherd's Bush; but I cannot imagine any sane person petitioning the citizens of Munich to provide the stern warriors of the Ægina pediment with petticoats. Yet it is precisely on these pre-Pheidian examples, and not on the more

25

luxurious models with which we are surrounded, that Mr. Epstein's art is based.

Those to whom appeals are now being made will doubtless consult educated opinion before any action is taken, and there can be no doubt what that opinion will be. Mr. Epstein must finally triumph as he deserves to do, and as the pre-Raphaelites did before him. For the moment these attacks have placed him in a position of grave difficulty; and for that reason, although I have not the privilege of his personal acquaintance, I have ventured to say on his behalf what will be a commonplace to those who know anything of the history of sculpture.

I am, Sir,

Yours faithfully,

C. J. HOLMES.

Slade Professor of Fine Arts, Oxford.

Ricketts and Shannon wrote as follows:

24th June, 1908.

SIR,

The Evening Standard and St. James' Gazette has devoted three articles to the censure of the statues now decorating the new building of the British Medical Association. The editor admits in his issue of June 20th that "many letters" have been received in defence of these works. These letters have not been published.

Would you allow two artists to express their astonishment that these austere and beautiful statues should have been questioned on moral grounds. We would urge that it is unfair to suppress all expert opinion on this matter, since it is manifest that the writer in *The Evening Standard* is unacquainted with the degree of nudity allowed in the decorations of public buildings in England, or on the Continent, such as the Sistine Chapel for instance.

C. RICKETTS.

CHARLES SHANNON.

Lansdowne House,
    Lansdowne Road,
      Holland Park,
        W.

The following letter came from Laurence Binyon:

To the Editor of *The Times*.

SIR,

A public and persistent attack has during the last few days been made upon certain sculpture on the outside of the new building of the British Medical Association in the Strand. These sculptures are represented to be

26

indecent and calculated to corrupt public morals; it has been, at the same time, denied that they are "artistic in any sense of the word." The accusation seems to have been so far so successful that the question of modifying or removing the statues is, so it is said, to be debated by a Committee of the Association on Wednesday next.

In the interest of British sculpture, may I be allowed to protest against this attack—an attempt to enthrone ignorance and prejudice as the final authority on questions of public art?

The conception of these statues is grave and austere. Those figures which are nude are treated in what might be called the Biblical spirit, from which all thought of offence seems totally absent. Anything less calculated to appeal to the average sensual man could not be imagined.

The charge of indecency is a grave one, as I think it gravely wrongs both the sculptor's intentions and the effect his work produces on men and women of healthy mind.

Competent judges will doubtless not entirely agree as to the precise merit of these sculptures as works of art. If I am not mistaken, it is just their lack of sensuous charm which, to many, will seem their chief defect. But none will deny their seriousness and sincerity; I believe few will fail to see in them a remarkable original power. Such qualities usually provoke hostility from "the man in the street", now appealed to as Judge.

It is a common cry that we have no sculptor capable of monumental work. If, when a young sculptor arises who shows himself possessed of the capacity to treat such a work in an adequate manner, far removed from the enfeebled conventions too characteristic of British sculpture in the past—if he is treated with ignominy and his work suppressed, the reproach will recoil upon the public itself.

I am, Sir,
Your obedient servant,
LAURENCE BINYON.

The following paragraph appeared in *The Times* of June 25th:

A meeting of the Premises Committee of the B.M.A. was held yesterday afternoon. The committee will report to the Council on July 1st. The terms of the report are private, but it is understood that the committee is favourable to the work being allowed to proceed.

In *The Times* of July 2nd the following article appeared:

DECISION OF THE BRITISH MEDICAL ASSOCIATION

A meeting of the B.M.A. was held yesterday afternoon at the office of the Metropolitan Asylums Board. Mr. Edmund Owen, chairman of the

Council, presided and there were present about sixty members from all parts of the British Empire. The proceedings were private, but we have been officially informed by the General Secretary, Mr. Guy Elliston, that the matter of the statues on the premises of the Association in the Strand was discussed. A report was presented by the Premises Committee recommending the Council to let the work proceed. The Committee further resolved: "that it be an instruction to the General Secretary to write and invite Sir Charles Holroyd to ask him to associate with himself three or four other members, who are skilled in art, to furnish the Committee with a report as to whether, in their opinion, the statuary on the façade of the new premises is indecent."

SIR CHARLES HOLROYD'S LETTER

DEAR SIR,

In reply to your letters of 25th and 26th June, 1908, in which you ask me for my opinion on the merits of the sculpture on your new building, I desire to say that although as Director of the National Gallery I do not give advice about works of art in private possession, yet in this case, and as my opinion is entirely favourable to the works in question, I can say what I think about them as a private citizen. In my opinion the sculptures are very interesting. They are dignified and reverent in treatment, and the sculptor has expressed ideas in a way unusually suitable to the material in which he has worked, and both ideas and workmanship harmonize with the building. I do not know the sculptor, but I believe he is a young man. From the works I have seen I believe the British Medical Association will be proud of having given him this work to do, in the future when he has made the name for himself which his work promises.

Faithfully yours,
CHARLES HOLROYD.

Sturdie House,
Beckwood Avenue,
Weybridge.
30/vi/08.

The decision of the Council of the British Medical Association with regard to the statues upon their new building in the Strand will commend itself to all who have considered the matter without prejudice and in the light of common sense.

The Council, as will be seen from the report of their meeting, which we publish to-day, have resolved, with practical unanimity, to instruct their architect to proceed with the work.

It remains to be seen whether this decision will bring to an end a controversy which ought never to have been begun. That it ought to do is sufficiently evident from the expressions of opinion which have come from those best qualified to speak on a question of this kind. Some of these expressions have appeared in our own columns, while others have been received by the Association, whose sculptor's work has been attacked with so much vigour and so little discrimination.

An attempt to obtain the interference of the London County Council in a sense hostile to the statues has also met with a discouraging reception, so that, on the whole, it may be hoped that an effectual check has been given to a purely fictitious agitation.

I felt like a criminal in the dock, and this unexpected hubbub in 1908 ushered me into a publicity I have always detested. To accuse me of making sensations is the easiest way of attacking me, and in reality leaves the question of sculpture untouched. For, whatever an artist does, or fails to do, whatever his reputation, the work is always there for all to see.

The attacks on the Strand Statues brought me many friends, some of whom later, when they found that I was really independent in my judgments, fell off.

I had to discover for myself how superficial is the world of art, and what a wretched lot of log-rollers, schemers, sharks, opportunists, profiteers, snobs, parasites, sycophants, camp-followers, social climbers, and what my dear old American artist friend, "Brandy Bill", called "four-flushers", infest the world of Art. It is a jungle, into which the artist is forced periodically to bring his work and live.

In 1935, the Southern Rhodesian Government took over the British Medical Association building, and the High Commissioner at once announced that the statues were to be removed, as the new occupants thought them undesirable. The tone of this announcement in the Press was of so insulting a nature that I was moved to write in protest, and I explained my position in a letter to *The Observer* of May 5th, 1935:

Sir,

In your issue of April 28th, your "Observator", in alluding to my statues at the corner of the Strand and Agar Street, refers to them as "topical" and thereby laying themselves open to a charge of unsuitability to the new and present owners of the building, the Government of Southern Rhodesia. Might I point out that they were never intended to be "topical" and perhaps that is the most far-fetched charge that could be brought against them. The figures were intended to have a universal appeal, even perhaps understood in South Rhodesia. The High Commissioner for South Rhodesia has taken no trouble, so far as I know, to consult Mr. Charles Holden, the eminent architect, or myself. The statues are an integral part of the building, and are actually built into the fabric (actually carved in situ), and to remove them would be risking damage to the statues.

The vandalism consists in removing and putting a price upon a decoration, the battle for which was fought out twenty-seven years ago, but the spirit of Philistinism dies not, and united to ownership dictates what shall and shall not be done to a decoration on a London building. We think dynasties that destroyed and mutilated the works of previous generations vandals, and do not hesitate to call them vandals. How is this different in spirit and intention? Ownership does not give the right to remove and destroy, or even the right to sell.

Yours, etc.,

JACOB EPSTEIN.

An acrimonious discussion broke out and the High Commissioner aggressively declared that as they had paid for the building, they could do as they pleased with the statues. This gentleman expressed surprise that I should object to this, as I had been paid for my work and the statues no longer belonged to me. I had pointed out the vandalism of removing from a building a decoration which was a part of its fabric, and which would mean the ruin of the statues. I was requested by *The Manchester Guardian* to report upon them, and with Mr. James Bone, I paid a visit to the site. We got as near the statues as we could from opposite buildings, examined them through glasses and photographs of all of them were taken. Mr. Bone reported upon the statues, giving my views.

In an interview with *The Daily Telegraph* I said:

This is the latest attempt to dictate London taste in sculpture. This time from Rhodesia. They proposed the removal of the British Medical Association sculptures which twenty-seven years ago won against the Philistines. To-day we have a victory of the Philistines from the outposts of Empire.

For the Southern Rhodesian Government, Mr. A. T. Scott, of the firm of Sir Herbert Baker, R.A., architects to Southern Rhodesia House, said:

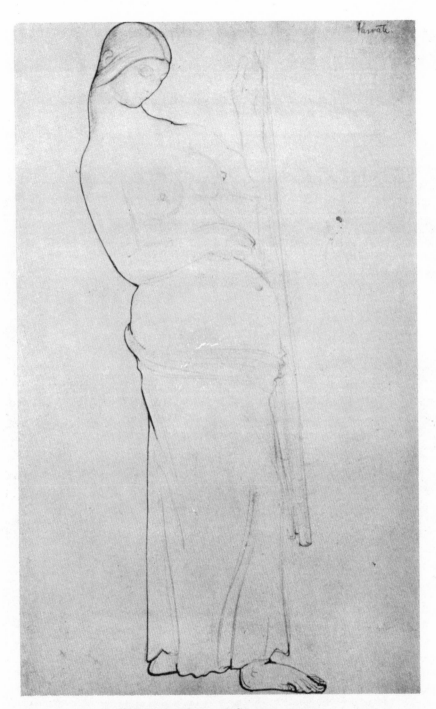

Study for Strand Statue, 1907

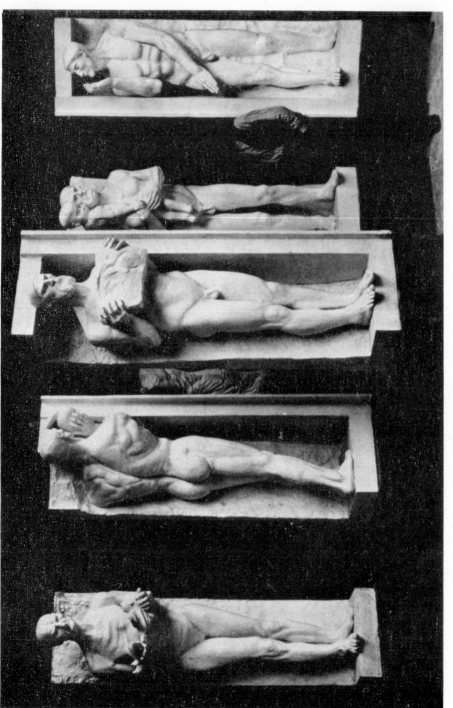

Some of the original plaster models for the Strand Statues, 1907

One of the Strand carvings *in situ*, 1907

Detail from Oscar Wilde Tomb, 1911

The position has been misunderstood. What we feel is that the figures, which were all very well, and indeed very appropriate, round the British Medical Association building, are quite out of place as decoration to a Government Office. Anatomy for the British Medical Association, yes. But do these figures indicate the produce of Southern Rhodesia? No. It is a question of what is appropriate.

Mr. Richard Sickert, R.A., wrote to *The Daily Telegraph* as follows:

As the writer of a letter published in 1908 on the subject of the Epstein statues in the Strand, I should be grateful if you would allow me to add a few words in 1935.

The 18 statues form part of the architecture of the former home of the British Medical Association. Your phrase in brackets, "although field-glasses were necessary to view them properly", should perhaps have run, "to view them improperly".

The merit of the statues we recognise as consisting in the fact that they 'form part of the architecture, and are inseparable from the architecture.

As I should be, as a matter of common sense, prepared to listen with sincere humility to the Rhodesians on all the infinite subjects on which they have a call to be heard, I would beseech them to grant us some authority on matters to which we may have given for generations and life-times some thought and feeling.

The whole building is planned to "tell", viewed from the road. The convention of movement, life and growth is a miracle of genius and accomplishment. I can hear the flowers of rhetorical respect that would be draped, at banquets, on this work if the sculptor were dead instead of alive and kicking.

You must not ask of sculpture that it should be a shop-sign or trade-mark.

The Government of Southern Rhodesia cannot possibly consider that the fact that they are to be housed in an august building once a medical centre is anything to be ashamed of.

> Yours, etc.,
> RICHARD SICKERT.

St. Peter's-in-Thanet.
May 9th.

Sir Eric Maclagan, Director of the Victoria and Albert Museum, and an influential committee circulated a petition for the preservation of the statues. The following letter from them appeared in *The Times* of May 10th:

MR. EPSTEIN'S STATUES

PROPOSED REMOVAL FROM STRAND BUILDING

SIR,

When Mr. Epstein's statues on what was then the new building of the British Medical Association in the Strand were attacked in June, 1908, *The Times* came to their defence in a leading article (published on the 24th of that month), and associated itself thereby with the views expressed in its columns by a number of distinguished correspondents.

It is now reported that the government of Southern Rhodesia, having acquired the building, is proposing to remove the statues, which formed an integral part of its design, although we understand that it would, in all probability, be impossible to cut out eighteen large Portland stone statues from their granite niches without destroying them. Apart from this, the statues were carved for their present situation, and it is difficult to imagine how they could be satisfactorily displayed in any other position.

We ask the hospitality of your columns to urge that even at the cost of some change in the plans of the new occupiers, Mr. Charles Holden's building in the Strand should be preserved intact with its nobly planned and executed sculptural decoration. If the statues are removed, and still more if they are irreparably damaged in the course of removal, we find it difficult to believe that this generation will be acquitted by our successors of a charge of grave vandalism.

KENNETH CLARK, W. G. CONSTABLE,
CRAWFORD AND BALCARRES, W. REID
DICK, H. S. GOODHART-RENDEL, G. F.
HILL, ERIC MACLAGAN, J. B. MANSON.

The signature of the President of the Royal Academy, Sir William Llewellyn, was sought, but Sir William refused to sign.

The Evening Standard of May 10th commented thus on his refusal:

MISSING SIGNATORY

Sir William Llewellyn, President of the Royal Academy, was not one of the many distinguished signatories to a letter in the Press this morning appealing against the proposed removal of the Epstein statues from the Southern Rhodesian Government building in the Strand.

I understand that Sir William was approached by Sir Eric Maclagan, Director of the Victoria and Albert Museum, for his signature, but declined to add it on the ground that the appeal was "not an Academy affair". His attitude had nothing to do with Mr. Epstein. On the contrary, he would like to see the statues preserved.

A dramatic development of the situation occurred when Richard Sickert indignantly repudiated the President's attitude and resigned his membership of the Royal Academy. Consternation reigned, and the President begged Sickert to reconsider his resignation. Sickert adhered to his decision, and in *The Daily Telegraph* was quoted as saying:

The Academy ought to have summoned an emergency meeting, and sent a request asking to be allowed to make a representation to the King on the subject. But they did not do so. It is not the President's fault. He sticks to his ship and does what he has got to do. But I am not an official. I am very fond of him and all my colleagues, who have been most extraordinarily kind to me, but sloppy sentimentality does not enter into it. They are in a sense Public Trustees, as a dignified representative body of art, and as such should have taken up the matter.

The President and Royal Academy's action was analysed by another President of another Academy, in *The Times*, of May 21st, 1935, after the Royal Academy had met and further action was expected:

SIR,

A statement issued by the Royal Academy explains that Sir William Llewellyn declined to support Sir Eric Maclagan's appeal because "whatever his own feeling may be, it is not possible to keep his personal attitude distinct from his official position as President of the Royal Academy."

I cannot imagine that Sir William was requested to sign the letter on behalf of the Royal Academy, any more than Mr. Clark was requested to sign it on behalf of the Trustees of the National Gallery, or Professor Constable on behalf of Cambridge University, or Lord Crawford on behalf of the House of Lords. Much, however, as the signatories of that letter may regret that Sir William's name could not appear with ours, his delicacy throws into relief an inaction on the part of the Royal Academy itself that it would be discourteous not to consider surprising. The proposal against which protest is being made is not that of taking loose statues out of niches, but of cutting away integral sculpture from an architectural design by one whom many of us consider to be the first English architect of our day. Against such needless mutilation of fine architecture the Royal Academy, which includes architects in its membership, might reasonably be expected to make some public appeal. Sir William Reid Dick has supported Sir Eric Maclagan, Mr. Richard Sickert has retired from membership, but no official voice has been heard beyond the statement on various internal matters that was published to-day.

I am, Sir,

Your obedient servant,

H. S. GOODHART-RENDEL.

Travellers' Club,
Pall Mall,
S.W.I.

President of Royal Institute of
British Architects.
Director of Architectural Associa-
tion School of Architects.

I myself, in commenting on the President's refusal to sign the memorial in support of the statues, recalled that a former President of the Royal Academy signed a memorial for the removal of my Hudson Panel in Hyde Park. One President signs a memorial against one of my statues, and another refuses to sign for. This is the spirit of the Royal Academy!

Further letters were written to *The Times* and to *The Daily Telegraph* and to *The Manchester Guardian*.

I reproduce a letter from the architect of the British Medical Association's building, Mr. Charles Holden, which appeared in *The Manchester Guardian* of May 15th, 1935:

MR. CHARLES HOLDEN'S APPEAL TO SOUTHERN RHODESIA

SIR,

When I first heard of the proposal to remove the statues from the building recently occupied by the British Medical Association, I assumed that it was the intention of the Rhodesian Government to pull down the building and erect a new building to suit their special needs. Such a desire, though lamentable, might not be considered unreasonable; but when, as it now appears, there is no such intention and it is proposed to remove the sculptures for some imaginary and doubtful gain to the efficiency of the building, the position is indeed very different.

These sculptures were defended in the first instance by a large body of influential and serious art-lovers who were undisputed authorities on these matters, and the fact that after all these years an equally formidable defence has been raised against their removal must carry conviction to any reasonable person. The sculptures are, in fact, works of first importance.

In my opinion, there is a universal quality about the work which is not only rare in our own times but in the whole history of sculpture, and I would plead with Southern Rhodesia to protect these treasures which they appear to have acquired inadvertently and without the full knowledge of their importance.   Yours, etc.,

CHARLES HOLDEN.

9 Knightsbridge,
    Hyde Park Corner,
        London, S.W.1.   29th *May*, 1935.

This is a letter from Mr. Van Dieren about the right to destroy the statues.

From *The Daily Telegraph:*

NO LIBERTY TO DESTROY ART

To the Editor:
SIR,

Will you allow me, as the author of the first book on Epstein's work, to reaffirm a principle which some participants in the recent controversy disregard or deny.

Most correspondents agree about Epstein's great gifts and personality. Both are sufficiently extraordinary to cause violent reactions. As Mr. Sickert put it, Epstein is very much alive, "and kicking". This disturbs numerous critics who would publicly worship him if only he were conveniently dead, preferably for some centuries.

Meanwhile, representatives of bluff and sturdy commonsense have wanted to know what the fuss is about. They indignantly ask whether the man who buys a work of art is to be in a different position from one who acquires any sort of commodity. Cannot he do with it as he likes?

The answer is: Most emphatically not! No more than you may discharge your own gun in the street or kill your own wife. Shylock could not even maintain his proprietary rights in that single pound of flesh.

The buyer of a work of art takes on a trust, which implies duties as well as rights. He is a patron whose responsibilities are his privileges. French and Italian law permits private ownership of art treasures, but their removal or exportation only within strict limits. In any country a claim of buyers to chop them up would be promptly met by legislation. Acts of vandalism are everywhere against public policy.

It is true that Epstein is not an Old Master. Not yet! But he will be one day. By that time the Strand building, with the statues in the particular position that was part of the sculptor's conception, will rank as a national monument.

We do not concede to the man who buys a piece of land the right to remove or destroy anything on it that might displease him, and which might happen to be Stonehenge or Salisbury Cathedral. The buyer of valuable sculpture as part of a building incurs the ethical obligation to preserve both in good condition.

The logic of the position, therefore, is perfectly clear. If the Rhodesian Government disapproved of the statues (it is immaterial for what reasons), the building simply was unsuitable for their requirements and they might have looked round for one to which no similar problems or controversial features were attached.

Yours, etc.,
BERNARD VAN DIEREN.

St. John's Wood,
   N.W.

This letter, from Sir Muirhead Bone, was published in *The Manchester Guardian* of May 16th:

SIR,

I am glad that *The Manchester Guardian* feels concerned about the strange proposal of the Southern Rhodesian Government to remove the famous statues by Mr. Epstein from the building they have acquired in the Strand.

It is a proposal to tear an important page from the art history of England. These statues are truly landmarks in that history. Taken away from the building for which they were designed (they are indeed its only ornament, as the architect, Mr. Charles Holden, kept his whole façade severely plain in order to emphasise them to the utmost), they would lose most, if not all, of their meaning, and London would lose the most successful, perhaps, of all its modern art monuments. And we art-lovers would feel such a robbery keenly. The monument I speak of is the perfect combination of the building and its statuary.

The history of sculpture—that most difficult of arts, the one most deserving of public encouragement and endowment—is strewn, as every student knows, with pathetic fragments, reminders of noble projects which age or death overtook before a complete conception could be brought to fruition. Such were the half-hewn, weed-grown torsos of Michelangelo's one used to come across in the dark alleys of the Boboli Gardens and gaze at with awe and an overwhelming sense of the pathetic grandeur of this art with its resolute claim to everlastingness. In the old British Medical building in the Strand a happily complete thing came into existence—an achievement uniting one of the very first buildings to show the real style of modern architecture with the earliest, and perhaps the happiest, public work by our chief English sculptor.

So I entreat the Southern Rhodesian Government to pause while there is time and realise the depth of feeling in the whole of our art world against such vandalism. Their proposal creates a grave precedent which I am sure they would hesitate to inflict on the London public who care for such matters, as their first welcome in our midst showed. This great series of sculptures was once before in danger of removal, but the art-lovers of London united to fight for them, and they stand above the Strand to this day as a testimony of a notable victory over Philistinism and misunderstanding. To hew them down now would be a serious discouragement to English art, and a disheartening setback to its progress in England. Even were it possible to remove the sculptures safely, their whole purpose would be entirely frustrated by this hacking out of the "eyes" of the building, and dispersing them for ever to the twilight of collections. I do not think it is too much to say that this building has proved a real "academy" to sculptors and architects, for the difficult art of sculpture applied to architecture is here seen to perfection. All this would be gone, and it would prove a real loss to the public good.

If the Southern Rhodesian Government would act as one is sure Rhodes himself would have acted—for no one was keener, Sir Herbert Baker makes plain in his book, in recognising and encouraging dignity in architecture and sculpture—they would magnanimously hold their hand now; a great work of art is in their power. For there is no question that such destruction as they propose will be considered unthinkable by anyone (including their own Government) a few years hence. For Mr. Epstein is graduating rapidly to classic rank and to the respect that is due to the work of a classic.

MUIRHEAD BONE.

The following letter came to me from the Secretary of the Royal Fine Arts Commission:

Royal Fine Arts Commission,
6 Burlington Gardens,
W.1.

R.F.A.C. 167/4a.
19th July, 1935.

SIR,

In reply to your letter of June 6th, I am directed by the Royal Fine Arts Commission to state that, from enquiries made from the Southern Rhodesian authorities, it appears to be certain that your sculpture will not be removed from Agar House.

I am, Sir,
Your obedient Servant,
H. C. BRADSHAW.
Secretary to the Commission.

Jacob Epstein, Esq.,
18, Hyde Park Gate,
S.W.7.

Under this combined pressure of intelligent opinion the day was won, and the statues were left in peace for two years.

In 1937, immediately after the coronation of George VI, removal of some of the decorations which had been attached to the statues caused a small portion of the work to fall. A head was reported to have fallen, and it was alleged that a woman was hit, or narrowly missed. A vague statement! With this as a proof of the danger of the statues to the public, scaffolding was erected, and a process of demolishing the greater part of every statue took place. My demand that I be allowed to examine and make a report on the state of the statues was refused. What is left of the statues now is a portion of the torso here, and a fore-leg there, and an arm somewhere else. Not a single head remains. The mutilation was complete.

For the dissolution of the stone after only twenty-nine years, two explanations can be given, one of which seems to me to be of major importance, although not accepted by the architect of the building. But what I alleged was never investigated. When I was working on the statues I noticed that, when rain fell, the water that dripped directly on to the statues caused greenish and blackish streaks such as I had never seen on stone before. This I believe was brought about by a metal plate which in each case protected a jutting out cornice immediately above each of the eighteen statues. I was told that the plates were of lead, but this I doubt because of the nature of the discoloration, which began at the time of the carving of the statues in their site. My opinion is that this liquid, with some chemical property in it, deteriorated the stone, and this process had continued for twenty-nine years, causing serious damage to the statues. One other reason can be given for the rapid destruction of the surface of the stonework, and that is that the single blocks out of which the statues were carved were set up in the wrong position from the point of view of weathering, that is, contrary to their bed positions.

The builders already had the blocks fixed in the building when I arrived there for the carving. Whatever the cause, some parts of the statues had rotted, but that the wholesale removal of nine-tenths of each statue was necessary—of that I am not at all convinced.

Many letters were written to show that others shared my doubts about the executions. I give the letters of T. W. Earp, Muirhead

NAN, 1909

NAN, 1909

Strand Statues: 1908

Bone, and Edwin Lutyens, on different points of view on the tragedy of the statues.

The following letter by T. W. Earp appeared in *The Daily Telegraph* of June 23rd, 1937:

S<small>IR</small>,

The demolition of Epstein's statues on the front of Rhodesia House entails more than the loss of a now familiar London landmark. It blots out eighteen works by one of the greatest sculptors of his time. Epstein's earliest achievement of importance and the basis of his fame, they were the key to future estimates of his art.

A special aspect of the statues' destruction is the light it throws on the function of the Royal Fine Arts Commission. Two years ago that body gave Mr. Epstein an assurance that his works would not be removed, yet last week they were doomed without reprieve by the owners of Rhodesia House.

The Commission has proved powerless, for its warrant gives it only consultative and advisory action. In France its equivalent can actually save the country's monuments of art and history from demolition. Here the Commission is limited to pious aspirations and ineffective reproofs.

In view of increasing vandalism this is not enough. We lose prestige along with beauty. The Royal Fine Arts Commission needs authority to back its word. By giving it uselessly in the case of the Strand statues, it has weakened even the little force that it possesses.

Yours faithfully,
T. W. E<small>ARP</small>.

Sir Muirhead Bone wrote as follows to *The Times*:

28th June, 1937.

S<small>IR</small>,

It will, I think, be generally agreed that the disappearance of the famous series of statues by Mr. Epstein from the building in the Strand now belonging to the Government of Southern Rhodesia would be a serious loss to the public art of London—not a city which can well spare any sculpture of merit from its buildings. I venture to appeal to their owners rather to restore any decayed stones among the eighteen figures than order their wholesale destruction.

Decayed stonework is no new or, indeed, difficult problem. The colleges of Oxford, for instance, tackle the same sort of thing year in, year out; but I have never yet heard of them completely obliterating an admired series of sculptures on their buildings when faced with the restoration of a few ailing pieces. It is difficult to credit that entire destruction is the solution proposed by the present owners of this fine building, and I know I speak for many art lovers in entreating them to reconsider the matter. There must certainly be a better way, and the respect due to works of real genius —for these famous figures have been widely accepted as that—claims a serious attempt to find it. A careful survey by the original architect, Mr. Charles Holden, would seem a natural preliminary.

I am, Sir,

faithfully yours,

MUIRHEAD BONE.

Burlington Fine Arts Club,
W.I.

In *The Daily Telegraph* of August 23rd, Sir Edwin Lutyens, R.A., wrote:

SIR,

The discussion that has taken place, and is yet taking place, over Mr. Epstein's unfortunate sculptures at Rhodesia House, in the Strand, gives food for thought and makes one wonder as to its sincerity.

Nothing is more distressing to an artist than that his work should collapse, even though he may be in no way responsible for the obvious cause of failure.

In the case of a living artist the loss is not irreparable; and in that he is still alive and in the full vigour of work and imagination, and with the faith he has in himself, he surely knows that within his wider power he can yet achieve better than he did years ago. Real tragedy occurs when the work of a dead genius perishes and the spark that created it is no longer existent. Such loss is irreparable. The rapidly changing character of London, and, indeed, of the whole of our countryside, gives daily evidence of this tragedy that is overwhelming us, and, with the exception of a few personal cases, is there any effective action being taken on the part of the general public to avert a climax of calamity?

Yours faithfully,

EDWIN L. LUTYENS.

5, Eaton Gate,
S.W.I.

This letter of Sir Edwin Lutyens is grotesque with its talk of the sculptor in the "full vigour of work and imagination", etc., etc., in view of the fact that this eminent and busy architect has never once even approached me with a request for sculpture during his long life.

Before the mutilation of the statues, Sir Muirhead Bone, wishing to preserve something of them, proposed making casts. I sent my moulder, an expert, to see what could be done. He was received with discourtesy by the Southern Rhodesian officials and told that he would not be given facilities, not even in the matter of water, to get on with the work. On that account Sir Muirhead had to go ahead with other moulders, who hustled through a wretched job and made moulds which were complete travesties of the originals. The battle was lost. I had made my protest on æsthetic and spiritual grounds. Naturally, in a court of law I had no case, and so my earliest large work ended tragically.

Anyone passing along the Strand can now see, as on some antique building, the few mutilated fragments of my decoration.

5

IT was at the time immediately after my decoration of the Strand building, that I again took in hand my development as a Sculptor. After so much that was large and elemental, I had the desire to train myself in a more intensive method of working; and, with that in view, I began a series of studies from the model, which were as exact as I could make them. I worked with great care, and followed the forms of the model by quarter-inches, I should say, not letting up on any detail of construction of plane; but always keeping the final composition in view. These studies included the various works I made from Nan, one of which is in the Tate Gallery, and also studies from Euphenia Lamb, and a model called Gertrude. I look upon this period as still formative. Also at that time I did a bust of Lady Gregory, and Mrs. Ambrose McEvoy, and several busts of my wife.

The Lady Gregory was a commission from Sir Hugh Lane, and he intended it for the Dublin Art Gallery. The bust progressed to my own satisfaction, and it was about completed, when one morning Lady Gregory turned up with the most astonishing head of curls: she had been to the hairdresser and wished me to alter the head. I was not inclined to do this, as the bust had up to then been planned to give Lady Gregory the air of the intellectual, somewhat "school-marmish", person that she was, and her usual appearance was all of a piece and quite dignified. Also she announced that if I came to the theatre that evening I would see her in evening clothes and would then see how much finer she appeared with bare shoulders. It is amazing how English women of no uncertain age fancy themselves dressed as Venus. On both points I told Lady Gregory that I could not imagine the bust any better if I altered it as she wished and in my headstrong way kept to my guns: this practically terminated the sittings.

When Sir Hugh Lane saw my bust of Lady Gregory for the first time, he threw up his hands in horror and exclaimed, "Poor Aunt Augusta. She looks as if she could eat her own children." Later I was to get accustomed to this sort of reception of a work, but at the time it nonplussed me, for I had put many days of work with long sittings, and much labour into it. Nevertheless, Sir Hugh Lane hurried the bust over to Dublin in time for Horse Show week.

I began at this time to do commissioned portraits of people. The artist who imagines that he puts his best into a portrait in order to produce something good, that will be a pleasure to the sitter and to himself, will have some bitter experiences.

I was also to meet for the first time in my life the hostility of a leader of a clique of artists who arrogated to themselves the sole possession of superior taste in matters of Art.

At one time a group of artists was got together under Roger Fry's management and they were assured of a yearly subsidy and patronage. This very good arrangement lasted for some years, of course to the benefit of that particular clique: when this group became somewhat stale, Matthew Smith and I were asked to join it but we discovered that the subsidy had just been withdrawn and would not be available for us.

These gentry never hesitate to go out of their way to damage and undermine an artist, even if he is only a beginner. They use the Press, especially the weeklies, and their social activities naturally help them to influence people. They are adepts at organisation and never lose opportunities. People are not generally aware that these amateurs and busybodies are often dealers, using their homes to show off and to sell works on commission.

It was at this period that I was proposed for membership of the Royal Society of British Sculptors, by Havard Thomas. I was rejected. The Royal Society represents officially British sculpture, and later on their attitude towards me was further emphasised. At an annual dinner of the Society, their guest of honour, Sir Herbert Samuel (now Lord Samuel), gave his opinion on my work, and said:

We are living in an age, to some extent of intellectual confusion, when there are no great standards in many things and when eccentricity has full scope. While, to many of us, the portrait busts of Epstein have upon them the authentic mark of genius, some of his monumental works, such as "Genesis", the one now on exhibition, "Behold the Man" and the Hudson Memorial, seem to be an aberration of genius.

For my own part, while sculpture of the early inhabitants of Easter Island and Benin may be quite interesting from the point of view of anthropology, I am not sure they ought to be models for present-day art.

Later, at the time when the Hudson Memorial was erected, Sir John Lavery as a gesture proposed me for membership of the Royal Academy. He asked me if I would allow him to put my name up and, in a moment of weakness, I consented to his doing this. I felt uneasy about it, regretting I had consented, but I need have had no fears about the matter, for on asking the secretary of the Royal Academy to remove my name from the list of candidates, I was told that after seven years' lapse one's name was automatically struck off. In more recent years I was approached again, this time by the President in the person of Sir Gerald Kelly. I told him that the offer had come too late to appeal to me in any way.

In 1911, while I was at work on the Oscar Wilde tomb in my Chelsea studio, a young fellow called on me one Sunday morning and asked if he could see the carving. It was Gaudier Brzeska* a picturesque, slight figure with lively eyes, and a sprouting beard. He was very pleasant, I thought, and he gave Ezra Pound an account of this first meeting. He declared to Pound that I asked him if he carved direct, and that, afraid to acknowledge that he hadn't, he hurried home and immediately started a carving. This was very characteristic of him.

Gaudier wished to be always in the vanguard of the moment. Not a bad thing in a very young man, but likely to lead him later into "anything for up-to-dateness"; he had any amount of talent and great energy. He awoke very early in the mornings and immediately set to work, finishing something right off in some particular style, but his volatile nature caused him to change his style from week

* Henri Gaudier was his original name. He added the name of Brzeska when he lived with Sophie.

44

to week. I say this, as critics now, not knowing the sources of all these styles, are inclined to speak of him as an innovator in sculpture.

His early death in the Great War gave him, in their eyes, an immediate status, which was out of proportion to his achievements. This is apt to happen in such circumstances, especially when the first appraisers are distinguished by their knowledge of literature rather than by their knowledge of art. Far from innovating, Gaudier always followed. He followed quickly, overnight as it were, and in the short period of his working life, he tried out any number of styles, not sticking long to any one. There have been some picturesque lives written about him and Sophie Brzeska who lived with him.

His life lent itself to dramatisation, and a play was written about him in America. Gaudier himself was young enough to wish to startle people, and I remember his declaring that he was homosexual, expecting us to be horrified. He wore a cloak over his shoulders and tried to grow a beard, and got his eyes blacked or nose punched in fights with Cockneys. My relations with Gaudier were very friendly. We were interested in each other's work. In the French fashion of the younger to the older artist he wrote to me and addressed me as Cher Maître.

I visited Gaudier at his workshop in Putney. He occupied one of a number of large workshops that were constructed under the railway arches leading to Putney Bridge. Gaudier was at that time working on his portrait of Ezra Pound in marble. (Pound had asked him to make it virile and this Gaudier was endeavouring to do, explaining to me the general biological significance.) Every ten or fifteen minutes the trains roared overhead, but Gaudier said he had quite got used to this—in fact, liked it. We went over to supper at the tenement where he lived near by with Sophie Brzeska. Gaudier got at the kitchen stove and made a stew, very strong, with heaps of all kinds of things in it. Sophie sat by and talked. We got on very well, although Sophie had it always in the back of her mind that I was standing in Henri's light. She forgot that I was much older than Gaudier, and got started long before him. She had complained about Henri not getting so well paid for his things as I was. The fact was that in her partisanship for Gaudier she trod on everyone's toes.

After Gaudier's death, John Quinn of New York asked me to get into touch with Sophie Brzeska and see if I could purchase works for him. I visited her in her place and saw what she had, and arranged that she should write to Quinn and tell him what things she had and at what prices. At the end of the talk she asked me to have a piece of Gaudier's work, which I refused on account of her peculiar nature.

The last time I saw Gaudier was at Charing Cross Station when he left for France the last time. The turmoil was terrible. Troops were departing and Sophie was in a state of hysterics and collapse. Gaudier's friends, including Hulme, Richard Aldington, Tancred and Ethel Kibblewhite, were there to see him off, and Gaudier himself, terribly pale and shaken by Sophie's loud sobs, said good-bye to us.

During the period in Paris in 1912, while I was engaged with the erection of the Oscar Wilde Tomb, I made the acquaintance of Picasso, Modigliani, Ortiz de Zarate, Brancusi, and other Montparnasse artists. This was a period of intense activity amongst the artists of Montparnasse. Certainly there were more men of talent who came to the cafés then than at any subsequent period. Later a tough element invaded the quarter. Cabarets sprang up and it became a haunt of night-club sightseers. Models and negro boxers became artists over-night and held exhibitions. None of these new-found geniuses turned out to be Rousseaus or Modiglianis. The present gatherings on the Terrace of the Dome are mostly holiday-makers, or at best, amateur artists who are attracted by the notoriety of the quarter. Modigliani I knew well. I saw him for a period of six months daily, and we thought of finding a shed on the Butte de Montmartre where we would work together in the open air, and spent a day hunting around for vacant grass plots for huts, but without result. Our enquiries about empty huts only made the owners or guardians look askance at us as suspicious persons. However, we did find some very good Italian restaurants where Modigliani was received with open arms. All Bohemian Paris knew him. His geniality and *esprit* were proverbial. At times he indulged himself in what he called " engueling". This form of violent abuse of someone who had exasperated him was always, I thought, well earned by the pretentiousness and imbecility of those he attacked, and he went for them with gusto. With friends he was charming and witty in conversation, and without any affectations. His studio at that time was a miserable hole within a courtyard, and here he lived and worked. It was then filled with nine

46

or ten of those long heads which were suggested by African masks, and one figure. They were carved in stone; at night he would place candles on the top of each one and the effect was that of a primitive temple. A legend of the quarter said that Modigliani, when under the influence of hashish, embraced these sculptures. Modigliani never seemed to want to sleep at night, and I recall that one night, when we left him very late, he came running down the passage after us, calling us to come back, very like a frightened child. He lived alone at that period, working entirely on sculpture and drawings. In appearance Modigliani was short and handsome, and, contrary to general belief or the impression given by his pictures, robust and even powerful. Later he had any amount of the girls of the quarter after him. His brother, at his death, arrived in Montparnasse to look after a child said to be Modigliani's, but so many girls came claiming maternity to Modigliani's children that the brother gave it up in despair.

When I knew him he had not attained fame outside Montparnasse, and only rarely sold a work. Drawings which he had made in the morning he would try to sell at café tables for anything he could get for them. We had our meals at Rosalie's, the Italian woman who had once been a beautiful model, and there Rosalie would admonish Modigliani. She had a motherly love for her compatriot and would try to restrain him from his "engueling" her other clients. She tried to make Modigliani settle down and be less nervy and jumpy. He was peculiarly restless and never sat down or stayed in one spot for long.

Rosalie had a large collection of Modigliani's drawings in a cupboard, set against multitudes of free meals, I suspect, because, as I have said, the old Italian had a very kind heart for him. When he died in 1921, she naturally turned to this cupboard for the drawings, as dealers were after them, but, alas! for Rosalie's hopes, the drawings, mixed with sausages and grease, had been eaten by rats.

A painting by Utrillo, which I remember on her walls, was later cut out of the plaster and sold to a dealer. Modigliani would say, "A beef steak is more important than a drawing. I can easily make drawings, but I cannot make a beef steak."

Hashish, he believed, would lend him help in his work, and cer-

47

tainly the use of it affected his vision, so that he actually saw his models as he drew them. Also he was influenced by *Les Chants de Maldoror*, which he carried in his pocket and to which he would refer as "une explosion".

I was amazed once when we were at the Gaîté Montparnasse, a small popular theatre in the rue de la Gaîté, to see near us a girl who was the image of his peculiar type, with a long oval face and a very slender neck. A Modigliani alive. It was as if he had conjured up one of his own images. Modigliani's liveliness, gaiety, and exuberant spirits endeared him to hosts, and his funeral was characterised as "Une Funéraille en Prince". Artists, tradesmen, and café waiters joined in the long procession. *Les Agents* stood at the salute as the long *cortège* passed. Picasso seeing that, and recalling that Modigliani and the police had not got on well together during his lifetime, called the funeral "La revanche de Modigliani".

I was in London when Modigliani died. At that time in Shaftesbury Avenue, Zobourovsky, Modigliani's dealer, had a gallery. I was in this gallery in 1922, when a telegram came through from Paris saying, "Modigliani dying. Sell no more of his works. Hold them back." These works had been very inexpensive up to his death. From then on the prices rose to the amazing figures they have reached now.

In 1912 I went also to the studio of Brancusi, with Ortiz. Brancusi never went to the cafés. He was in the habit of keeping a number of bottles of milk "maturing", and rows of these bottles were in the passage of his studio. He would exclaim against café life and say that one lost one's force there. No matter when one called on Brancusi, he was at work, and yet he always found time to be genial. He is, in his simplicity, truly saintly. He now drinks only hot water, of which he says, "It cures you of everything, even of love". Brancusi and Modigliani were not friendly when I first knew them, but later became so. I remember Brancusi telling me of how at one period he had rescued Modigliani out of the clutches of a rapacious dealer, who had practically immured him, in order to exploit him, in a cellar. He was without decent clothing and ashamed to go out. Brancusi had gone and bought a pair of trousers and a jersey, so that he could make a get-away.

Brancusi's sculpture has in many quarters too great an influence, and he is the origin even of much commercial art, influencing the mannequins that one sees in the shop windows. Strange that what seemed then so novel should become banal through its popularity in Fifth Avenue, and later in Regent Street shops. Through their imitation and commercialisation, seemingly new and æsthetic forms became in their turn quite commonplace. Brancusi is not to be blamed for this, and I think he looked with dismay on this imitation and spreading of his doctrine. African sculpture, no doubt, influenced Brancusi, but to me he exclaimed against its influence. One must not imitate Africans, he often said. Another of his sayings was directed against Michelangelo, for his realism. He would pluck at the back of his hand and pinch the flesh, "Michelangelo", he would say, "beef steak!"

This period in Paris was in itself, from the point of view of working, arid. For one reason or another I did little work, and in the end got very exasperated with Paris, and determined to go back to England —if possible get into some solitary place to work. This was actually an intense reaction to my life in Paris which, more than at any other period that I can recall, was one of fruitless attempts to settle down and carry through some new work. I remember that when I had taken a studio and started carving, no sooner had I got started than my neighbour, who lived below, complained of my hammering. He was a baker who only slept during the day. The landlord explained that it was a painter's studio and not a sculptor's. These rows and continual interruptions finally decided me to leave Paris for good, and coming to England I rented a bungalow on the Sussex coast at a solitary place called Pett Level, where I could look out to sea and carve away to my heart's content without troubling a soul. It was here I carved the "Venus", the three groups of doves, the two flenite carvings and the marble "Mother and Child", now in the possession of Miss Sally Ryan of New York who has lent it to the Museum of Modern Art. This was a period of intense activity and were it not for the war and the impossibility of living in the country and making a living, I would have stayed there forever. With the war came difficulties. A sculptor living on the coast was beyond the understanding of the military authorities, and I had several visits from inspectors who were puzzled as to why I should choose to live there and occupy myself with something they could not quite make out. As one official put it suspiciously in questioning me, "You are an alleged sculptor, are you not?" These petty vexations and a bombing raid by Zeppelins decided me to move away altogether, and I shipped my sculpture to London with regret, giving up a place where I had been very happy and where I had had a very fruitful period of work.

6

THE TOMB OF OSCAR WILDE: 1912

I HEARD of the commission to do the tomb of Oscar Wilde the day
after it had been announced at a dinner given to Robert Ross by
his friends at the Ritz. I neither knew of this dinner nor of its
being made the occasion for an announcement that I was to receive
a commission to design a tomb for Wilde. In the morning when
friends rang me up to congratulate me I imagined a hoax was being
played upon me. The rumour was confirmed later in the day, and I
believe the secrecy with regard to me can only be explained by the
fact that other sculptors knew of the commission and expected it to
be given them, and the trustee for the monument, Robert Ross, was
too timid to let it be known that I would be offered the work for fear
of what these sculptors might do to hinder the plan.

Ross was Wilde's literary executor, and the secrecy maintained
with regard to me is otherwise inexplicable. I had only just finished
the British Medical Association figures, and this important commission, following immediately after, was a matter of some excitement. It took me some time to get started on the work. I made
sketches and carried them out, but I was dissatisfied and scrapped
quite completed work. Finally I determined on the present design,
and I went to Derbyshire to the Hopton Wood stone quarries where
I saw an immense block which had just been quarried preparatory
to cutting it up into thin slabs for wall-facings. I bought this mono-
lith, weighing twenty tons, on the spot, and had it transported to my
London studio. I began the work immediately and without hesitation
continued to labour at it for nine months. I carved a flying demon-
angel across the face, a symbolic work of combined simplicity and
ornate decoration, and no doubt influenced by antique carving. For

me its merit lay in its being a direct carving and on a grand scale. When it was finished I threw open my studio and had it shown, and what notice there was in the Press was singularly favourable. I never looked forward to the reception the work was to receive at the hands of the Paris authorities. *The Evening Standard,* which had attacked my Strand Statues with such virulence, took a different tone and even headed its article, "Mr. J. Epstein's dignified sculpture".*

The work was transported to Paris and erected in its place over the remains of Oscar Wilde. It actually is a tomb and not just a grave monument. On the back of the tomb is carved the inscription:

> *And alien tears shall fill for him*
> *Pity's long-broken urn*
> *For his mourners will be outcast men,*
> *And outcasts always mourn.*

When I arrived at Père Lachaise cemetery and saw the monument finally in place, I was suddenly confronted with a formidable apparition in the shape of a certain Comtesse de Brement, who upbraided me for what she considered a horrible insult to her dear dead friend Oscar. At the same time she informed me that she had come to get a story for the Paris *Daily Mail,* of course a story that would not be to my credit. I recall that this Comtesse de Brement, an American lady, very large, and very blonde, had been brought to my studio in London to see the finished carving, and had with difficulty been persuaded to leave the studio. Her admiration was such that she had asked me if she could see the monument at midnight, and preferably by moonlight. I of course refused this, and here she was filled with indignation. As I remained calm her hysteria died down, and when I left she was kneeling at the foot of the carving crossing herself and murmuring prayers.

I was still at work putting the finishing carving to the head at the cemetery, when arriving one morning I found the tomb covered with an enormous tarpaulin, and a gendarme standing beside it. He informed me that the tomb was banned. I would not be allowed to work on it. I waited, and when the gendarme moved off I removed the tarpaulin and started working. The gendarme, returning from his stroll, gravely shook his head and replaced the tarpaulin, ex-

* This article will be found in the Appendix: The Tomb of Oscar Wilde: 1912.

pressing his disapproval of my conduct. Thereafter the gendarme stayed with the work. I returned a few days later with a company of French artists to show it to them, and I had again to remove the tarpaulin with the usual protests from the gendarme who came hurrying up.

Artists and writers who heard of the ban on the tomb took the matter up, and manifestoes and protests in the Paris Press followed. I was given to understand by Robert Ross that the work was considered indecent, and he asked me if I would modify it. There was no indecency in the monument, and I refused to do anything that would admit I had done an indecent work. Thereupon Ross set about finding someone who would do as he wished. In the meantime, the French artists and writers had produced a very remarkable protest against the action of the Prefecture of the Seine. Articles and letters by famous writers, Remy de Gourmont and Laurent Tailhade, appeared.

I think the story of this French protest—a protest by famous men of letters and artists—so important that a reproduction of these articles becomes a matter of historic documentation, and I give them in an Appendix,* more or less in the order of their appearance.

While this tremendous protest was being made, the great Rodin himself failed the supporters of the monument for reasons peculiar to himself. A beautiful Russian-English girl, who knew Rodin, volunteered to go as an emissary to solicit his support with photographs of the tomb. Without looking at the photographs, Rodin started to upbraid her for bringing to his notice the work of a young sculptor who, he imagined, was her lover, and declared he would do nothing to help her. A plain girl would have been a better emissary to Rodin.

It only remains to add that a petition organised by Lytton Strachey to have the money refunded which I had had to expend on duties to take the monument into France failed of its object. The petition was as follows:

31st July, 1912.

The sculptor, Epstein, has just completed the Tomb of Oscar Wilde which is going to be placed in the cemetery of Père Lachaise. It is estimated that the customs duty will amount to £120 at the least, in consequence of the value of the stone which the artist used. The monument

* See Appendix: The Tomb of Oscar Wilde: 1912

is a serious and interesting work of art, destined for public position in Paris.

It is dedicated to the memory of the famous English poet and author, Oscar Wilde. Given these circumstances, it is suggested to us that we should make some approach to those concerned in the French Government in order to obtain an exemption from Customs duty. The æsthetic merit of this work by Mr. Epstein and the public interest it has awakened lead us to hope that the artist could be freed from this onerous charge. We think that the favour of such an exemption would be in full conformity with the fine tradition of the French nation, which is so justly renowned for its attitude of enlightened munificence towards the arts.

GEORGE BERNARD SHAW, H. G. WELLS, JOHN LAVERY, ROBERT ROSS, LEON BAKST.

The monument was altered. Robert Ross had a large plaque modelled and cast in bronze, and fitted to the figure, as a fig-leaf is applied. A band of artists and poets subsequently made a raid upon the monument and removed this plaque; and one evening in the Café Royal a man appeared wearing this affair suspended from his neck, and approaching me explained its significance. The monument remained covered by the tarpaulin until the outbreak of the war, when it was removed without remark.

I have only to add to the foregoing account of the Oscar Wilde tomb that my relations with Robert Ross were on the whole very cordial. On one or two occasions there were slight disagreements over the length of time I took to do the monument, and this affected the payments on account. These disputes were settled in my favour, but as rumours magnifying every incident connected with Wilde or the tomb were rife, I was told that Ross had deposited a memorandum at the British Museum concerning the working out of the tomb, which gives his version of any disputes which arose. I can regard any memorandum with equanimity, if one really exists, and my account, I hope, will stand against any perversion of the facts.

Robert Ross saw the tomb while it was in the course of carving, and when it was finished visited my studio several times. Never once did he find anything wrong with it, and he wrote to *The Pall Mall Gazette* a witty letter defending the work which I give here.

Portrait of the Sculptor, 1911

MASK OF MEUM, 1918

The Tomb of Oscar Wilde: 1912

Sir,

I will be much obliged if you will kindly correct the statement of *Le Journal* reproduced in *The Observer* and the London evening papers of Saturday.

M. Lepine cannot have ordered any postponement of the unveiling of Mr. Epstein's beautiful monument to Wilde for the very good reason that no date had been fixed for the ceremony. Even the police cannot postpone an unfixed date. The monument would in ordinary course have remained veiled at my own instructions until the ceremony. It is true that the police have taken official possession of this unique work of art, of which I am sure they will take the greatest care.

I regard the arrest of the monument by the French authorities simply as a graceful outcome of the Entente Cordiale and a symptom on the part of our allies to prove themselves worthy of political union with our great nation, which, rightly or wrongly, they think has always put Propriety before everything. I hesitate to say that the rest lies in the lap of the gods, because that is precisely the part of the statue to which exception is taken.

Yours, etc.,

London, *Sept.* 28.   ROBERT ROSS.

7

ROCK DRILL: 1913–1914

IT was in the experimental pre-war days of 1913 that I was fired to do the rock drill, and my ardour for machinery (short-lived) expended itself upon the purchase of an actual drill, second-hand, and upon this I made and mounted a machine-like robot, visored, menacing, and carrying within itself its progeny, protectively ensconced. Here is the armed, sinister figure of to-day and to-morrow. No humanity, only the terrible Frankenstein's monster we have made ourselves into. I exhibited this work complete in plaster at the London Group, and I remember Gaudier Brzeska was very enthusiastic about it when he visited my studio in 1913 with Ezra Pound to view it. Pound started expatiating on the work. Gaudier turned on him and snapped, "Shut up, you understand nothing!"

Later I lost my interest in machinery and discarded the drill. I cast in metal only the upper part of the figure.

In reviewing this period and its concern with abstract forms, I cannot see that sculptors who took up abstraction later and used it made any advance on the 1913–14 period, or produced more novel forms, although with surrealism came in the use of mannequins from shop windows and castings from life; also the incorporation of loaves of bread, lunatic collections of nails, and bird-cages. Actual movement is not novel either, for I had thought of attaching pneumatic power to my rock drill, and setting it in motion, thus completing every potentiality of form and movement in one single work. All this I realised was really child's play, and was like those toy circuses that children get going and which fill them with such excitement. This kind of excitement is far removed from the nature of the æsthetic experience and satisfaction that sculpture should give. In our attempts to extend the range of sculpture we are led into extravagance and puerility. What is sad is to see the younger generation adopting these out-worn originalities, thinking they are doing so where we left off; and, with conceit of youth, imagining themselves innovators who have inherited, and are surpassing, the achievements of their elders. When I returned to a normal manner of working, and was so bold as again to carve and model a face with its features, the advanced critics spoke of my having "thrown in the sponge". I was lost to the movement. I feel easy about this. The discipline of simplification of forms, unity of design, and co-ordination of masses is all to the good, and I think this discipline has influenced me in my later works like the "Behold the Man" and the "Adam". But to think of abstraction as an end in itself is undoubtedly letting oneself be led into a cul-de-sac and can only lead to exhaustion and impotence.

EZRA POUND'S ESTIMATE FROM "THE EGOIST",
16th March, 1914

The exhibition of new art now showing at the Goupil Gallery deserves the attention of everyone interested in either painting or sculpture. The latter art is represented by the work of Epstein and of Gaudier Brzeska. I endeavoured to praise these men about a month ago, and shall again so endeavour.

Jacob Epstein has sent in three pieces: a "Group of Birds" placid with an eternal placidity existing in the permanent places. They have that greatest quality of art, to wit: certitude.

"A Bird Pluming Itself" is like a cloud bent back upon itself—not a woolly cloud, but one of those clouds that are blown smooth by the wind. It is gracious and aerial.

These things are great art because they are sufficient in themselves. They exist apart, unperturbed by the pettiness and the daily irritation of a world full of Claude Phillipses and Saintsburys and of the constant bickerings of uncomprehending minds. They infuriate the denizens of this superficial world because they ignore it. Its impotences and its importances do not affect them. Representing, as they do, the immutable, the calm thoroughness of unchanging relations, they are as the gods of the Epicureans, apart, unconcerned, unrelenting.

This is no precious or affected self-binding aloofness. Mr. Epstein has taken count of all the facts. He is in the best sense, realist.

The green flenite woman expresses all the tragedy and enigma of the germinal universe: she also is permanent, unescaping.

This work infuriates the superficial mind, it takes no count of this morning's leader; of transient conditions. It has the solemnity of Egypt.

It is no use saying that Epstein is Egyptian and that Brzeska is Chinese. Nor would I say that the younger man is a follower of the elder. They approach life in different manners.

Brzeska is in a formative stage, he is abundant and pleasing. His animals have what one can only call a "snuggly", comfortable feeling, that might appeal to a child. A very young child would like them to play with, if they were not stone and too heavy.

Of the two animal groups, his stags are the more interesting if considered as a composition of forms. "The Boy with a Coney" is "Chow", or suggests slightly the bronze animals of that period. Brzeska is as much concerned with representing certain phases of animal life as is Epstein with presenting some austere permanence; some relation of life and yet outside it. It is as if some realm of "Ideas", of Platonic patterns, were dominated by Hathor. There is in his work an austerity, a metaphysics, like that of Egypt—one doesn't know quite how to say it. All praise of works of art is very possibly futile—were it not that one finds among many scoffers a few people of good will who are eager for this new art and not quite ready.

It is perhaps unfitting for a layman to attempt technicalities, the planes of Mr. Epstein's work seem to sink away from their outline with a curious determination and swiftness.

Last evening I watched a friend's parrot outlined against a hard grey-silver twilight. That is a stupid way of saying that I had found a new detail or a new correlation with Mr. Epstein's stone birds. I saw anew that something masterful had been done. I got a closer idea of a particular kind of decision.

EZRA POUND.

THE LONDON GROUP AND FUTURISTS

The London Group gathered together before the war the best of the English artists, and looking back at it, I contrast it with present-day groups who must stick together like thieves for self-protection, in a "united we stand" attitude, rather than for any respect they have for each other, or enthusiasm for the common weal of Art. There was an integrity about the painters and sculptors in the London Group which is lacking to-day. In fact, it was the incursion into the Group of the Abstractionists that caused the Saturday afternoon gatherings to break up.

It was at this period that Mr. Marinetti turned up with his futurists.

ADMIRAL LORD FISHER, 1915

LILLIAN SHELLEY, 1919

They were pre-Fascists, and with true Fascist impertinence they went from city to city spreading themselves and their silly gospel, and showing their incompetent paintings and sculpture. In England we are very ready to receive what seems novel and exciting, on condition that it is superficial enough and entertaining enough. So these Italian charlatans were received with open arms. At an exhibition of Futuristic Art, I remember Marinetti turned up with a few twigs he had found in Hyde Park, and a tooth-brush and a match-box tied together with string. He called this "The New Sculpture", and hung it from the chandelier. This was the beginning of those monkey tricks we see elaborated to-day in Paris, in London, and in New York. Marinetti, when reciting his own poems, used an amount of energy that was astonishing, pouring with perspiration, and the veins swelling, almost to bursting-point, on his forehead. Altogether an unpleasant sight. Before beginning his own poems he would recite a poem of Baudelaire and demolish it as he thought. He would then proceed to imitate the chatter of machine-guns, the booming of cannons, and the whirr of aeroplane engines. On this occasion, one of our "rebels" beat a big drum for him at appropriate moments. Apart from these unusual antics, Marinetti's "poems" were of a commonplaceness and banality that was appalling. He was a stupid-looking man, and his impudence was as great as his energy. Of course, he was the model for our own English futurists, abstractionists, and careerists. Personally, I had no sympathy with his nonsense and show. It became very tiresome, as all spoofy and artificial entertainment does, and the novelty soon wore out. Marinetti went back to give birth to Mussolini, and our own rebels have since made frantic efforts to enter the Royal Academy.

T. E. HULME AND HIS FRIENDS

At this period (1912) I got to know T. E. Hulme very well. His evenings, always on Tuesdays, at a house in Frith Street, were gatherings that attracted many of the intellectuals and artists. Hulme was a large man in bulk, and also large and somewhat abrupt in manner. He had the reputation of being a bully and arrogant, because of his abruptness. He was really of a candid and original nature like that of Samuel Johnson, and only his intolerance of sham made him feared.

Personally I think he was of a generous and singularly likeable character, and with artists he was humble and always willing to learn. In his own subjects of philosophy and religion he was a profound student, and he made short shrift of the pretentious when it came to discussing philosophy. Of this side of him I understood little, although I often listened to his argumentative exegesis.

He had translated Bergson for the first time into English, and had written on Sorel and Croce, and the many violent discussions in Frith Street interested and amused me. Mrs. Kibblewhite and her sister Dora were the hostesses at the parties, and their old father, who was a designer in stained-glass windows, sometimes looked in.

The company, mostly workers in intellectual fields, included Ford Madox Hueffer as he was then called, later Ford Madox Ford (I remember him as a very pontifical person), Ashley Dukes, A. R. Orage, editor of *The New Age*, Douglas Ainslie, Richard Curle, Sir Edward Marsh, Wyndham Lewis, Ezra Pound, Richard Aldington, Ramiro de Maeztu, who later became Spanish Ambassador to the Argentine, and many others. Among artists, Charles Ginner, Harold Gilman, Gaudier Brzeska, and Spencer Gore, Madame Karlowska, and Robert Bevan. I remember having an amusing argument on one occasion with Stanley Spencer concerning a statue of Buddha on the mantelpiece. When Spencer was asked what he thought of it, he shuddered and said he knew nothing of Asiatic art, as he was a Christian. I asked him what part of the world Christ came from. Spencer was of that school of philosophers who will not drink coffee because it is not grown in England. Hulme, to attract so large and varied a company of men, must have had a quality, I should say, of great urbanity, and his broad-mindedness, I maintain, only ceased when he met humbug and pretentiousness.

Someone once asked him how long he would tolerate Ezra Pound, and Hulme thought for a moment and then said that he knew already exactly when he would have to kick him downstairs.

From Gaudier Brzeska he commissioned some small works which Gaudier thought it great fun to do. These were small brass carvings in a somewhat abstract style, and Hulme would carry them about in his pocket and handle them while talking. Hulme excluded women for the most part from his evenings, as he said the sex element interfered with intellectual talk. A confession of his own weakness. Although certain women frankly detested him, he was a virile type of man, and he once humorously confessed that his extensive knowledge of the geography of outlying parts of London came entirely from his suburban love-affairs.

I remember his astonishment when a book of D. H. Lawrence appeared which was entirely concerned with sex. To his mind this was inexplicable. He attributed this book, not without reason, to a lack of virility on the part of the author. Hulme, although he never lived to fulfil the great promise his remarkable mind and character foreshadowed, yet has aroused tremendous interest by what are really only fragments of his projected works. He was a great conversationalist, and he admitted to being lazy, and always said that as he had plenty of time to do his work in, he was in no hurry. He also projected a large family, and felt he had plenty of time for that too. He was killed by a German shell while serving in the Royal Marine Artillery at Nieuport in Flanders on September 27th, 1917. A book he had written on my sculpture, and which he had with him in manuscript, disappeared from his effects, and has never turned up. Later I met a naval man by accident in a train, who belonged to Hulme's unit, about a year after his death, and I questioned him. He remembered Hulme very well, and recalled that during one of the recurring bombardments, a shell came over which Hulme, apparently absorbed in some thoughts of his own, failed to hear. He kept standing up, paying no attention, when all the others in his company had thrown themselves down flat.

The news of his death, when it reached London, caused widespread pain and sorrow; he had been so much and so strongly alive. It was difficult, for a long time, to believe that he was physically dead. We all felt a personal loss.

I had modelled a head of him which was in the possession of Mrs. Kibblewhite, and it passed, I believe, to Ashley Dukes.

Orage was a man of extraordinary mental vigour. He had a magnetic personality, attracting people by his conversation. His charm of voice and manner drew listeners to him, and he went about like a Greek philosopher or rhetor, with a following of disciples. Hulme also had this following. As between the two, Hulme was the more solid man—the more profound mind. Orage was undoubtedly greatly under the influence of him at onetime. After Hulme's death Orage came under the influence of the Russian Gurdjieff, who had a house near Versailles where he gathered men and women together to lead a new life, and learn a new philosophy. Many mysterious stories were told of this place. In any case, Orage later went to America as a fisher of men, as it were, and also women—in all cases, wealthy men and women for this establishment.

I recall that I had not been long in New York in 1927 on my visit there, when I ran into Orage, and he took me along to a cocktail party where I met Carl Van Vechten and Paul Robeson.

Orage was there lecturing, and gathering the pupils for the Versailles Abbaye Theleme. One poor old lady I met at Orage's flat complained that she had wished to join the sacred group, but was afraid that her bank balance was not large enough, and she had, for that reason, been rejected. I noticed there, around Orage, cranks of all sorts. I believe this mission came to an end, and Orage returned to England to try and resuscitate *The New Age*, but it was finished beyond recall. *The New Age* was no longer new. The life had gone out of it. The lovable spirit that was Orage also took flight suddenly.

In closing this note on Hulme and his friends, I have not mentioned that on many an occasion Hulme very effectively defended me against what he considered unfair attacks. Hulme in controversy wielded a trenchant pen, and was never taken in by rhetoric, however distinguished the person was who resorted to it. I remember he had been listening to Frank Harris one night in the Café Royal; Frankie, as his friends called him, had been going on in his usual high-falutin, bombastic manner for a long time; Hulme turned to me and said, "The poor man! He has stopped thinking".

T. E. Hulme's keenly discerning articles in *The New Age* about the direction of the First World War, written for good reasons under the *nom de plume* "North Staffs" will be of very vivid and present-day interest to anyone who now cares to dig them up.

His death was a loss to England. The fine measuring instrument that was his mind would, in the last thirty-five years, have shown up many a dark patch of pretence and sham and pomposity, and cleared away many weeds that have penetrated from being only troublesome undergrowths into the high places in the world of art and literature and philosophy.

Rock Drill: 1913–1914

The New Age, December 25th, 1913:

MR. EPSTEIN AND THE CRITICS

By *T. E. Hulme*

I begin with an apology. All through this article I write about Mr. Epstein's work in a way which I recognise is wrong, in that it is what an artist would call literary. The appreciation of a work of art must be plastic or nothing. But I defend myself in this way, that I am not so much writing directly about Mr. Epstein's work as engaged in the more negative and quite justifiable business of attempting to protect the spectator from certain prejudices which are in themselves literary. This is an article, then, not so much on Epstein as on his critics. When I see the critics attempting to corrupt the mind of the spectators and trying to hinder their appreciation of a great artist, I feel an indignation which must be my excuse for these clumsy, hurriedly written and unrevised notes.

An attack on critics could not have a better subject matter than the Press notices on Mr. Epstein's show. They exhibit a range and variety of fatuousness seldom equalled. It is not necessary to spend any time over notices which, like that of "C. B." in *The Athenæum*, are merely spiteful, or that in *The Illustrated London News*, which compared him unfavourably with the Exhibition of Humorous Artists. I propose rather to deal with those which, in appearance, at any rate, profess to deal seriously with his work.

Take first the merely nervous. Their method is continually to refer to Mr. Epstein as a great artist and at the same time to deplore everything he does. It reminds one of the old philosophical disputes about substance. Would anything remain of a "thing" if all its qualities were taken away? What is the metaphysical nature of an artist's excellence that seems to manifest itself in no particular thing he does? The truth is, of course, that they dare not say what they really think. The particular kind of gift which enables a man to be an art critic is not the possession of an instinct which tells them what pictures are good or bad, but of a different kind of instinct which leads them to recognise the people who do know. This is, of course, in itself a comparatively rare instinct. Once they have obtained a "direction" in this way, their own literary capacity enables them to expand it to any desired length. You can, however, always tell this from a certain emptiness in their rhetoric (cf. Arthur Symons' article on Rodin). There is no one to give them a "direction" about Mr. Epstein's drawings, and they are at a loss. They seek refuge in praise of the "Romilly John", which has been universally admitted to be one of the finest bronzes since the Renaissance.

I come now to the most frequent and the most reasonable criticism; that directed against the "Carvings in Flenite". It is generally stated in a rather confused way, but I think that it can be analysed out into two separate prejudices. The first is that an artist has no business to use formulæ taken from another civilisation. The second is that, even if the formula the artist uses is the natural means of expressing certain of his emotions, yet these emotions must be unnatural in him, a modern Western. I shall attempt to show that the first objection really has its root in the second, and that this second prejudice is one which runs through almost every activity at the present time. These "Carvings in Flenite", we are told, are "deliberate imitations of Easter Island carvings". This seems to me to depend on a misconception of the nature of formulæ. Man remaining constant, there are certain broad ways in which certain emotions must, and will always naturally, be expressed, and these we must call formulæ. They constitute a constant and permanent alphabet. The thing to notice is that the use of these broad formulæ has nothing to do with the possession of or lack of individuality in the artist. That comes out in the way the formulæ are used. If I or the King of the Zulus want to walk, we both put one leg before the other; that is the universal formula, but there the resemblance ends. To take another illustration, which I don't want to put forward as literally true, but which I only use for purpose of illustration. A certain kind of nostalgia and attenuated melancholy is expressed in Watteau by a formula of tall trees and minute people, and a certain use of colour (I am also aware that he got this feeling, in the Gilles, for example, by a quite other formula, but I repeat I am only giving a sort of hypothetical illustration). It would be quite possible at the present day for a painter, wishing to express the same kind of emotion, to use the same broad formula quite naturally, and without any imitation of Watteau. The point is, that, given the same emotion, the same broad formula comes naturally to the hands of any people in any century.

I have wandered into this bypath merely to find therein an illustration which will help us to understand the repugnance of the critic to the "Carvings in Flenite". It is, says the critic, "rude savagery, flouting respectable tradition-vague memories of dark ages as distant from modern feeling as the loves of the Martians". Modern feeling be damned! As if it was not the business of every honest man at the present moment to clean the world of these sloppy dregs of the Renaissance. This carving, by an extreme abstraction, by the selection of certain lines, gives an effect of tragic greatness. The important point about this is that the tragedy is of an order more intense than any conception of life. This, I think, is the real root of the objection to these statues, that they express emotions which are, as a matter of fact, entirely alien and unnatural to the critic. But that is a very different thing from their being unnatural to the artist. My justification of these statues would be then: (1) that an alien formula is justifiable when it is the necessary expression of a certain attitude; and (2) that in the peculiar conditions in which we find ourselves, which are really the breaking up of an era, it has again become quite possible for people here and there to have the attitude expressed by these formulæ.

I have dealt with these in rather a literary way, because I think that in this case it is necessary to get semi-literary prejudices out of the way, before the carvings can be seen as they should be seen, i.e. plastically.

To turn now to the drawings which have been even more misunderstood by the critics than the carvings. I only want to make a few necessary notes about these, as I am dealing with them at greater length in an essay elsewhere. I need say very little about the magnificent drawing reproduced in this paper, for it stands slightly apart from the others and seems to have been found intelligible even by the critics. I might, perhaps, say something about the representative element in it—a man is working a Rock Drill mounted on a tripod, the lines of which, in the drawing, continue the lines of his legs. The two lines converging on the centre of the design are indications of a rocky landscape. It is the other drawings which seem to have caused the most bewildered criticism; they have been called prosaic representations of anatomical details, "medical drawings", and so on. It is perfectly obvious that they are not that. What prevents them being understood as expressions of ideas is quite a simple matter. People will admire the "Rock Drill", because they have no preconceived notion as to how the thing expressed by it should be expressed. But with the other drawings concerned with birth the case is different. Take, for example, the drawing called "Creation", a baby seen inside many folds. I might very roughly say that this was a non-sentimental restatement of an idea which, presented sentimentally and in the traditional manner, they would admire— an idea something akin to the "Christmas crib" idea. If a traditional symbol had been used they would have been quite prepared to admire it. They cannot understand that the genius and sincerity of an artist lies in extracting afresh, from outside reality, a new means of expression. It seems curious that the people who in poetry abominate clichés and know that Nature, as it were, presses in on the poet to be used as metaphor, cannot understand the same thing when it occurs plastically. They seem unable to understand that an artist who has something to say will continually "extract" from reality new methods of expression, and that these being personally felt will inevitably lack prettiness and will differ from traditional clichés. It may also be pointed out that the critics have probably themselves not been accustomed to think about generation, and so naturally find the drawings not understandable. I come now to the stupidest criticism of all, that of Mr. Ludovici. It would probably occur to anyone who read Mr. Ludovici's article that he was a charlatan, but I think it worth while confirming this impression by further evidence. His activities are not confined to art. I remember coming across his name some years ago as the author of a very comical little book on Nietzsche, which was sent me for review.

I shall devote some space to him here then, not because I consider him of the slightest importance, but because I consider it a duty, a very pleasant duty and one very much neglected in this country, to expose charlatans when one sees them. Apart from this general ground, the book on Nietzsche is worth considering, for it displays the same type of mind at work as in the article on art.

What, very briefly then, is the particular type of charlatan revealed in this book on Nietzsche. It gave one the impression of a little Cockney intellect which would have been more suitably employed indexing or in a lawyer's office, drawn by a various kind of vanity into a region the realities of which must for ever remain incomprehensible to him. Mr. Ludovici, writing on Nietzsche, might be compared to a child of four in a theatre watching a tragedy based on adultery. The child would observe certain external phenomena, but as to the real structure of the tragedy, its real moving forces, it would naturally be rather hazy. You picture, then, a spruce little mind that has crept into the complicated rafters of philosophy —you imagine him perplexed, confused: you would be quite wrong, the apperceptive system acts like a stencil, it blots out all the complexity which forms the reality of the subject, so that he is simply unaware of its existence. He sees only what is akin to his mind's manner of working, as dogs out for a walk only scent other dogs and as a Red Indian in a great town for the first time sees only the horses. While thus in reality remaining entirely outside the subject, he can manage to produce a shoddy imitation which may pass here in England, where there is no organised criticism by experts, but which in other countries, less happily democratic in these matters, would at once have been characterised as a piece of fudge. I have only drawn attention to this in order to indicate the particular type of charlatan we have to deal with, so that you may know what to expect when you come to consider him as an art critic. I want to insist on the fact that you must expect to find a man dealing with a subject which is in reality alien to him, ignorant of the aims of the actors in that subject and yet maintaining an appearance of adequate treatment with the help of a few tags.

That a man should write stupid and childish things about Nietzsche

MASK OF MRS. EPSTEIN, 1916

MRS. EPSTEIN, 1918

does not perhaps matter very much; after all, we can read him for our-selves. But when a little bantam of this kind has the impertinence to refer to Mr. Epstein as a "minor personality—of no interest to him", then the matter becomes so disgusting that it has to be dealt with. The most appropriate means of dealing with him would be a little personal violence. By that method one removes a nuisance without drawing more attention to it than its insignificance deserves. But the unworthy sentiment of pity for the weak, which, in spite of Nietzsche, still moves us, prevents us dealing drastically with this rather lightweight superman. To deal definitely, then, with his criticism. He dismissed Mr. Epstein with the general principle "Great art can only appear when the artist is animated by the spirit of some great order or scheme of life." I agree with this. Experience confirms it. We find that the more serious kind of art that one likes sprang out of organic societies like the Indian, Egyptian, and Byzantine. The modern obviously imposes too great a strain on an artist, the double burden of not only expressing something, but of finding something in himself to be expressed. The more organic society effects an economy in this. Moreover, you might go so far as to say that the imposition of definite forms does not confine the artist, but rather has the effect of intensifying the individuality of his work (of Egyptian portraits). I agree, then, with his general principle: we all agree. It is one of those obvious platitudes which all educated people take for granted, in conversation and in print. It seems almost too comic for belief, but I begin to suspect from Mr. Ludovici's continued use of the word "I" in connection with this principle, that he is under the extraordinary hallucination that the principle is a personal discovery of his own. Really, Mr. Ludo, you mustn't teach your grandmother to suck eggs in this way. That you should have read of these truths in a book and have seen that they were true is so much to the good. It is a fact of great interest to your father and mother, it shows that you are growing up; but I can assure you it is a matter of no public interest.

Admitting, then, as I do, that the principle is true, I fail to see how it enables Mr. Ludovici to dismiss Mr. Epstein, in the way he does, on *a priori* grounds. The same general principle would enable us to dismiss every artist since the Renaissance. Take two very definite examples, Michelangelo and Blake, neither of whom expressed any general "scheme of life", imposed on them by society, but "exalted the individual angle of vision of minor personalities".

The whole thing is entirely beside the point. The business of an art critic is not to repeat tags, but to apply them to individual works of art. But, of course, that is precisely what a charlatan of the kind I have just described cannot do. It is quite possible for him in each gallery he goes to to find some opportunity of repeating his tags, but when (as he was in his book on Nietzsche) he is entirely outside the subject, when he is really unaware of the nature of the thing which artists are trying to do, when he gets no real fun out of the pictures themselves, then, when he is pinned down before one actual picture and not allowed to wriggle away, he must either be dumb or make an ass of himself. It is quite easy to learn to repeat tags about "balance", but put the man before one picture and make him follow with his finger the lines which constitute that "balance" and he can only shuffle and bring out more tags.

That a critic of this calibre should attempt to patronise Mr. Epstein is disgusting. I make this very hurried protest in the hope that I may induce those people who have perhaps been prejudiced by ignorant and biased criticism to go and judge for themselves.

8

PORTRAITS

I N my portraits it is assumed that I start out with a definite conception of my sitter's character. On the contrary, I have no such
conception whatever in the beginning. The sitter arrives in the
studio, mounts the stand, and I begin my study. My aim, to start
with, is entirely constructive. With scientific precision I make a quite
coldly thought out construction of the form, giving the bony forma-
tions around the eyes, the ridge of the nose, mouth, and cheek-bones,
and defining the relation of the different parts of the skull to each
other. As the work proceeds, I note the expression, and the changes
of expression, and the character of the model begins to impress itself
on me. In the end, by a natural process of observation, the mental
and physiological characteristics of the sitter impose themselves upon
the clay. This process is natural and not preconceived. With close
and intensive study come subtleties and fine shades. From turning
the work round so as to catch every light, comes that solidity that
makes the work light-proof, as it were. For in a work of sculpture the
forms actually alter with the change of light, not as in a painting or
drawing, where the forms only become more or less visible. In Ibsen's
When We Dead Awaken there is a sculptor depicted as a disillusioned,
embittered man, who is, I should say, the contrary of what a sculptor
should be. I will quote what he says of his sitters (Act 1):

MAIA. Do you think it is better then—do you think it is worthy of you
to do nothing at all but a portrait-bust now and then?

PROF. RUBEK (*with a sly smile*). They are not exactly portrait-busts
that I turn out, Maia.

MAIA. Yes indeed they are—for the last two or three years—ever since
you finished your great group and it got out of the house . . .

PROF. RUBEK. All the same they are no mere portrait-busts, I assure you.

MAIA. What are they then?

PROF. RUBEK. There is something equivocal, something cryptic, lurking in and behind these busts—a secret something, that the people themselves cannot see.

MAIA. Indeed?

PROF. RUBEK (*decisively*). I alone can see it. And it amuses me unspeakably. On the surface I give them the striking likeness, as they call it, that they all stand and gape at it in astonishment—(*lowers his voice*)—but at the bottom they are all respectable, pompous, horse-faced, and self-opinionated donkey muzzles, and lop-eared, low-browed dog-skulls, and fatted swine-snouts—and sometimes dull brutal bull-fronts as well.

MAIA (*indifferently*). All the dear domestic animals in fact.

PROF. RUBEK. Simply the dear domestic animals, Maia. All the animals which men have bedevilled in their own image—and which have bedevilled men in their turn. (*Empties his champagne glass and laughs.*) And it is these double-faced works of art that our excellent plutocrats come and order of me. And pay for in all good faith—and in good round figures too —almost their weight in gold as the saying goes.

Naturally, a sculptor like this could never arrive at the truth about a person. It is said that the sculptor as an artist always depicts himself in his work, even in his portraits. In only one sense is this true, that is in the sense in which the artist's own nature colours his outlook. To illustrate what I say, take a portrait of Franz Hals. We observe that his outlook on humanity is cold and detached, he observes his models without any emotions, and never warms to them. He seemed unfortunate in his sitters; as human beings they evidently aroused in him no feeling of sympathy, and he turned to their clothes with greater pleasure than he got from their faces. He obviously enjoyed his own technique and revelled in his marvellous skill.

With Rembrandt the opposite seems the case. His great heart seemed to warm towards the men and women who sat for him, and he seemed to penetrate into their inner selves, and reveal their very souls—in children their lively joy, and in grown-ups the burden of living, their sorrow and disappointments. There is a great wisdom in him, and his people look out of his canvases, human beings whose trades and businesses you cannot tell, but they have deep human thoughts; they are not just tradesmen and shrews, as in Hals. A

JOSEPH CONRAD, 1924

PROFESSOR ALBERT EINSTEIN, 1933

beggar in the hands of Rembrandt is some ancient philosopher, a Diogenes content in his tub; a manservant in a borrowed cloak becomes a King of the East with splendour wreathing him round. So with the portraits of Goya. His men are witty, cynical, brutal, and his women lovely, gallant, and lecherous.

Rarely have I found sitters altogether pleased with their portraits. Understanding is rare, and the sitter usually wants to be flattered. How Goya ever "got away" with his superb portraits of the Spanish Royal Family is still an inexplicable mystery.

I recall the naïve expression of one of my sitters who asked me if his nose was as I depicted it, and when I assured him that it was so, cajolingly exclaimed, "Can't you cheat nature a little?"

Another will feel the bump at the back of his neck and look ruefully at my bust. On the whole, men sitters are more vain than women sitters. Shaw was terribly nervous about his bust, so was Priestley, and I have found that rarely does a wife see eye to eye with the artist. Always the artist "has just missed something" that she wants in or he has "put in something" that she has never observed.

My best portraits, of course, have been those of friends and people I have asked to sit for me. The model who just sits and leaves the artist to his own thoughts is the most helpful one. Not the model who imagines she is inspiring the artist. It seems to me that Mona Lisa said nothing, that "enigmatic" smile was quite enough for Leonardo to bother about.

I should like to say here that with most of my men portraits, I have been asked to work from them when they were very old, the reason for that being, I suppose, that they had not attained a fame worthy of commemoration earlier. What a relief it would be were I to be asked to do some notable person, say, in the hey-day of his physical and mental powers. Often my models, after a few minutes on the stand, go to sleep, and all I can see of them is the tops of their bald heads.

For the art of the portrait, I have noticed on the part of art critics a certain contempt. Sculptors themselves do not feel this contempt. On the contrary, it is the ambition of many sculptors to do a fine portrait, which they know is not easily arrived at. It is well not to be too dogmatic as to what is sculpture and what is not, for one must estimate as the highest expression of sculpture those Egyptian works, which were never meant to be anything but portraits; the Cephren in Cairo, or the Sheik El Beled. Personally I place my portrait work in as important a category as I place any other work of mine, and I am content to be judged by it.

The successful portrait sculptor or painter for that matter needs a front of brass, the hide of a rhinoceros, and all the guile of a courtier. While I have done a certain number of portraits, the history of those portraits is for the most part a story of failure to please the sitters or their relatives. Even my dealers are distrustful, and in one instance where I had exhibited the bust of a man and an inquiry was made with a view to purchasing a replica, the gallery was so sceptical about the sincerity of this inquiry that they coolly informed me they had not even taken the address of the inquirer. This, mind you, was one of my best portraits. When it comes to the statue of a famous man for commemoration, I will instance the Thomas Hardy memorial. When this memorial was under consideration I was approached informally by a member of the committee, with whom I discussed the project, and undertook to do the work, stating my fee. I heard nothing further about it, and one morning read in *The Times* that the memorial had been entrusted to a sculptor. A memorial to Thomas Hardy would have been a work that would test all the powers of the portrait sculptor, and I had really looked forward to the commission. To have portrayed the great novelist, so that not only his essential physical characteristics were shown, but also some sense of the over-burdening pessimism of his soul, something of the feeling of human frustration, was a work to call out all one's forces of evocation, also some suggestion of that elemental nature that is the background for Hardy's tragic characters. The statue produced was more than unfortunate. Hardy was represented as a dejected market gardener, with a trilby hat, seated, as he might appear on a Sunday morning, deploring a bad crop of spinach. Colonel T. E. Lawrence, who was on the Committee of the memorial, wrote early on to Sir Sidney Cockerell of Cambridge (August 29th, 1927) concerning the proposed memorial to Hardy. "Statues are so difficult, unless some-one quite first-rate does them. Epstein is the obvious choice." Yet after the first half-hearted approach I was passed over.

Sometimes the sitter impresses his or her own conception of them-

selves upon the artist. This can never result in a successful work—
one that renders the character of the model. Sir Hugh Walpole was
one of these sitters. He insisted in sitting to me like a Pharaoh, with
head held high and chin stuck out. In reality, Sir Hugh was the most
genial of men with sparkling, twinkling, humour in his eye, and his
mouth wreathed in a kindly and genial smile. But with the rigidity
of Sir Hugh's pose I could do nothing. I knew that the head was well
modelled, but as for a portrait of my model's real self, I never
thought it was that for a moment. It was Sir Hugh Walpole in the
rôle of Benito Mussolini.

JOSEPH CONRAD

Muirhead Bone had arranged that I should do a bust of Conrad
for him. I had desired, ten years before, to work from him and had
spoken to Richard Curle about it, but had been informed by him
that Conrad could not sit for me owing to the intervention of a
painter "friend". At the time I was deeply disappointed and dropped
the idea, but in 1924 the commission was finally arranged. My admiration for Conrad was immense, and he had a head that appealed
to a sculptor, massive and fine at the same time, so I jumped at the
idea of working from him at last. After a meeting in London it was
arranged with him that I should go down to his place at Oswalds.
near Canterbury, and—at my suggestion—should live in an inn in
a nearby village while working on the bust. This arrangement always
suits me best, as I prefer to be free outside my working hours.

I set out from London on a cold March morning, feeling somewhat ill and down-hearted. I hated working away from my studio,
amidst uncertain and perhaps disagreeable conditions. Before beginning a work I am timid and apprehensive. What will the lighting be?
A good start is everything, and with a subject like Conrad I wanted
to do justice to myself. My taxi contained my working materials,
stands, clay, and working tools. It seemed a long journey to Kent,
I arrived towards dark with snow falling. Conrad met me and we
arranged the room in which I should work, where I unpacked my
baggage. I was then conducted across a park to the village of Bridge
and the inn where I was to stay. This inn seemed to be of the gloomi-
est and coldest type. The whole mood of the place, with the sodden
country-side, promised a cheerless beginning.

The next morning I began the work. At the end of the sitting I did not know what to think of it, and felt altogether wretched. In the evening I wired for my five-year-old Peggy Jean to come. The second day, on the arrival of Peggy Jean, things looked better. Conrad was an absorbing study. He took posing seriously and gave me good long sittings until one o'clock, when we lunched and talked. Conrad from the beginning called me Cher Maître, embarrassing me by this mode of address from a much older man who was a great master of his own craft. His manners were courtly and direct, but his neurasthenia forced him at times to outbursts of rage and irritability with his household which quickly subsided. I already had a fairly clear notion as to how I should treat the bust. A sculptor had previously made a bust of him which represented him as an open-necked, romantic, out-of-door type of person. In appearance Conrad was the very opposite. His clothes were immaculately conventional, and his collar enclosed his neck like an Iron Maiden's vice or garrotter's grip. He was worried if his hair and beard were not trim and neat as became a sea captain. There was nothing shaggy or Bohemian about him. His glance was keen despite the drooping of one eyelid. He was the sea captain, the officer, and in our talks he emphasised the word "responsibility". Responsibility weighed on him and weighed him down. He used the word again and again and one immediately thought of *Lord Jim*—the conscience suffering at the evasion of duty. It may have been because of my meeting him late in life that Conrad gave me a feeling of defeat; but defeat met with courage.

He was crippled with rheumatism, crotchety, nervous, and ill. He said to me, "I am finished". There was pathos in his pulling out of a drawer his last manuscript to show me that he was still at work. There was no triumph in his manner, however, and he said that he did not know whether he would ever finish it. "I am played out," he said, "played out."

We talked after the sittings, mostly in the afternoons when we had tea together and Conrad was full of reminiscences about himself. We were usually alone. There, in this country house, he seemed to live alone although the house was filled with servants. A few visitors came at the weekends, but he appeared a lonely, brooding man, with none too pleasant thoughts.

He was a good sitter, always strictly punctual, and he stuck to the

GEORGE BERNARD SHAW, 1934

HAILE SELASSIE, EMPEROR OF ABYSSINIA, 1936

stand, giving me plenty of opportunity for work and study. I was with him for twenty-one days. Once, while posing, he had a heart attack, and felt faint. His manservant brought him a stiff whisky and he insisted on renewing the sitting. I had no hesitations while at work, owing to his very sympathetic attitude. A doubtful, or critical attitude of the sitter will sometimes hang like a dark cloud over the work and retard it. Conrad's sympathy and good-will were manifest, and he would beam at me with a pleased expression and forget his rheumatism and the tree outside the window at which he railed. The tree was large and beautiful, but to Conrad it was a source of misery.

The house was roomy, and set among low hills. To Conrad it was a prison set in a swamp. He must move. He must find another house He would set out in his car. One step from the door to the sealed vehicle to search for the new house. No outdoors for him. The sea captain hated out of doors, and never put his nose into it.

To return to the bust; Conrad had a demon expression in the left eye, while his right eye was smothered by a drooping lid, but the eyes glowed with a great intensity of feeling. The drooping, weary lids intensified the impression of brooding thought. The whole head revealed the man who had suffered much. A head set on shoulders hunched about his ears. When he was seated, the shoulders gave the impression of a pedestal for the head. His gnarled hands were covered with woollen mittens, and his habit of tugging at his beard when in conversation or in thought gave me the idea of including the hands in the bust, but Conrad recoiled from so human a document.

On anything connected with the plastic arts Conrad frankly confessed ignorance, although perhaps to flatter me he attempted to draw a parallel between the processes of building up a work of sculpture and that of writing a novel. Of music he said he knew nothing, nor did it interest him; but he admitted being impressed by the sound of drums coming across the waters in Africa at night.

The walls of his house carried a few indifferent family portraits in oil. He turned over lovingly the family portrait album of his ancestors. His father, Korzeniowski, was a distinguished literary Pole, who had suffered under the Czar, photographs of himself very young; these showed him as being extremely handsome.

We usually had tea in his small, cosy study. On one occasion, as there was company, I recall having tea in a large, grand, shuttered room with French furniture very conventionally arranged. Conrad was strongly feudal in his ideas and when I complained of the servile attitude of the villagers round about, he said that they were happier so. My reference to the villagers was occasioned by an incident which happened at Bridge. I had remarked on the astonishing velocity of a racing-car which had driven through the village at race-track speed scattering children and chickens. At the local barber's I mentioned this, and ventured to remark that the children were in danger of their lives. The barber said that in fact several children had been killed, but that the racing magnate had paid the parents handsomely, and all the villagers looked to him for employment. The report that Conrad refused a knighthood because it was offered by a Socialist Government, would, if true, bear out my observation about his feudal cast of mind.

I looked at Conrad's bookshelf. He had not many books. In no sense a library. A complete edition of Turgeniev in English. We talked of books and, expecting him to be interested in Melville's *Moby Dick*, I mentioned it, and Conrad burst into a furious denunciation of it. "He knows nothing of the sea. Fantastic, ridiculous," he said. When I mentioned that the work was symbolical and mystical: "Mystical my eye! My old boots are mystical." "Meredith? His characters are ten feet high." D. H. Lawrence had started well, but had gone wrong. "Filth. Nothing but obscenities." For Henry James he had unqualified admiration. Of his own novels he said it was a toss up at one time as to whether he would write in English or French. He emphasised the amount of labour he gave to a novel to get it to satisfy himself.

At a few of the sittings Conrad dictated letters to the secretary. His English was strongly foreign with a very guttural accent, so that his secretary frequently failed to get the right word, which made Conrad growl. I would try to detach myself from the work to listen. His composition was beautiful. Sentence followed sentence in classic "Conrad", totally unlike his conversational manner, which was free, easy, and colloquial.

The work on the bust was nearing completion. One day at the end of the sittings, Mrs. Conrad appeared at the door to see it. She gave one glance and fled. A wife, a lover, can perhaps never see what the artist sees. The fact, at any rate, is that they rarely ever do. Perhaps a really mediocre artist has more chance of success in this respect. When George Bernard Shaw was sitting to me, I asked him why he had given sittings to a very incompetent artist. Shaw exclaimed: "Why, he is a fine portrait painter—my wife, on entering the room where the portrait was, actually mistook it for myself."

Conrad's own opinion about my portrait of himself was conveyed in a letter he wrote to Richard Curle, his biographer and literary executor. "The bust of Ep. has grown truly monumental. It is a marvellously effective piece of sculpture, with even something more than a masterly interpretation in it. . . . It is wonderful to go down to posterity like that." Later Sir Muirhead Bone offered the bust to the National Portrait Gallery. It was refused.

At last the bust was completed. I wired my moulder to come and carry it away to London to be cast. I said good-bye to the old Master and travelled with the bust. Five months later I opened a newspaper and read that Joseph Conrad was dead.

ALBERT EINSTEIN

In 1933 rumours of the intended assassination of Einstein caused his flight to England. He left Belgium and was a refugee under Commander Locker-Lampson's care, at a camp near Cromer. I had some correspondence with Commander Locker-Lampson about my working from Einstein, and we arranged for a week of sittings. I travelled to Cromer, and the following morning was driven out to the camp situated in a secluded and wild spot very near the sea.

Einstein appeared dressed very comfortably in a pullover with his wild hair floating in the wind. His glance contained a mixture of the humane, the humorous, and the profound. This was a combination which delighted me. He resembled the ageing Rembrandt.

The sittings took place in a small hut, which was filled with a piano, and I could hardly turn round. I asked the girl attendants, of whom there were several, secretaries of Commander Lampson, to remove the door, which they did; but they facetiously asked whether I would like the roof off next. I thought I should have liked that too, but I did not demand it, as the attendant "angels" seemed to resent a little my intrusion into the retreat of their Professor. After the third day they thawed and I was offered beer at the end of the sitting.

I worked for two hours every morning, and at the first sitting the Professor was so surrounded with tobacco smoke from his pipe that I saw nothing. At the second sitting I asked him to smoke in the interval. Einstein's manner was full of charm and *bonhomie*. He enjoyed a joke and had many a jibe at the Nazi Professors, one hundred of whom in a book had condemned his theory. "Were I wrong," he said, "one Professor would have been quite enough." Also, in speaking of Nazis, he once said: "I thought I was a Physicist, I did not bother about being a Jew until Hitler made me conscious of it."

At the end of the sittings he would sit down at the piano and play, and once he took a violin and went outside and scraped away. He looked altogether like a wandering gypsy, but the sea air was damp and the violin execrable and he gave up. The Nazis had taken his own good violin when they confiscated his property in Germany.

Einstein watched my work with a kind of naïve wonder, and seemed to sense that I was doing something good of him.

The sittings unfortunately had to come to a close, as Einstein was to go up to London to make a speech at the Albert Hall and then leave for America. I could have gone on with the work. It seemed to me a good start, but, as so often happens, the work had to be stopped before I had carried it to completion.

Later I exhibited the head in London, in December, 1933. During the exhibition, while the Gallery was without attendants for a short time, it was discovered on the floor, fortunately only bent on to its stone pedestal which could easily be remedied. Who had overthrown it? This version was bought by the Chantry bequest, and is at present in the Tate Gallery.

BERNARD VAN DIEREN

1915–1937

I worked from Bernard Van Dieren on first meeting him in 1915. He was strikingly handsome and the head I did of him resembled superficially one of Napoleon's generals; but there was a quality of force allied to something mystical, far different, and beyond the vulgar good looks of the dandy generals of the First Empire, at any rate as they are depicted outside the Louvre. The head expresses this mystical quality, and later I worked from him in 1919 as he lay ill in bed. One of his periodical lyings-up which sometimes lasted months on end. I was only visiting him, but as we talked, the desire came over me to work from him. I hurried home and collected some clay in a bucket and came back. I made a mask. The mask was filled with suffering, but it was so noble and had such a high quality of intellectual life, I thought of him as the suffering Christ, and developed the mask into a head, then into a bust with arms, and extended it again, and so made my first image of Christ in bronze.

I made a third study from Van Dieren in 1936, about a year before he died. He was very ill, and by turns hot and cold, and very faint, and yet he had a noble emperor's air which is in the bust.

There is bitterness in the head, frustration. A genius neglected, misunderstood. One whose work will have to wait in our welter of vulgarity, noise and opportunism, before it comes to be understood, for qualities that our age does not care for.

I think of his quartets, and can only compare them to Beethoven's posthumous quartets. Not that they are influenced in any way, but that they contain a similar quality of pain, so intense, so beautiful in expression, that in our own period they are unique.

LORD ROTHERMERE

I met Lord Rothermere on the *Aquitania* on my return from New York in January, 1928, and he then asked me if I would do his bust in London. Of this meeting with Rothermere on the *Aquitania*, I recall a dinner which he gave on board, at which the great steel magnate, Charles Schwab, and P. G. Wodehouse, the English humorist, were present. Schwab was asked by Lord Rothermere how much he thought his fortune amounted to, and Schwab answered very impressively that he "really couldn't compute it". I was, of course, referred to as the "greatest" sculptor in the world, and in the eyes of these moneyed men that meant the sculptor who made most money. Wodehouse discussed stocks and shares, and altogether I got a strange impression of the values that rich and successful men place on things, and of how they are interested in wealth, which to an artist is only a means to finer ends. Lord Rothermere, although he prided himself on owning a fine collection of old masters, answered, when I asked him naturally enough what Rembrandts he possessed: "But Rembrandt isn't any good, is he?"

The sittings in London for the bust characteristically began with a film company making a film of myself and the sitter at work, and altogether the proceedings went on, as it were, in public, as Rothermere liked company and conducted his various businesses in my studio. I did not mind this, as it showed the sitter animated by subjects that really interested him. I have long ago been forced into the habit of ignoring those around me when at work and thinking only of the work in hand. Financiers and millions of pounds were discussed. Rothermere was monumental and offered strange psychological problems to the artist. Also he possessed a natural sense of humour and did not expect me to flatter him. He jocularly remarked that I was not making an Ivor Novello of him. The work progressed, but my model had a disconcerting habit of leaving for foreign parts suddenly, and sending me a wire that he would turn up in about a week or fortnight and "join me in the clay bin", as he put it.

This habit of the wire finally decided me to call it a day, and the bust was declared finished.

Rothermere pretended to no knowledge of Modern Art, but collected Old Masters. I will say that when he showed me these, apart from fine collections of Guardi and Canaletto, I was not very much impressed. A critic called Konody had collected them for him. This Konody was a razor-nosed little person, who showed me that he was eager that I should not criticise the pictures. On the occasion when the collection was shown to me, one evening at dinner at Lord Rothermere's at Sunningdale, Konody waylaid me previously and made a personal appeal to me not to decry the pictures to Lord Rothermere. To my amusement Konody added that Lord Rothermere could be very useful to both of us. The use of "us" made me laugh.

The occasion of this dinner was the placing of Rothermere's bust in the Sunningdale house, which took place five years after I had finished the work. Rothermere had apparently forgotten the bust for that period. This bust, with its somewhat formidable character, seemed to have to be handled carefully, for when I had proposed exhibiting it on some previous occasion, I was advised not to do so, as a general election was coming on and it might possibly exert some baneful influence on events.

Lord Rothermere's secretaries seemed particularly upset by the work. This I take as a tribute to the sincerity and truth of the rendering of the character. What these "yes men" expected me to do, I do not quite know, but their hostility was expressed quite frankly. I think of the bust as one of my best portraits.

LORD BEAVERBROOK

Isodore Ostrer wished to make a birthday present to his friend, Lord Beaverbrook, and the Canadian peer entered my studio one morning very like the stage hero in a musical comedy, dramatic and breezy. At the time I had the floor covered with newspapers, as a moulder was in working. Instantly Beaverbrook asked petulantly: "I do not see my papers here." I replied: "Do you imagine I would have your papers on the floor to be trodden on?"

We started work. He had a secretary with him, and had his own papers read out to him from first to last inch, so I saw the man in action. Like Rothermere, he also had a good sense of humour, and would express astonishment now and then that he gave up so much of his time to an artist.

Then he would jump up and make as dramatic an exit from the studio as his entrance had been.

I succeeded in making a sketch of him, which he shows in the entrance of *The Daily Express* Office in Fleet Street. When the head was finished, he asked the editor of *The Daily Express* to come and see it. Beaverbrook pointed to the head and said meaningly: "A present from a friend." The other just replied: "Humph," and they left the studio.

During the sittings, Lord Beaverbrook, in looking at the works in the studio, professed to see a diabolical spirit in them, as if my sole mission was to express evil. This attitude amused me, as some of the works are as candid and innocent as the models themselves.

GEORGE BERNARD SHAW

Shaw sat on condition that I was commissioned to do the work. He thought I ought to benefit materially and not just do his bust for its own sake. Orage arranged a commission for me from Mrs. Blanche Grant, an American. Shaw sat with exemplary patience and even eagerness. He walked to my studio every day, and was punctual and conscientious. He wise-cracked of course. In matters of Art he aired definite opinions, mostly wrong, and I often had to believe that he wished to say smart, clever things to amuse me. On seeing a huge block of stone, unworked in the studio, he asked me what I intended to do with it. Not wishing to tell him exactly what my plans were, I merely remarked that I had a plan. "What," he exclaimed, "you have a plan! You shouldn't have a plan. I never work according to a plan. Each day I begin with new ideas totally different from the day before." As if a sculptor with a six-ton block to carve could alter his idea daily! Shaw believed that sculptors put into their portraits their own characteristics, and of a bust done of him by a prince, he remarked that it contained something very aristocratic. This was amusing in view of the fact that this particular bust was peculiarly commonplace.

One day Robert Flaherty brought along the Aran boatman, Tiger King, who was the chief character in the film, *Man of Arran*, written about fishermen. In the studio, when Tiger King was introduced, Shaw immediately started talking to him on how to sail a boat, what happened in storms, and generally instructed him in sea-lore.

Shaw was puzzled by the bust of himself and often looked at it and tried to make it out. He believed that I had made a kind of primitive barbarian of him. Something altogether uncivilised and really a projection of myself, rather than of him. I never tried to explain the bust to him, and I think that there are in it elements so subtle that they would be difficult to explain. Nevertheless, I believe this to be an authentic and faithful rendering of George Bernard Shaw physically and psychologically. I leave out any question of æsthetics, as that would be beyond Shaw's comprehension. When the bust was finished, we were filmed, and Shaw was wonderful as an actor, taking the filming very seriously.

In 1934, when the work in bronze was done, I offered Shaw a copy of the bust through Orage, but was told that Shaw could not think of having it in his house. This, I believe, was due to Mrs. Shaw's dislike of it.

Throughout my life in England, Shaw was an outspoken

ROBERT B. CUNNINGHAME GRAHAM, 1923

DOLORES, 1923

champion for my work, on several occasions giving the great British public lively smacks on my behalf. I will not say that he understood what I have made. He seemed deficient in all sense of the plastic, but had a lively notion of how stupid the newspapers can be over new works of sculpture or painting. He was generous to young talent, but always likely to be taken in by cleverness or pretence. I would say that Shaw was not really interested in the plastic Arts, although he could be got to take a passing or journalistic interest in controversial work. On one occasion, on visiting an exhibition of paintings of Epping Forest, not knowing what to say, he asked me if I had done the paintings with brushes.

THE EMPEROR OF ABYSSINIA

Haile Selassie had arrived from Jerusalem an exile, and Commander Locker-Lampson asked me to do a study of the Emperor which might be used to further the cause of Abyssinia. The Commander fondly believed that I might do a work which in reproduction would be popular and raise funds for the heroic struggle. As it turned out, my bust had no popularity, and was only a matter of great expense to myself.

I arrived at the Abyssinian Legation with my clay and things, prepared to work. The hall was filled with a strange hubbub and excitement, and a dispute was going on with a chauffeur who was insisting on a payment down for car hire. Alas! The finances of the Emperor were not of that fabulous size reported in newspapers.

I knew Haile Selassie's appearance from photographs, but when I saw him advancing through the rooms of the house next door to the Abyssinian Legation, at which I worked, I was astonished at his calm air of dignity. A cream-coloured shirt garment of very soft Abyssinian material showed where it appeared swathed about his neck, and over this was the beautiful cloak either of dark blue or dove grey. His suite followed him. I had already produced my model's throne (a box, used by all of my sitters), and I am afraid the only throne the Emperor was to occupy for some time until he was once more re-instated in his own country.

On our meeting we delivered deep bows to each other, and without further preliminaries, Haile Selassie ascended the box and I started to work while the Court stood around. Whilst I worked, I noticed that the Emperor had the habit every few minutes of casting nervous glances behind him over one shoulder or the other. This apprehension on his part was most suggestive. His fine, handsome features were lit by a pair of melancholy eyes which seemed tired and strained, and at the time I worked from him he still suffered from the effects of recent harassing and painful events. His youngest son was much amused at my pellets of clay and called them *maccaronis*.

For my purpose, Haile Selassie was at his best talking in Amharic to his immediate followers, Ras Kassa, a tremendous giant of a man with an immense bald head, and Herouy, who was dressed in European clothes. At times the Emperor wrote in fine Amharic characters. All his movements were distinguished and firm. It was strange to me to be, as it seemed, at an African Court when in mid-Kensington. His people on approaching him prostrated themselves to the ground.

One morning on arriving, there was no Emperor, and I hunted through the house for someone to let me know of his whereabouts. Meeting a handsome blonde girl on the staircase I asked for the young medical man, an Abyssinian who usually arranged the sittings for me. She answered in German and said that she would find "der schön doktor".

When she found my intermediary, he laughed nervously and conducted me to the door of the Emperor's apartments, where his suite were mostly seated on the ground or on the staircase, and he let me know that the Emperor was still in his dressing-gown, but would be with me immediately. I liked and just accepted this mixture of formality and easy-going patriarchal casualness, and only hoped to get on with my study. The Emperor's hands especially attracted my attention. They were fine, even feminine. He was altogether delicately fashioned, although this delicacy was tempered with a Semitic virility. I made what I considered an interesting study, although an unfinished one.

This work is now owned by a collector in the North of England who has a large collection of my work. It was lent to the Tate Gallery for the retrospective exhibition of my sculpture there in 1952.

Portraits

J. B. PRIESTLEY

I am always aware of the feelings of my sitters towards the work. Sometimes they say frankly what they think, and if they do not say anything, their regard often betrays their feelings. Naturally, a critical and unfavourable attitude makes it difficult for me, and I wish to God I hadn't begun or rather that I hadn't the necessity for taking on a portrait. In the case of the bust of Mr. Priestley, he seemed none too pleased with the progress of the work, but one morning he came into the studio briskly and said:

"It's this way, Epstein. I look upon this bust as an insurance for both of us against getting forgotten. If you get forgotten, there is your bust of *me*. If I am forgotten there is *your* bust of me."

When Mrs. Priestley came to see the bust, she was evidently dissatisfied, but said nothing until she moved round to the back, when she said: "Well, at any rate the back is unmistakable."

This was not so crushing as a sculptor who, looking at a small head of Enver that I had brought into an exhibition, exclaimed: "What a beautiful bronze casting!"

CLARE SHERIDAN'S LUNCHEON PARTY

When I arrived, Clare Sheridan was engaged on a statuette of H. G. Wells. Wells was sitting on a stand rolling a pellet of clay in his hands, a procedure which would have maddened me, had I been working from him.

The sculptor asked me what I thought of the sketch, and I pointed out that one of the essentials of Wells's facial makeup was his overhanging eyebrows, which she had not put in. That addition in modelling gave it the Wellsian look. The luncheon that followed was made up of quite a large gathering, and had some interesting personalities. Opposite me sat Lord Birkenhead. He seemed to look duller than any man I had ever seen, with his cigar sticking out of the corner of his mouth. A Lady Michelham, who was reported to be very wealthy, and was involved in an inheritance case, known as the Michelham Millions, shouted over at me: "And when am I going to sit for you, Mr. Epstein?" I answered gallantly: "Will to-morrow do?" Immediately my hostess shouted out: "You are sitting for me to-morrow, Lady Michelham." I then said: "Will Thursday do?" A painter whose name I forget shouted out: "You are sitting for me on Thursday, Lady Michelham." I suggested Friday, and Mr. Ambrose McEvoy, the painter, then said: "You are sitting for me on Friday, Lady Michelham." With that I gave up. A very striking-looking lady, the Marchesa Casati, was at the luncheon, and I asked her to sit for me, which she consented to do the next day.

The Marchesa arrived in a taxi-cab at two o'clock and left it waiting for her. We began the sittings and her Medusa-like head kept me busy until nightfall. It was snowing outside, and a report came in that the taxi-man had at length made a declaration. He did not care if it were Epstein and if it were a countess, he would not wait any longer. On hearing this Casati shouted: "He is a Bolshevik! Ask him to wait a little longer." He was given tea and a place by the fire and shown the bookshelf.

The winter light had failed, and I had many candles brought in. They formed a circle round my weird sitter with the fire in the grate piled high to give more light. The tireless Marchesa, with her over-large blood-veined eyes, sat with a basilisk stare, and as if to bear out her epithet of "Bolshevik", her taxi-man picked out for himself *The Brothers Karamazov* to read, and ceased to protest.

The Medusa-like mask was finished the next day.

The Marchesa had strange tastes. She loved snakes, and had a python who crept into an oven. Inadvertently the oven was shut and lit up, and the poor python was baked. Then a young man at her home in Capri was to be an Antique God and he was gilded all over, so legend says. This modern type who was sitting to me was, at the same time, sophisticated and childish. Her clothes were bizarre and original. Once she appeared in a frock composed of white feathers, which as she moved rapidly along, left stray feathers floating behind her.

At dinner she wore white silk pyjamas and a peacock's feather rose from her shoulder, parallel with her head. She was determined to be unnatural, and would argue for any perversity rather than countenance normal behaviour. In art, of course, her taste was also for the perverse, and she was enamoured of a mask I had done of Meum and coveted it, but was determined to have it in some odd material, glass lit up, from within.

RABINDRANATH TAGORE, 1926

The Sculptor with Rabindranath Tagore, 1926

Portraits

Early during the War, Francis Dodd, R.A., asked me to do a bust of Lord Fisher for the Duchess of Hamilton. It was to be begun that very morning and "would I get my clay and other things together and start?" I packed everything into a cab and was taken to the Duchess of Hamilton's flat in the St. James's district.

Fisher had an extraordinary appearance. His light eyes, with strange colours, were set in a face like parchment ivory, and his iron grey hair was cut short and bristled on his head. He was short, but had the appearance of combative sturdiness.

In posing he was tireless. He began at ten every morning. We lunched at one and resumed sittings immediately after lunch, and went on until six o'clock in the evening.

During the afternoon, Fisher would take a short nap of about five minutes, and waken refreshed and full of vigour. He talked incessantly and watched the progress of the bust through a looking-glass, when he was turned away from the clay.

I asked him why he wanted me to do his bust, and he replied that when Francis Dodd suggested me, he asked my nationality, and on hearing that I was of Polish origin, said that one of his greatest inventors at the Admiralty was a Pole, and that was sufficient for him.

He was the typical man of war. He made no bones about it. War was terrible, and should be terrible, and some of his characteristic sayings bear out his ruthless outlook. Of an enemy he would say that "he would make a wife a widow, and his home a dunghill". He continuously quoted scriptures, but characteristically only from the Old Testament. Proverbs fell from his lips copiously.

I was impressed by his mental energy and there was a look in his eyes that was dangerous. At the time I worked from him he had been forced out of office, and seemed pleased at the unsatisfactory conduct of Naval affairs. One morning he came into the room where I worked, filled with sardonic satisfaction. The Battle of Jutland had just been fought. Fisher read out to me "a message from Lord Nelson" on the event which he said he had received. It did not spare the Jacks-in-Office who, he alleged, had allowed the German Fleet to skedaddle back to harbour. I enjoyed working from him and he understood and appreciated my active interest in the bust.

87

When it came to his shoulders and uniform, completely covered with decorations, he referred to himself as a "Christmas Tree". He was proudest of his Order of Merit. In his luncheon talks he would often speak of himself as a poor man. He could have been rich, opportunities were offered to him outside the Navy, but he considered that he had given his life to the Navy, and he was satisfied with that.

I finished, aided by Fisher's intensive methods of work, a large bust in a week. He seemed very pleased with it. This bust belongs to the Duchess of Hamilton. A version of it is in the War Museum.

Some years later, walking along Piccadilly, opposite Green Park, I saw Lord Fisher being wheeled along in a bath-chair by a nurse. He was looking very changed, and very ill, a sharp and painful contrast to the vigorous man I had modelled.

"DON ROBERTO"

Imagine Don Quixote walking about your studio and sitting for his portrait! This was R. B. Cunninghame Graham, and you could see him on horseback any day in Hyde Park on his small American mustang, seated in a high saddle, riding along Rotten Row in a bowler hat. He was no *poseur*, as many imagine. His distinguished appearance and bearing were natural. No man with easier manners, more debonair and courteous. At my studio he was always the centre of a group, and his anecdotes and conversation were delivered in the same incisive and stylistic manner that he wrote in. His candour was refreshing, he had been in Parliament years before, but the probity of his character could not stand an assembly where conformity and chicanery were the order of the day. I should have gone on with his head and made it into a bust and full figure and mounted it on a horse, and had it set up in Hyde Park, where his ghost now rides. He had been instrumental in getting me the commission for the Hudson memorial, and when I was at work on it in Epping Forest, he came to see it, and afterwards we walked through Monk Wood and Don Roberto with astonishing agility jumped the brooks at the age of seventy-three. You imagined around his belt (he scorned braces) Colt revolvers, and with his air of Hidalgo of Spain, he carried also a whiff of the American Wild West into London studios and drawing-rooms. In the head I modelled he seems to sniff the air, blowing from

88

the Sierras, and his hair is swept by a breeze from afar. Cunninghame
Graham was a great friend of Conrad, and when I had made the
bust of the latter, he brought along the Polish Ambassador to see it,
and proposed there and then to start a fund for its purchase for
Poland with a contribution of his own, but his enthusiasm was not
catching and nothing came of it. Salud! Don Roberto Quixote.

AUGUSTUS JOHN

John sat to me in my Guildford Street studio. I had wanted to do a
head of him for some time, and as he had made two etchings of myself and several drawings, I was eager to do him justice. He had sat to
a number of artists, including a sculptor who had made him look, as
I told John, like a future president of the Royal Academy, all dignity
and well-trimmed beard; John's head had plenty of dignity, but
there was much more to it than that, and I wanted to capture a certain wildness, an untamed quality that is the essence of the man. I
made a sketch and then something interfered—I forget what—and
so the work remained a sketch, but a vital one. Of some persons I
feel that one work is not enough to represent them, and that is what
I feel about John's head. What a miserable collection of works for the
most part is that of the National Portrait Gallery! Were you to try
and find an authentic portrait of your hero there, you would only
come across someone's silly flattery. Lord Byron is the "corsair" of
stage limelight, and Shelley looks a most "ineffectual angel" depicted by a most ineffectual limner. For reality, you have to go to
Holbein and look at that straightforward portrait of Henry which
stares at you in all its unblinking brutality. Reynolds's heroics, and
Gainsborough's idealisms, and the whole port-wine-complexioned
school of Raeburn, and the pink nymphs of Romney, are totally
divorced from reality. Romney and most of his colleagues give one
no real picture of the men and women of the period, skilful as the
painting often is, particularly that of Thomas Lawrence, who preceded our Sargent and Lazlo.

There should be a special fund to engage artists who are capable
of doing so to paint portraits or model busts of our "great" ones, if
greatness can be spotted anywhere; or if that is too responsible a task
for a committee, there might be a ballot for the members of our

"Hall of Fame". I do not know what qualifies a candidate at present for that august distinction.

DOLORES. 1921–1923

My first work from Dolores I abandoned and thought a failure, and yet years afterwards, when I came across the plaster again, I realised that it was a very vivid and spontaneous sketch of her, and I cast it in bronze. It became instantly popular.

The second study was again a failure, I thought, but this I followed up with a bust which was tragic and magnificent; Dolores was a model who was extremely suggestionable, and after I made this bust, she always strutted about, keeping her arms folded in the pose of the bust, and with the same tragic and aloof expression fixed upon her face, and she took great care that she never relaxed into those careless smiles of the first head. In the studio she was the devoted model, never allowing anything to interfere with posing, taking it seriously; a religious rite. She became the High Priestess of Beauty, and this rôle she carried to ridiculous lengths. She even gave as an excuse to a magistrate, before whom she appeared for some indiscreet conduct in Piccadilly, that my being in America had disorientated her, and this was taken as sufficient excuse, together with a small fine, by a magistrate indulgent to a Phryne of modern times.

In 1923, I made one more head of her, which I think is the best work I did from the beautiful and fantastic Dolores. Later I can remember how, passing through Piccadilly, a strange vehicle of period 1840 or so met my gaze; complete with high-stepping horses, coachman with whip, and footman. Dolores was mounted on a high seat with folded arms and the air of a Queen as she passed majestically to advertise some perfume or cosmetic. Her sang-froid carried her into some strange adventures, but the use she made of my name was sometimes embarrassing, as when she married a coloured gentleman and sent out the invitations to the reception in my name. Her endless amours were a boon to Fleet Street journalists, and when she died of cancer, suddenly, they must have regretted the passing of a character so colourful and so accessible.

Her *Memoirs* published by the Hearst Press in America were packed full of inventions conceived by the not very scrupulous brains of the scribblers who seized on her notoriety and exploited it.

HIS GRACE THE 9TH DUKE OF MARLBOROUGH, 1923–1925

J. RAMSAY MACDONALD, 1934

Portraits

One day a girl passing in the street attracted my attention by her delicate and aristocratic beauty. The girl was of African origin, and she did not resent my asking her to pose for me, which she did with a naturalness that was explained when she told me of her engagement to marry a French painter.

She was a Senegalese, and she said her name was Madeleine Bechet. She told me she was the daughter of a French officer married to a Senegalese. I spoke to her of a book I had just read because her name astonished me. The book was called *A Travers le Sudan*, and was written by a French officer called A. Bechet. This story recounted how the officer, watching a caravan of captured slaves, had rescued a girl of twelve, who was the daughter of a Senegalese chief. He bought her off, and looked after her, educated her, and finally married her. This model of mine was the daughter of this French officer by the slave girl who later became his wife.

I gave the name, "The Girl from Senegal", to the bust. Later, she became a governess for a short time to Peggy Jean, but the English climate was too cold for her. In midsummer she would be wrapped up in everything she could wear, and still shiver. I was glad for this reason when she determined to go and join her fiancé in Tunis.

MOSHEH OVED

The poet-jeweller was sitting to me for his head. My models, more especially Sunita, would go to his cameo corner shop, which was like Aladdin's Cave, and Mosheh would deck them out in oriental jewellery. Sunita would appear like the Queen of Sheba, and an amusing story was told by Mosheh himself of how, one sunny day, he and Sunita were in a taxi-cab in the city, and as they were caught up in some ceremonial procession, were mistaken for royalty itself, and Sunita bowed her regal way through crowds.

I liked working from him and transferring to clay his sensitive, nervous features. There was something fluttering and naïve about his expression, like a charming child.

One morning he seemed more than usually nervous, and I noticed his face getting more and more pale. The strain of sitting is

harder on some persons than on others, although I try to put sitters
at their ease. The truth is that the steady gaze of the sculptor is somewhat disconcerting. I asked Mosheh Oved what was the matter with
him, and he said: "I am not used to sitting here and doing nothing.
Can't I sell you something?" Some of his books have this same
whimsical humour. His bust is one of the most successful I have done,
and is now, I believe, in the Museum of Tel-Aviv.

RABINDRANATH TAGORE

"I am he that sitteth among the poorest, the loneliest, and the
lost."

This quotation from Gitanjali was strangely contradicted by my
sitter, whose handsome, commanding presence inspired in his followers awe and a craven obedience. On entering my house I brought
to him for presentation a little Indian boy, Enver, who was living
with me, He was the son of Sunita. Tagore looked at him and asked:
"A Hindu?" I said: "No, a Moslem", whereat Rabindranath
lifted his eyes to the ceiling and passed on.

He posed in silence and I worked well. On one occasion two
American women came to visit him, and I remember how they left
him, retiring backwards, with their hands raised in worship. At the
finish of the sittings usually two or three disciples, who waited in an
ante-room for him, took him back to his hotel. He carried no money
and was conducted about like a holy man. On one occasion the disciples did not turn up until too late, and I had my handyman take
him back to the Hyde Park Hotel in a cab. I can imagine the wrath
visited on the heads of those disciples. His indignation could be em-
phatic. A flock of them were on the hotel steps when the cab arrived.

The manners of Tagore were aloof, dignified and cold, and if he
needed anything only one word of command escaped him to his
disciples.

It has been remarked that my bust of him rests upon the beard, an
unconscious piece of symbolism.

A K.C.

I had undertaken to do a portrait of a K.C. during the war. He
was a man of handsome appearance, somewhat Spanish in features,

and I remarked on his Jewish characteristics, which he did not deny. In working from him I sensed cruelty and the legal mind. One day I remarked on what seemed to me to be a savage sentence pronounced on an old woman for throwing some crumbs of bread out to the sparrows, a sentence of imprisonment. My sitter said: "Yes, and quite right too. I would have given her a heavier sentence." I felt so sick at this that I would not go on with the portrait.

"OLD SMITH"

Often in Bloomsbury where I live, I see an old, bareheaded, bearded man with a hand-organ. His savage apostle's head attracts my attention. He turns and says: "Take another look!" I ask him to sit for me, and he consents. He sits, a silent character, revealing only that he had been in the Army on service in India.

He is determined to keep out of the workhouse, and is glad of the opportunity of making a little extra. His head is bronzed with his outdoor life, and I suspect he is a gypsy. I like his rugged defiant character, and I think of doing a life-size figure of him, or of using him for a group. I am planning a "Descent from the Cross". I never carry out this plan, and Old Smith disappears from Bloomsbury.

I never see him again.

"OLD PINAGER"

He is a different character. He sits with his matches every evening on the doorstep of a shop labelled "Old Masters". His head is bowed. He is the image of abject patience. He is quite pleased to sit in the same position in my studio where it is warm.

He speaks of himself, of how he had never been able to make a living for himself at anything. He accepts himself as a natural failure, and is even content to be that. He lives in a "doss house". It seems that the girls of the quarter are his best friends, and with good-hearted generosity drop pennies or "tanners" into his box on a cold winter's night.

"Pinager." His bust with the gnarled patient hands is in the Aberdeen Art Gallery.

He also has disappeared.

KRAMER

The Leeds painter, Kramer, was a model who seemed to be on fire. He was extraordinarily nervous. Energy seemed to leap into his hair as he sat, and sometimes he would be shaken by queer tremblings like ague. I would try to calm him, so as to get on with the work. He was the typical Bohemian, and I recall his waking me up one morning to ask me to go to the Marlborough Street Police Court to speak for his model, Betty May, who had, in a café dispute, thrown a glass at my enemy. I went, and there was the model with all her friends in court. Betty was excited and happy at the situation and smiled to everyone. I said in answer to the magistrate that Betty May was to my knowledge most gentle but temperamental, and must have been provoked. The magistrate repeated: "Gentle but temperamental. Three pounds." With that the happy band of Bohemians went to the Café Royal for drinks.

THE 9TH DUKE OF MARLBOROUGH
1923–1925

A description of the genesis, duration, and finish of a bust of this nature is of interest, as it exhibits very clearly the relation of the sculptor to the sitter of the ordinary sort. My reading of the Duke's character, the study of his appearance, and regard for the destination of the bust, brought about a series of characteristic events. The bust was to decorate a niche in the entrance hall of Blenheim Palace, and it was thought that sittings given in the Palace itself would materially help to solve the problems involved. I made fairly good progress with the head, which I wanted to get first go off, before beginning the bust. I completed the head and started on the bust, and that was where the trouble began.

The Duke thought he would look best as a Roman bust with nude shoulders, but to my mind it was best as a man of his period and I was not particular as to what the costume should be as long as it was something that he wore. The Duchess agreed with me, but we came to no understanding, and I gave up working on the bust, after an acrimonious debate which ended in ill-temper on both sides.

Two years later, the Duchess asked me to resume work on the portrait, and it was agreed that the Duke should be depicted in his Robes of the Garter with the hands included.

The entrance hall at Blenheim Palace is a vast, lofty place, and there was sculpture of other Marlboroughs in it, mostly in marble. I had planned a bronze, and resumed the sittings in London, and all went well. The Duke brought along his Garter Robes. To help the sittings along, a manservant of mine called Sydney wore the Robes at times, as his size and figure were very like the Duke's.

Sydney was a typical Cockney ne'er-do-well, and later I saw him dressed in sandwich boards in Piccadilly where we had a talk together, and I reflected on the different costumes a man can wear in his time.

My stay in Blenheim Palace in 1923 was quite pleasant because of the beautiful park land, mostly wild, that surrounded the Palace. In my careless working costume, so unlike the usual plus-fours, etc., of a Palace guest, I was more than once called upon by the gamekeepers to explain my presence. My assertion that I was a guest at the Palace always produced a comic forehead salute of flunkeys and apologies.

Also the Duchess of Marlborough had an organist to come and play the organ for me, which was built by a former Duke, and the day began with an hour of Bach. The Duke disliked Bach. After the organ recital I began work. In the evening there was more Bach; the Duke was bored by it and asked why we did not care for jazz or night-club music. His idea of a great man, he freely said, was someone like Luigi, who ran a fashionable club.

One day the Duke asked me to see the Chapel of Blenheim. We entered a building totally devoid of Christian symbolism or Christian feeling. I said: "I see nothing of Christianity here." The Duke said: "The Marlboroughs are worshipped here."

On this visit I tried to make a second study of the Duchess, but only succeeded in making a sketch. I had earlier made a study of the Duchess which I still have. This bust, which is somewhat stylised, was the cause, I was told when exhibiting it, of great uneasiness amongst English patronesses of artists, who expect a work to be entirely lacking in any character and would rather have a portrait lacking all distinction than one which possessed psychological or plastic qualities, and a combination of these qualities is abhorrent to those ill-educated snobs who run about London airing their money-bag opinions, and who dominate with their loud-voiced arrogance the exhibiting world.

The Duchess, at whose instigation the portrait of the Duke was undertaken, was a woman of great discrimination in Art, and owned works by Rodin and Degas, and had known both these artists, and thoroughly understood what an artist was aiming at.

Blenheim Palace, when I was there, had been denuded of its fine Rubens, and I thought the pictures, of which there were quantities, were mediocre. A large and vulgar Sargent dominated one room, and in another the place of honour was occupied by a flashy Boldini.

The modern artist has the ambition of rivalling the great Renaissance masters and imagines himself in the place of Titian or Mantegna decorating Palaces, and given the opportunity to do honour to his craft and give immortality to the great. Alas! Practical experience dispels these illusions and he finds himself out of spirits, and out of pocket over the results, as a rule.

THREE PORTRAITS

I made this portrait of my wife in 1912. Leaning upon her hand, she looks toward the future with serene confidence. In the composition itself, I attempted movement which, while very natural, I abandoned in later work, and severely restricted myself to the least possible movement. This I practised as a kind of discipline so that my construction would be more firm. I have always intended returning to the portrait of movement. It is a pity that I have not started on this new departure ere this, but there is time yet for new developments.

1916

In this mask, I immediately made what I think is one of my subtlest and most beautiful works. The serenity and inward calm is there, and from the point of view of style, the simplicity is that achieved by antique sculpture. I can recall that I worked at this mask without effort, achieving it happily, and was pleased with the result. It is worth remarking of this mask that two versions of it were bought by Japanese, one of them a young sculptor who, on visiting me, immediately wished to acquire it, and took it away with him.

Portraits

1918

This bust, I think, is the most profound of the three works, and it has that quiet thoughtfulness that I had unconsciously striven for in the other two; or most likely, as I matured in my work, I naturally brought into full play all my powers of observation and expression, and so made this one of my gravest, and I think one of my most beautiful busts.

This work was unhurried and brooded over, and the drapery was worked with great care. The lines, all running downwards like the rills of a fountain, are essential to the effect of the bust, and help to express its innermost meaning.

I think of this bust as a crowning piece, and I place it with any work I have done. There is a version of it in New York owned by Stevenson Scott, the dealer in Old Masters, and when I visited his gallery I was pleased to see it, holding its own amongst paintings by Rembrandt and Hals. On the other hand, Lord Duveen saw it at my bronze moulders' on his discouraging visit with me to see the "Madonna and Child"; he looked at it indifferently, and just asked whom it was a portrait of. I suppose one ought to be indifferent to praise or blame, and yet the artist faced with indifference is always cut to the quick. I remember George Grey Barnard remarking about this indifference to works of art, when I was a student, and he ironically said that the killing of ten thousand pigs in Chicago was what interested Americans, and not the creating of sculpture. That was a case of pork butchers, but when it comes to experts and dealers in works of art, critics, professors, authorities on art . . .

BUST OF A LADY

The sculptor is to model a bust and the beautiful sitter has arrived. To give an impression of how the sculptor works, the state of mind, and the moods by which the successive stages are achieved, imagine him then in a state in which critical analysis of the form and emotional exaltation are present at the same time. To the exclusion of all else his vision is concentrated on the model, and he begins (a state of high nervous tension). His searching and loving eye roams over the soft contours of the face and is caught by the edges of the brow enclosing the eyes, and so to the cheek-bones, and then downwards past the mouth and nose. The mask is lightly fixed and the salient points established. This mask is arrested by the twin points of the ears. Behind the mass of hair from above, the brow and falling to the shoulders is then indicated, by broad and sketchy additions of clay, without particular definition, merely a note to be taken up later. Return to the mask, the expression of the eyes, and the shape and droop of the upper eyelid, the exact curve of the under-lid is drawn. Here great care is exercised and the drawing must be of hair-breadth exactness. The nostrils are defined, and for this a surgeon's sharp eye, and exactitude of observation and handling, are necessary; a trembling sensitiveness, for the nostrils breathe; and from thence to the contours of the lips and the partition of the lips. Then the contours of the cheeks, the faintest indication of cheek-bones, and the oval of the head never exactly symmetrical, must be shown, and when so much is achieved—a halt. A sonnet of Shakespeare, or Faust's invocation to Helen comes to mind. Return to work. Inward fire must be translated to clay. The mind and hand of the sculptor must work together, an embracing mind, an active and translating hand, a conjunction of material and spiritual From the model who sits quietly, unconscious of the absorbed worker, the sculptor draws out wizard-like the soul, and, by a process almost of incantation, builds up the image. Now the head is formed and takes on life, by ever so slight gradations. The movement of the head is finally resolved on, and by ceaseless turnings of the stand, the planes are modelled and related. The subtle connections between plane and plane knit the form together. The forms catch the light, emphasis is placed, now here, now there, the shapes are hunted, sought after with ardour, with passion; there is no halt in the steady building up and progress of the work. Strange metamorphosis, incarnation, and consummation. Now the shoulders are formed, they are related to the cheeks, the back is studied, the arms and hands come into being, the hands flutter from the wrists, like flames, a trembling eagerness of life pulsates throughout the work. What a quartet of harmonies is evoked in this bust! Head, shoulders, body, and hands, like music. Turn the stand, pace round the clay, study from a thousand angles, draw the contours, relate the planes, evoke the immortal image—sculptor of eternal images.

DR. CHAIM WEIZMANN, 1933

DR. CHAIM WEIZMANN, 1933

9

MY FIRST STATUE OF CHRIST: 1917–1920

I HAD made during the war a statue in bronze of Christ, and exhibited it at the Leicester Galleries. Immediately a most hellish row broke out. The statue was reviled, attacked by the Press, the Clergy, R.A.s, Artistic Associations, and Social bodies. Father Bernard Vaughan wrote as follows:

I feel ready to cry out with indignation that in this Christian England there should be exhibited the figure of a Christ which suggested to me some degraded Chaldean or African, which wore the appearance of an Asiatic-American or Hun, which reminded me of some emaciated Hindu or badly grown Egyptian.

I was astounded at the reception of this figure, and still am. George Bernard Shaw came out in defence of it, and it was eventually bought by Apsley Cherry-Garrard, who was a member of Scott's South Polar Expedition.

To-day Ecclesiastical authorities fight shy of any work which shows any religious intensity of feeling, and merely wish for innocuous "furniture" that will not disturb the mind of the beholder. For the Ecclesiastical authorities especially there exists by now a whole school of copyists of early religious work. They love to work in a washed-out, slightly Gothic, somewhat Byzantine style, and by this "copy cat" business, imagine that they are in the great Christian tradition. They have even banded themselves together and have workshops, showrooms, and agents, to sell their products. In fact they find religious sculpture a fruitful field for exploitation.

They would, if they could, prevent any other artist from invading what they consider their province—religious art—monopolists, of course, of what they have copied.

There are in fact a number of artists ripe for Fascism, who, if they had their way, would ban and burn as readily as any Nazi. Intolerance is as rife amongst the artists and writers as amongst business people, although those who are engaged in the intellectual pursuits are supposed to be free of such feelings as trade jealousy, bigotry, and narrow-mindedness.

In attempting to explain the motives, and my methods of work, and the progress of my major works such as the "Christ", "Genesis", "Day and Night", and "Consummatum Est", I find myself at a disadvantage as, although my aims and methods of work are clear enough to myself, yet not having had the advantage of ever being asked to teach anybody, I lack the habit of giving verbal expression to my efforts or aims in sculpture. There is a language of form which is sufficient to itself, as there is the language of music, and my inarticulateness is not due to any vagueness in my own mind, but only to lack of experience in explaining, and as an outgrowth of that, my tendency of mind not to care to explain what I find so clearly expressed in the work itself.

Years ago I chose as a heading for my catalogue the sentence, "I rest silent in my work". I thought that a superb and complete attitude towards those who are continuously asking the artist to explain himself: for it has been my experience to find that those artists who have taken the greatest trouble to explain themselves, in fact, who have been the most verbose and "high-falutin", have mostly been the feeble, the pedantic, and the impotent. At school at the Beaux Arts, during one of the "treats" by new students, I recall how a Swiss sculptor, who was almost the worst student in the atelier, when asked to speak, began: "I will now give you a discourse on the history of art in Europe from A.D. 1100 to ——"; at which we all howled him down. I still have this aversion from lengthy and scholarly "discourse".

Cézanne, whom all the scholars now worship, is a good example of this dislike inherent in the really creative artist. Cézanne never gave out more than simple sentences or somewhat terse aphorisms which can be variously interpreted. I am most often bored to death by the artist who in front of his work, when showing it, starts groaning out his explanation of what he had attempted to achieve. One look at the work is enough. Also I consign to the waste-paper basket the missives, mostly of extraordinary length, sent to me to explain to me my own works. Artists of all kinds write to me, religious cranks, theologians, clergymen, and women eager to express themselves, crazy people who write threatening letters, and journalists. I have even been told by one enterprising American, quite clearly in a schedule, just when he and his party travelling through Europe would pay a visit to my studio! My language is form, in all its variety and astonishing wealth, and that is my native language. Sometimes the motive for beginning a work is obscure even to myself, or the genesis of it may be partly accidental. This in no way diminishes the final importance of the work, as a composer beginning with some simple theme or melody expands and fills out a work until it becomes a symphony or opera: so with my first "Christ", the one cast in bronze. I began it as a study from Bernard Van Dieren when he was ill. I went to his bedside to be with him and talk. Watching his head, so spiritual and worn with suffering, I thought I would like to make a mask of him. I hurried home and returned with clay and made a mask which I immediately recognised as the Christ head, with its short beard, its pitying accusing eyes, and the lofty and broad brow, denoting great intellectual strength.

You will say—an accident. That was no more an accident than the event recorded in some short sketch of Turgeniev, when he records how, standing in the crowd somewhere, he instantly felt, in some man beside him, the presence of the Christ Himself and the awe that overcame him. So with the Disciples of Emmaus, as represented by Rembrandt in the unforgettable Louvre picture of that name. The Disciples have met a stranger at an inn who has sat down with them and broken bread. In a flash the divine head is lit up, and in awe and astonishment the Redeemer is revealed to them.

I saw the whole figure of my "Christ" in the mask. With haste I began to add the torso and the arms and hand with the accusing finger. This I then cast and had, as a certainty, the beginning of my statue. So far the work was a bust. I then set up this bust with an armature for the body. I established the length of the whole figure down to the feet. The statue rose swathed in clothes. A pillar firmly set on the two naked feet—Christ risen supernatural, a portent for all time. I remember that I was interrupted on this work for a considerable period, a whole year in fact, and it stood in the centre of my studio in Guildford Street unfinished. When I resumed work on it, it was only to finish the feet.

My original model at this time lay on a sick bed in Holland. I had Kramer, the artist, and Cecil Gray, the musician, pose for the unfinished parts. Throughout, my conception was clear, yet the fact that live people pose and are helpful to a sculptor in finishing a work which has a symbolical or religious import shocks some people. They look upon even the remotest resemblance to someone they know as a sort of impiety, something sacrilegious—so with the "Christ". Before the work was cast in bronze, a woman visiting the studio looked upon the "Christ", and knowing that Van Dieren was a model for the head and torso and arms and, not approving of him personally, immediately exclaimed against it, and in a horrified tone declared that I had committed something "evil". This extraordinary and personal view of the statue of course did not enter into the minds of those who later condemned the statue. I must maintain that my statue of Christ still stands for what I intended it to be. It stands and accuses the world for its grossness, inhumanity, cruelty, and beastliness, for the First World War and for the later wars in Abyssinia, China, and Spain which culminated in the Second World War.

How prophetic a figure! Not the early Evangelical Christ of Byzantium and Rome, nor the condemning Apollonian Christ of Michelangelo, or the sweet rising and blessing Christ of Raphael, but the modern living Christ, compassionate and accusing at the same time. I should like to remodel this "Christ". I should like to make it hundreds of feet high, and set it up on some high place where all could see it, and where it would give out its warning, its mighty symbolic warning to all lands. The Jew—the Galilean—condemns our wars, and warns us that "Shalom, Shalom", must be still the watchword between man and man.

Now I return in thought to my "Christ" of 1917–1920, and recognise how well I worked. How in this work I realised the dignity of man, his feebleness, his strength, his humility, and the wrath and pity of the Son of Man.

The attack upon the "Christ" came from all quarters. Editors of newspapers, clergymen, and the "man in the street". I will reproduce part of Father Bernard Vaughan's article in *The Graphic* for February 14th, 1920.

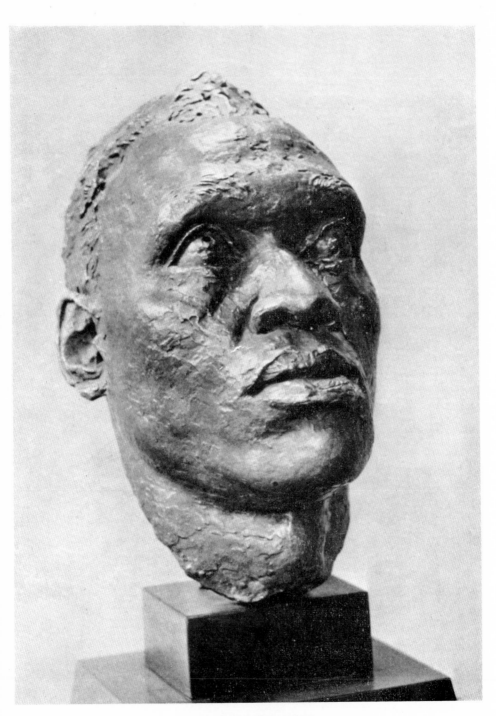

PAUL ROBESON, 1927

THE BLESSING. 1927

After a long prelude he goes on:

Since Cimabue's day till our own Holman Hunt's, sculptors and artists have followed the traditional idea about the features and expression of our Divine Lord. No artist, not even the saintly Fra Angelico, dared to innovate upon what was handed down as the embodiment, as far as might be, of the Divine character which has been revealed to us by tradition and in the Gospel stories. Any "portrait" of Our Lord that fails to express tenderness, dignity, calmness and sweetness, with overwhelming majesty —in a word, any so-called "likeness" which does not manifest a countenance in which are united an expression intensely human, yet altogether Divine, must be ruthlessly set aside as sinning against the canons of correct taste and as running counter to the conceptions which even non-Christians, as well as Christians, have formed of the unique character of Jesus Christ.

Listen to this consensus of opinion with regard to Christ's surpassing goodness and greatness. Before Him Kant feels constrained to bow as "the Ideal of perfection", in Him Hegel sees "the union of the Divine and the Human"; in Him again Spinoza recognises "the symbol of Divine Wisdom". To the scoffing Renan Jesus Christ "is the most beautiful Incarnation of God in the most beautiful of human forms". Of Him Napoleon said, "I know men. I tell you Jesus Christ was not a mere man." To the German Strauss Our Lord "is the brightest object we can possibly imagine with respect to religion, the Being without whose presence in the mind perfect piety is impossible." To Lecky, our British historian, Jesus Christ is "the highest pattern of virtue and the strongest incentive to its practice", while to John Stuart Mill, Christ "is charged with a special express and unique mission from God to lead mankind to truth and virtue".

With this established tradition, profane as well as sacred, literary as well as artistic, about the pre-eminent character and riveting personality of Jesus Christ, one could not, in wildest dreams, imagine any self-respecting artist to quarrel, still less to be so insolent as to strike out of metal a figure of the Risen Christ in which neither the man in the street nor the normal artist can discover any redeeming feature. Yet this has been done, and the painful result may be seen in Mr. Epstein's work, which is at present being exhibited at the Leicester Galleries, Leicester Square.

I have stood in front and at the back elevation of this gross and grotesque thing, with nose turned up and feet turned in; I have stood on the right and the left of this offending and hurting caricature; I have studied the unshapely head, the receding brow, the thick lips, the untipped nose, the uncanny eyes, the poorly built body, with its ugly feet and uglier hands, till I felt ready to cry out with indignation that in this Christian England there should be exhibited the figure of a Christ which suggested to me some degraded Chaldean or African, which wore the appearance of an Asiatic-American or Hun-Jew, which reminded me of some emaciated Hindu, or a badly grown Egyptian swathed in the cerements of the grave. I call it postively wicked and insulting to perpetrate such a travesty of the Risen Christ and to invite a Christian people, to whom the Founder of Christianity is the Man-God, to come and admire it.

Who is the man who, standing in presence of this shapeless specimen of humanity, could imagine coming from its brutally thick throat the words, "I am the Light of the World", or "I am the Way and the Truth and the Life", or "I am the Resurrection and the Life", or, lastly, "I am thy reward exceeding great"?

Someone has observed that if a hero were to come into a room, we should stand up and acclaim him, and if Christ should cross the threshold we should kneel down and revere Him; but let me add, if Mr. Epstein's horror in bronze were to spring into life and appear in a room, I for one should fly from it in dread and disgust, lest perhaps he might pick my pockets, or worse, do some deed of violence in keeping with his Bolshevik appearance. As I came out of the gallery I noticed that Mr. Epstein's statue stands near a certain type of shop round about Leicester Square. Whoever should succeed in sweeping such shops and such "art" into the Thames, to be carried out to sea and lost for ever, would do something to vindicate Christian morality and save us from the reproach of utter Pagan profligacy in our mammoth metropolis.

It is difficult to beat this for vilification, and it must be remembered that Father Bernard Vaughan, known as "The preacher of Mayfair", who castigated the "Sins of Society", was following out his rôle of modern Savonarola. Bernard Shaw undertook the answer to the reverend father the following week in *The Graphic*, and I reproduce his letter:

Father Vaughan is an unlucky man. He has a genius for mistaking his profession. The war tore off his cassock and revealed the spurs, the cartridge belt, the khaki beneath. And now that he is demobilised, his wandering star leads him into the profession of art critic.

When I was last at Lourdes I saw a cinema representation of the Passion. I think that Christ would have pleased Father Vaughan. He looked like a very beautiful operatic tenor. I have seen Victor Capoul and the late Lord Battersea; and he was as Christ-like (in Father Vaughan's sense) as both of them rolled into one. He was more the gentleman than the Christ of Oberammergau, who was in private life a wood-carver. The

My First Statue of Christ: 1917–1920

Church is so powerful at Lourdes that I do not think this exhibition would have been possible without its approval. That the approval was obtained is not to be wondered at. The Church knows its business at Lourdes. And the cinema actor knew his business, which was to study the most popular pictures of Christ, and to reproduce their subjects in his own person with the aid of his make-up box. He purchased the ambrosial curls and the eyebrows, and put them on with spirit gum. If his nose was not the right shape, he built it up with plastic material. The result was very pretty, and quite satisfactory to those whose ideal Christ is a stage lover. I did not care for it myself. The stage has no illusions (of that sort) for me; and I feel quite sure that Christ was no more like a modern opera singer than he was like Henry Dubb, the modern carpenter.

Now that Father Vaughan is going in for art, many terrible shocks await him. Imagine him in Bruges, looking at the Christs of the Netherland school (he can see some, by the way, in the National Gallery). He will almost forgive Mr. Epstein when he sees how Dierick Bouts and Hans Memling and Gerard David made Christ a plain, troubled, common man. Or he may go to Tunbridge Wells and walk to Speldhurst Church, where he will see a magnificent Morris stained window in which Burne-Jones, departing utterly from the convention which he himself had so often exploited, made the figure on the cross a glorious Greek God. Michelangelo did the same in his Last Judgment. Holman Hunt, after representing The Light of the World as an excessively respectable gentleman with a trim beard and a jewelled lantern, knocking at a door with the gesture of a thief in the night, lived to be reviled by the Vaughans of his day for representing Him in "The Shadow of the Cross" as a Syrian—actually as a Syrian Jew instead of an Oxford graduate. Raphael's unique Christ in His Transfiguration is a Tyrolese peasant. Rembrandt's Christ is a Dutchman. Von Uhde's Christ is a poor man who converses with men in tall hats, and women in nineteenth-century bonnets and shawls.

But there is no end to the varieties of type to be found in the Christs of the artists. We are only waiting for an advance in African civilisation for a negro Christ, who may be quite as impressive as any of the Aryan ones. The shallowest of all the Christs is the operatic Christ, just as the shallowest of the Virgins is the operatic Virgin. Father Vaughan, obsessed with the Christs of Guido, Ary Scheffer, Muller & Co., and with the Virgins of Sassoferrato and Bouguereau, was staggered by Epstein's Christ, just as he would be staggered by Cimabue's gigantic unearthly Virgin. He will soon know better. And if he will only read the Gospels instead of the despatches of the war correspondents, he will find that there is not a trace of "tenderness, calmness, and sweetness" in St. Matthew's literary portrait of Christ, and that the operatic Christ was invented by St. Luke.

All the Christs in art must stand or fall by their power of suggesting to the beholder the sort of soul that he thinks of as Christ's soul. It is evident that many people have found this in Mr. Epstein's Christ, and that Father Vaughan has not. Well, Father Vaughan will find his Christ in every Roman Catholic Church in the land, and in all the shops that furnish them. Let him choose the statue that is nearest his own heart; and I have no doubt that Mr. Cecil Phillips will place it beside Mr. Epstein's and leave every man to judge for himself which of the two is the more memorable.

BERNARD SHAW.

I remember on visiting the gallery one day with a friend, I noticed a man just emerging from the room where the "Christ" was shown, with clenched fists and an angry, furious face. I was told this was John Galsworthy, who ever after, in season and out, attacked my sculpture. I believe that in England it is his class, the upper-middle class, that has most resented my work. One might wonder at this, wonder what it is that strikes at them in my sculpture, what profoundly rooted beliefs and shibboleths are disturbed. I know that my work has become the sport of popular music-hall quips, and "man-in-the-street" jocularities, but this is due to a humorous association in their mental picture of sculpture with a comic figure like the little mannequin that ventriloquists use; but the class that Galsworthy represents really "sees red" when confronted with my imaginative works and even my portraits. A man entering my exhibition of drawings says to the gallery owner: "I should like to take Epstein out to a butcher's shop and have his hands chopped off." Matthew Smith overheard a man saying to a woman in front of a Bond Street dealer's window which showed a flower painting of his: "Those fellows Epstein and Smith ought to be in jail!" This fury over flower paintings, or paintings of still life, fruit, or landscape, or portrait busts, passes one's comprehension, and can only be understood by relating it to something fundamental, going far deeper than the sculpture or painting involved.*

* See Appendix: The First Statue of Christ.

The Sculptor in Epping Forest, 1924

THE HUDSON MEMORIAL; "RIMA", 1925

10

THE Royal Society for the Protection of Birds, including artists and writers, asked me to do a memorial to W. H. Hudson, author of *Green Mansions*, *The Purple Land*, and books on birds and the wild life of South America and England.

I was asked to do a panel in an enclosure which was to be called the Bird Sanctuary. I made two sketches showing Hudson himself, and was informed that the Office of Works would not accept a representation of a person, that is anything in the way of a portrait, in Hyde Park, and that I would have to make a design of a more symbolic nature.

In the meantime I was invited to attend a meeting of the Royal Society and hear their views on this matter. This meeting was a large one, and in the course of discussion John Galsworthy rose and declared that, in his opinion, I was not the right man to do the monument. He spoke, I thought, with some bitterness, and I was told later that he had proposed for the work another sculptor whom he knew personally. I agreed at this meeting to make a model which would incorporate the idea of Rima, the heroine of *Green Mansions*, and my particular supporters on this occasion were Muirhead Bone, Cunninghame Graham, and Holbrook Jackson. I made a sketch which was passed by the Office of Works, and I started at once in Epping Forest, in a shed, on the direct carving of the panel from a block of Portland stone. This took me seven months, 1924–1925, working through the winter, solitary, surrounded by silent and often fog-laden forest. In the spring, on a fine May morning, the memorial was unveiled in Hyde Park.

The ceremony, which was attended by a large crowd, was

preceded by speeches from Mr. Stanley Baldwin, the Prime Minister, and from Mr. Cunninghame Graham, and music was played and sung, and then the Prime Minister pulled the cord of the covering sheet. This small and inoffensive panel produced a sensation wholly unexpected on my part.

Cunninghame Graham would relate, with some humour, how he saw a shiver run down the spine of Mr. Stanley Baldwin. Immediately afterwards a "hullabaloo", unequalled for venom and spite, broke out in the Press. The monument was "obscene" and should be removed immediately. "Take this horror out of the Park", shrieked *The Dail Mail*. A letter to *The Morning Post* advocating its removal was signed by the President of the Royal Academy, Sir Frank Dicksee. A shabby gentleman turned up who held out-of-door meetings in front of the Memorial and attracted a large crowd by denouncing it. I was astonished to hear him harangue his audience thus: "Would you," he said pointing an accusing finger at the panel, "want your sister depicted in this manner?"

The Cockney crowd can get interested in anything in the way of entertainment. They are so good-hearted and good-humoured, and when this gentleman announced that he would speak from sunrise to sunset on his hymn of hate, and the papers had given him the publicity he sought, he was given victuals and drink as well. Finally the police removed him.

For a whole summer troops of Londoners and provincials wore the grass down into hard, beaten earth in front of the monument, seeking the obscenities that did not exist. A campaign of vilification more uncalled for never existed. There was nothing in the Memorial to shock anyone from the point of view of morals or art, and on my part no row was anticipated. I had my defenders and a memorandum was sent to the Office of Works by Muirhead Bone and others, and questions were answered in Parliament. A demand was made in Parliament that "the terrible female with paralysis of the hands called 'Rima' be instantly removed from the Park". Another M.P. characterised the panel as "this bad dream of the Bolshevist in Art". Bernard Shaw defended it and remarked on the meanness that could only afford a panel the size of a postage stamp, and wittily congratulated me on making this postage stamp size bulk so large that it caused high explosives of rage and hate in controversy.

Shaw was right about the size. When considering the monument with the Office of Works, three screens of different dimensions were put to judge its size, and, without consulting me, the smallest of the screens was chosen.

Cunninghame Graham defended the work with his usual brilliance and courage. Again and again he returned to the fight.

Finally the protests died down. The "muck-rakers" grew tired of their fruitless journeys to the Park, and the panel was left in its peaceful setting. The deserted spot could now be visited without alarm or interference. Grass grew again on the downtrodden soil.

Months after, the more scurrilous newspapers failing in their first attempt to remove the statue, continued, nevertheless, tactics of incitement. *The Morning Post* of October 7th, 1925, said:

Mr. Epstein's work in Kensington Gardens is so far from being the object of admiration that, were not the English a tolerant people, it would have long ago been broken into pieces.

On November 14th, *The Morning Post* had the satisfaction of reporting:

The inevitable has happened to Mr. Epstein's "Rima". She has been ingloriously daubed with green paint.

Again on November 18th *The Morning Post* announced triumphantly:

It is clear that there is some quality in the monument in Hyde Park that revolts the public.

A letter demanding the removal of the memorial with as little delay as possible now appeared in *The Morning Post*, signed by a number of noted persons, including Lady Frances Balfour, Hilaire Belloc, E. F. Benson, the Hon. Stephen Coleridge, the Hon. John Collier, Sir Arthur Conan Doyle, Sir Frank Dicksee, President of the Royal Academy, Sir Philip Burne-Jones, Sir E. Ray Lankester, Sir David Murray, R.A., Alfred J. Munnings, R.A., Sir Bernard Partridge, Sir Johnston Forbes-Robertson, Her Highness the Ranee Margaret of Sarawak, and H. Avray Tipping.

This manifesto declared that Epstein's design is "by universal consent so inappropriate and even repellent that the most fitting course open to the authorities would be to have it removed bodily. It would be a reproach to all concerned if future generations were allowed to imagine that this piece of artistic anarchy in any way reflected the true spirit of the age ".

The satisfaction of *The Morning Post* was almost complete.

With this encouragement, it resumed its campaign to remove the memorial, letters poured in (we know how these letters are engineered), which tended to show how this small carving upset the moral and æsthetic susceptibilities of London. Remember that the memorial is in an obscure corner of Hyde Park where only a chance visitor seeking quiet and solitude might occasionally venture.

Muirhead Bone wrote to *The Times* on November 23rd, 1925:

> Opinions will always differ about the artistic merits of works of art, and they are likeliest to differ about a work so modern and unconventional in style as Mr. Epstein's monument to W. H. Hudson (The Bird Sanctuary in Hyde Park). Due consent for the whole design (shown in a large model of the Panel by the sculptor) was obtained from the First Commissioner of Works, assisted by the advice of his Art Advisory Committee, and the memorial was then erected by subscriptions from all parts of the United Kingdom, the Empire and America. I have the agreement of the following signatories against any proposal to remove so completely authorised a work on the demand of a mere section of the public. So unprecedented an action as now seems to be proposed would, if carried out, inevitably open an era of hasty decision and reprisal in the region of our Public Memorials, which most of us would deplore and which all Committees responsible for them, and all sculptors would find intolerable.

The Times goes on:

> The following are the signatories referred to: Arnold Bennett, Laurence Binyon, Sir D. Y. Cameron, The Hon. Evan Charteris, S. L. Courtauld, Samual Courtauld, G. Eumorfopoulos, Lord Howard de Walden, Sir John Lavery, the Right Hon. J. Ramsey MacDonald, M.P., Ambrose McEvoy, Professor C. H. Reilly, Morley Roberts, Sir Michael Sadler, Lord Sandwich, C. P. Roberts, George Bernard Shaw, Ernest Thurtle, M.P., Sybil Thorndyke, Hugh Walpole, R. B. Cunninghame Grahame, Holbrook Jackson, Augustus John, George Moore, Henry W. Nevinson, Sir William Orpen, Ben Tillett, Hubert Wellington, Francis Dodd, R.A., etc. We have also received letters to protest against the removal of the panel from 170 students of the Royal College of Art, and from 85 students of the Slade School.

A question was asked in Parliament. Sir William Davison asked the Under-Secretary for Home Affairs what was the use of having a Fine Arts Commission if "Rima" were allowed to remain.

But the carving weathered this attack also. I discovered later that what had really saved the memorial was a memorandum sent to Viscount Peel, His Majesty's First Commissioner of Works, by Muirhead Bone. This document I now publish with the consent of Sir Muirhead.*

On the last two occasions when the monument was defiled, the letters I.F.L. (Independent Fascist League) and Swastikas were painted on.

Following this, an inspector from the Park police visited me. He asked me who I thought were the perpetrators of the defilement. When I suggested that they might, because of the Swastika signs, be of Fascist origin, he solemnly said: "We police make no difference between Fascists and Communists", and with that oracular remark, he departed.

* See Appendix: W. H. Hudson Memorial: 1925.

11

"THE VISITATION": 1926

IN 1926 in Epping Forest I modelled a life-size figure which I intended for a group, to be called "The Visitation". I can recall with pleasure how this figure looked in my little hut which I used as a studio. I should have liked it to stand amongst trees on a knoll overlooking Monk Wood. This figure stands with folded hands, and expresses a humility so profound as to shame the beholder who comes to my sculpture expecting rhetoric or splendour of gesture. This work alone refutes all the charges of blatancy and self-advertisement levelled at me.

It now occupies a niche at the Tate Gallery in such a position that it is easily missed on entering the Gallery. I am pleased it is in an obscure niche and that the statue is only discovered on leaving the Gallery; the jaded visitor may "turn perhaps with relief" (a phrase often used by the critics to my detriment) to this bronze which could also be called "Charity". When I exhibited the work at the Leicester Galleries, wishing to avoid controversy, I called it "A Study". By this disguise I succeeded for once in evading the critics, always ready to bay and snap at a work. A subscription was raised to purchase it, and I recall that Richard Wyndham gave the proceeds of an exhibition he was holding of his own work towards its purchase for the Tate Gallery. George Grey Barnard, who was passing through London at the time, came with me to the Gallery and was enthusiastic, and this from my old master moved me greatly. He declared that if I sent it to New York he would see that it went to the Metropolitan. On this visit I noticed a little man in the Gallery who seemed very upset at the figure, fretting and fuming. I asked who he was, and was told he was a well-known collector of the most modern art. What

112

opposite emotions were aroused by my modest and unassuming work!

CABARET DECORATIONS

Just before the First World War Madame Frida Strindberg turned up in London. She had been, I believe, the last of August Strindberg's wives, a little Jewish woman from Vienna. She intended starting a night club, the first of its kind in London. To pave the way for this venture Madame Strindberg gave a dinner, to which she invited artists and those she thought would be interested in her scheme. The meal was sumptuous, the champagne lavish. When the management presented the bill Madame Strindberg took it in her hand, and turning to the company said: "Who will be my knight, to-night?" There was no response from the company! The Club was situated in a basement off Regent street, and Madame Strindberg asked me to decorate it for her. Two massive iron pillars supported the ceiling, and I proposed surrounding these with sculpture. I proceeded directly in plaster and made a very elaborate decoration which I painted in brilliant colours. Gaudier Brzeska came down to see these decorations while I was at work on them. This Cabaret was intended to capture the youthful and elderly rich, and several of my models, amongst them Lillian Shelley and Dolores, sang and danced there.

I went there once or twice, but this sort of night life was distasteful to me, and I heard later that the place had been raided by the police, and my decorations and Madame Strindberg disappeared.

Of Lillian Shelley I made two studies, an early head, and later an elaborate bust. Of the head I remember that when I was exhibiting it, the model turned up while I was in the Gallery, leaning on the arm of a gentleman who turned to me and said self-righteously: "Yes, I can see that you have depicted the vicious side of Lillian." I answered that he "knew her perhaps better than I did". . . . In truth I had made a head expressive of innocence and sweetness. A short time later the gentleman who had so offensively rebuked me was kicked to death in Cornwall by the miner-father of a girl he had attempted to seduce.

For the morals and manners of my professional models I have never been responsible, and it is strange that an artist should have the odium of the somewhat erratic conduct of his models placed to his account. The charming and often *facile mœurs* of the model, if known, sometimes give the artist a lurid reputation.

I would prefer to work from models who are not known, but often a pestiferous journalist will nose around and get on familiar terms with the models. He mentions them in the Press. That very soon turns their head, and they become characters with "a public". They imagine themselves to be like actresses. Their opinions are quoted, and they make fools of themselves generally. That particular period in London has now passed with the passing of the old Café Royal. Lillian Shelley, the temperamental, was of course beautiful, and likewise Dolores was beautiful, but their devotion to Art ceased when they left the model's stand. Betty May also shared in their beauty and notoriety, and I did two studies of her. The notion that I only worked from models of this kind was severely commented on in the newspapers, and one of my exhibitions was characterised, I recall, as nothing more than an exhibition of semi-oriental sluts. How pharisaic! Perhaps as I exhibited these bronzes with the "Christ", these Magdalenes were in the right company. I have of course worked from every kind of man and woman, and it is amazing that to-day an artist can be criticised for following in the footsteps of Donatello and Rembrandt.

It was at this period that I met Frank Harris, who asked me to do his bust and work from him at a villa in the South of France, but he was a character so filled with bombast and conceit that I was careful about having anything to do with him, more especially as he was extremely large in his requirements of work, but when I mentioned money to him, he became the vaguest of the vague. I believe he later intrigued Gaudier to do his bust, and Gaudier, more trusting than I, or hard up at the time for funds, went some way with it, and then destroyed it. "Killed Frank Harris", as he said.

Accusations of wickedness in my work cannot affect my own judgment of it, which is that it is sound and healthy, more especially as there is now an Art which professes with pride its own viciousness.

Perhaps those artists are not so "devilish" as they believe themselves to be.

Had I an income I would like to live in the country and work, but I have found it impossible to work in the country and keep in touch with Galleries and others who might want my work. My three years,

THE VISITATION, 1926

"The Visitation" on a Scottish moor

1913–1916, at Pett Level, near Hastings, were productive of many carvings, but I had continually to run up to London to see if I could dispose of something or get a portrait to do.

My staying for so long a period in London I put down to a natural disinclination for moving about. Barnard said to me: "You can work anywhere in the world, I see," for he could not understand why I stopped in England when America held out so many more opportunities for me as a sculptor. In truth, I cannot think of my work as peculiarly of London or of my time. It had never, of course, troubled me whether I was of my time or not. Some critics and artists harp on this and discuss whether an artist represents his period or whether he has influenced his time. Such questions can be argued either way, without arriving at anything of value. This hair-splitting does not appeal to me. It is like the question whether an artist ought to be, or is, Classic or Romantic, Realistic, Academic, Abstract, or Revolutionary—all terms which can be construed differently and argued endlessly.

One of the sticks which was used to hit me during the First World War was the saying that my work smacked more of Dürer than of Leonardo—that I was really a Boche. But I took it as a compliment that I ever so remotely resembled Dürer. They thought also, when they said my work was more like Easter Island work, that they had accused me of barbarities unspeakable, the critics not realising that the carvings of Easter Island are sculptural and sensitive—far more so than our wretched imitations of Belgian Renaissance and French nineteenth-century decadence which disfigure London's squares.

This was a period when a strange character roamed about amongst the artists called Stuart Gray. He had been a respectable lawyer in Edinburgh, and "kicked over the traces", and had led a contingent of "hunger marchers" to London. He finally got hold of some sort of derelict house where the lease had not expired. It was facing Regent's Park. He turned it into a caravanserai for artists and models.

This refuge was without gas or electric light, so that candles were used, and it seldom had water. No room had a lock, as most of the metal work had been carried away. Here the artists lived, and there was a life class at which I sometimes drew, and sometimes the artists, among others Roberts and Bomberg, a mysterious Indian artist and some models would have parties. Whether Stuart Gray ever received any rent was a question, but the old man who resembled a Tolstoy gone wrong would prowl about at night in a god-fatherly fashion and look over his young charges.

The mysterious Indian died, it is said of eating a herring which he had kept too long in a drawer. Another lodger, a woman who had advanced views on the relations of the sexes and had written a play called *The Triumph of Venus* in which her ideas were incorporated, went on to the balcony in her dressing-gown and started declaiming her play to passers-by, until the police intervened. This fantastic place did not last long, however, and Stuart, under the guidance of Bomberg, became a painter, gathering his materials where he could and painting on old bits of rag. But he had no talent and finally went off to become "King" of some Utopian colony on an island where he reared another family.

At this time I became acquainted with Philip Heseltine (Peter Warlock in Music), and also got to know Cecil Gray, and I took them both to St. John's Wood one day to introduce them to Bernard Van Dieren, the Dutch composer. This introduction was to have an important influence on the lives of both Gray and Heseltine.

Heseltine later committed suicide. He was a restless and discontented character, but he certainly was devotedly attached to Van Dieren, and took his mental colour largely from him. He left a quantity of music which reflects Elizabethan work, at that period very much in vogue. His mentality was, I thought, warped by a very crude and childish streak, and practical jokes of a stupid sort satisfied him.

Cecil Gray's book is unfortunately a one-sided and idealistic picture of him. I met, through Gray and Heseltine, Frederick Delius, and we visited each other. This composer of sweet and melancholy music was argumentative, cranky, and bad-tempered, and we had many a set-to. Delius having very little sense of humour, the argument on his part became almost always acrid. For one thing he imagined himself a tremendous authority on Art. This was founded on the fact that in Paris, years ago, he had bought a picture of Gauguin's. Also Mrs. Delius was a painter. Delius would lay down the law on Art, and absurd laws they were too. He was only interesting when he spoke of his early days in Florida as an orange grower and crocodile hunter or related anecdotes about negroes or Paris life.

My picture of him is borne out by Richard Fenby's account of his four years' martyrdom at the house of Delius.

I should have liked to do a bust of Delius, for I think that all the drawings made of him are unbelievably sentimental, especially those made during his last illness. The artists imagined that a sick man must be a saint, and they drew him with a saint-like martyr's expression on his face.

I proposed the idea to Gray, but nothing came of it. It was the same with Busoni whom I met with Van Dieren, but at the time Busoni told Van Dieren he could not stay long enough in London to sit for me. In reality he did not think me good enough to work for him, and Van Dieren confessed later this was the true reason. With Busoni also I found that, when it came to the plastic arts, he was both arrogant and dogmatic, referring with disdain to Van Gogh and El Greco, and speaking of Greek works as "Wedding Cake Sculpture". He was an admirer of the Italian Futurists! Busoni was surrounded by an adoring crowd of worshippers who thought that every word falling from his lips was gospel, and this undoubtedly gave him a wrong proportion on things. He had a fine head, leonine and ravaged by illness, and I do not think that any artist did him justice. He looked best at the piano when he scowled at what was not always a friendly audience, for, as a pianist, his brilliant distortions of Beethoven and Bach caused murderous feelings in some, and Busoni seemed well aware of this. I thought him far more Teuton than Italian and no doubt his upbringing in Germany moulded his mind and music.

12

LIVERPOOL EXHIBITION, AND ALLEGED
FORGERIES: 1926

IN answer to an invitation from the Walker Gallery Committee, I
sent to the Liverpool Exhibition of 1926, in the Walker Gallery,
a bust of "Mrs. Epstein", and a bust called "Anita". At the
official opening, Lord Wavertree, who held an important position
in the Gallery, made some severe strictures in his speech, which were
widely reported in the provincial and London papers. He said: "If
these are Mr. Epstein's best, then a poor artist would have done better
if he had submitted his worst." Naturally, as I had been invited to
send my works, I now wished to withdraw them. The Committee
apologised for the rudeness of Lord Wavertree and asked me to allow
the works to remain. Lord Wavertree, true to his class and position,
remained unrepentant and revelled in the notoriety his words had
given him. Of course he spoke for a large section of the ignorant, and
to them to insult an artist was just being honest and straightforward.
In fact, the noble lord thanked, in an advertisement he had inserted
in *The Times*, the large number of persons who had written and
congratulated him.

An interesting sidelight on the foregoing is that an artist can be
libelled with impunity. The artist is supposed to enjoy and profit by
libellous notices in the newspapers. Certainly in my case this is a
fallacy. In America there exists the expression: "Every kick is a
boost." Architects and public bodies, however, will not give commissions to a man when the bullying newspapers have convinced
them that he is unsafe or dangerous. The bullying of the newspapers
has an adverse effect on the sales of an artist, and certainly on any
commissions that he may get.

THE SICK CHILD, 1928

LYDIA, 1928

Liverpool Exhibition: 1926

Archbishop Downey of Liverpool said in an interview when the new Roman Catholic Cathedral was started: "It would be a calamity if anything Epsteinish were found in the new Cathedral." I replied: "Where else could be found a sculptor to do justice to the spirit of Christianity to-day, in a world almost wholly bereft of Christian action?"

This brings me to another problem which artists have to face, namely, forgeries. When I returned from America I found that a number of works not made by me had been sold under my name. I traced the works to a certain company of dealers in works of art, and brought an action against them in the Courts. This case was tried before Mr. Justice Maugham (now Lord Maugham), and was decided against me. I quote from *The Daily Telegraph* of October 17th, 1930, an account of the case. It will be of interest to artists in a like predicament.

Mr. Jacob Epstein, the noted sculptor, was the unsuccessful plaintiff in an action brought before Mr. Justice Maugham in the Chancery Division to-day.

He claimed an injunction restraining the International Depositories Ltd., proprietors of the King's Galleries, King's Road, Chelsea, their servants, and agents, from selling, offering for sale, or describing any pieces of sculpture as his work, when in fact it was not his work at all.

The defendants denied ever having passed off, or attempted to pass off, any work of Mr. Epstein which was not his.

Mr. E. J. Herckscher, counsel, stated that in July, 1929, Mr. Epstein, his client, was informed by Lady Jones of Hyde Park Gate, wife of Sir Roderick Jones, that she had purchased at King's Galleries a bust carved by him of his wife. At her invitation he went to see it, and declared it to be not sculpture but a cement cast, and not his work.

Subsequently two other ladies went to the Galleries and saw four or five other pieces of sculpture or casts, which they were led to believe were the work of Mr. Epstein, but actually were not his work at all. Thereupon in July, Mr. Epstein started an action, and the defendants gave an undertaking in the terms of a notice of motion not to sell any casts as his work which were not his work. Since then further negotiations led to nothing. Mr. Epstein did not ask for damages, but was anxious to stop what he thought was a very improper use of his name.

Giving evidence, Lady Jones said that when she visited King's Galleries, she noticed five pieces of sculpture on a shelf, and was told by Madame Fredericke, a director of the defendant company, that they were

Epstein: An Autobiography

"Epsteins". On a second visit a week or a fortnight later, Madame Fredericke told her "she believed" they were Epsteins, and that she had bought them as such, but that she could not warrant them as Epsteins. She stated her belief that two of the pieces were "Lust" and "Vice", and that because of their extreme character, she had difficulty in selling them. The price of the lot was thirty pounds. Witness paid seven pounds fifteen shillings for the piece in question, believing it to be a work of Mr. Epstein.

Mrs. Ethel Kibblewhite, another witness, said that in June last she went to the Gallery at the request of Mr. Epstein, who was her friend, and on questioning Madame Fredericke about a head or mask was told that it was a "Portrait of Epstein by himself".

Mr. Cleveland Stevens, K.C. (for the defendants): "Madame Fredericke said that she never saw you before in her life. Did you see anybody else there?"—"No."

Another witness, Miss Jessie Briggs, also a friend of Mr. Epstein, said she saw a mask at the Gallery labelled "Epstein himself".

Mr. Epstein gave evidence himself, describing his inspection of the bust at Lady Jones' house and his denial on that occasion that it was his work. He had never seen it before.

Mr. Herckscher: "Was it a copy or imitation of any work of yours?"

"I should say that it was a faint imitation of a certain work of mine."

"Did it bear any resemblance to your wife?"—"None whatever."

Witness said that his object in bringing this action was to guard himself and other artists from a very dangerous form of trafficking in names, reputations, and false works.

Mr. Epstein stated that if the bust purchased by Lady Jones had been genuine, it might have fetched between two hundred pounds and three hundred pounds.

Mr. Stevens: "Do you say that your reputation has suffered with Lady Jones?"—"Certainly. She would have many persons of social distinction at her house, and if they saw a work of this kind, it would be bound to damage my reputation."

Madame Fredericke, giving evidence, said that she had bought seven pieces of sculpture, picture frames, canvas and pottery from a Chelsea artist who was in financial difficulties, paying him twenty-five pounds or thirty pounds for the lot. She thought the pieces of sculpture were interesting and odd shapes.

"The public," she added, "like these things to-day, they make good garden ornaments." When she asked the artist from whom she had purchased them where they came from he said they "might be Epsteins".

One was called "Grief", another called "A Pugilist" looked like a boxer's fist, and a third was something like a snail.

She gave two of the pieces to her sister. When Lady Jones visited the gallery, witness told her that she had never verified the authenticity of the pieces of work, and could not give a guarantee.

Giving judgment for the defendants with costs, Mr. Justice Maugham said that Mr. Epstein's motive in bringing the action was reasonable and proper, but it was a great pity that he had not taken more seriously a letter of the defendants from which it was plain that they had no desire to insist on any such statement as that they believed this bust to be his work.

On the evidence of Lady Jones alone, he was unable to find that the bust was said to be Epstein's. The true construction seemed to be that Lady Jones was left under the impression that it "might be" Epstein's, and that it was a speculative purchase, without any positive guarantee.

He did not think the words "Epstein—himself" would, standing alone, lead any person to believe that the bust was a portrait of the sculptor executed by himself. His Lordship was not satisfied to leave the case without saying that Madame Fredericke's observation with reference to the piece of sculpture in question was unwise and, in some respects, observations of which the Court did not approve.

The foregoing account does not give a picture of the grotesque situation in which I found myself at the trial. The Judge, who seemed to me to adopt a snubbing tone towards my lawyer throughout the proceedings, was perhaps impressed by the pathos of Madame Fredericke, who, dressed in a crinoline and with curls at the side of her head, complained bitterly of having her time wasted by this action. As she claimed also to be deaf, she was given special facilities by the Court, standing down amidst Counsel, rather in a martyr's attitude. From the way things went at this trial it looked as if I were the criminal, one who by his villainous accusations made other people suffer. I was strongly reminded of the famous account by Dickens of the trial in *Pickwick Papers*, except that I felt myself to be the "hass".

Note that this traffic in "good garden ornaments" went on while I was safely away in America!

My witnesses failed me. Lady Jones and Mrs. Kibblewhite were indefinite in their statements, whereas the Company's witnesses gave assured statements. A Court has a peculiar overawing effect on people who are not accustomed to the atmosphere. After the trial these two ladies apologised to me and could not understand why they had given such vague and unsatisfactory answers to questions. No account was taken of the fact that the Company, by ringing me up on the 'phone, could have found out in half an hour whether they were dealing in Epsteins or not. I was nonplussed by the verdict, which was a complete triumph for the King's Road Company. Apart from this case I have been asked on other occasions to verify bronzes not by me; and once even my name had been engraved on the base of the bronze.

Frequently newspapers have published articles advising architects not to employ me, This, you would think, is a direct libel, and I would have a perfectly legitimate case to bring to Court. I have refrained from bringing libel actions, knowing only too well that as the popular idea, high and low, in England is that if anything is really new and intense in Art it should be shot at first sight, I would not be given even the legendary farthing that Whistler received in his action against Ruskin. In any case, litigation is a costly business, as I found out in my action against the Company that sold the alleged Epsteins. Also, how can an artist have his time taken up with the details of Court claims and the intricacies of the Law?

THEO, 1930

MADONNA AND CHILD, 1926

13

"MADONNA AND CHILD", AND VISIT TO NEW YORK: 1927

I HAD worked for a year on the "Madonna and Child". An Indian woman, Sunita, and her son, Enver, posed for me. The model was of that eternal Oriental type which seemed to me just right for a work of this religious character. When I had finished the head the model remarked that she could not possibly "look as good as I had made her". She recognised that there was something eternal and divine in it and outside herself. Her boy, aged six, was another matter. He was restless, and for a boy to sit or rather stand quietly while I was working was out of the question. To interest or distract him I had him read to while I worked, but none of the stories interested him for long and, sensing that he was master of the situation, he kept constantly asking for new stories. My impatience at the time is responsible for the child's body being somewhat unfinished, but taking all in all it was a work I carried through with great concentration and continuity of thought and its complex linear plan and very elaborate secondary motives were dominated by my original idea of presenting a massive group that would go into a cathedral or religious sanctuary.

In connection with the "Madonna and Child" it is interesting to record that M. and Mme Maisky, the Soviet Ambassador and his wife, when visiting me were especially struck by this group. Madame Maisky thought the Soviet would be interested in it, although the title did not accord with the Soviet "Ideology", but it was a Mother and Child and might be accepted as a group of Motherhood. I gave Madame Maisky photographs of the group, but there was no result, and later the New York sculptor, Sally Ryan, bought the group and lent it to the Tate Gallery.

While the bronze was still at the foundry Lord Duveen asked me if he could see it and we motored to the workshop in Fulham. Looking at the work he turned to me and said: "If you had in mind to do a Madonna and Child, why did you not choose a beautiful model?" I was so astonished at this reception of the work that I turned away from him in disgust. This action as to what constituted beauty was typical of him. On one occasion I heard him say that had he not thought in his youth that Rembrandt's people were ugly, he would have made many more millions of money in his lifetime. Knowing that I was leaving for America, the great man got in one more shot. It was a piece of advice. "So you are going to America," he said. "Do not let it be thought that you are leaving England because of dissatisfaction with the manner in which you are received here." James Bone of *The Manchester Guardian*, in commenting on my departure for America, said that "England has been a bad stepmother to him". It was generally thought that I was shaking off the dust of England from my feet. That was not my intention. English artists often visited America. Some made it the habit of going yearly. I had been away from America for twenty-five years, so there was nothing unusual in my holding an exhibition of my work there. Nevertheless, every move I made was looked upon as significant, and so Duveen warned me to mind my step.

Before I arrived in New York Harbour a journalist who was on board asked me for an interview for a Jewish paper. His first question was: "What is your attitude towards Zionism?" At that time, 1927, Zionism was not the acute question it became later and I had not thought about it. I answered that I had no attitude. He then said with a belligerent air: "We will want to know your attitude, make no mistake about it." At that I left him.

Arrived at Sandy Hook, the American journalists had gathered in a cabin to receive and question me. They were courteous and their questions amused me. One said: "Have you come to debunk sculpture?" This "debunk" was explained to me, and I had to answer in the negative. I had no such evangelistic mission. Instead, I had to assert that I had come simply as a working sculptor to show some of my pieces. I got on very well with the newspaper men, but a leader in one of the papers cautioned me that the warmth of my reception depended upon my attitude to American art. This touchiness, I am afraid, is characteristic of American feeling towards artists who arrive from England. Why should they bother about what European artists think of them? The European artist usually goes to America to sell his wares and has no business criticising and fault-finding. The American artist resents an attitude of patronage or superiority assumed by the visitor.

I was returning to the country of my birth, and a peculiar feeling that I had deserted America to live and work in Europe was in the air. This feeling was somehow hostile and expressed itself in *The New Yorker*, which carried a weekly notice while I was exhibiting that "Epstein has come home to roost". I had not realised that I was as important as all that. I knew nothing of what had happened in America during my twenty-five years' absence. For my old master, George Grey Barnard, I had the greatest respect and I was prepared to see what there was that was new. I knew that American artists made frequent trips to Paris and absorbed the very latest "ism" long before the English artists did, though they were so much nearer. I felt that those who would interest me most would more likely be the artists who showed little or no Paris influence.

I revisited the haunts of my youth—the dockland along the lower East and West side of New York. I found it greatly changed. Gone were the wooden piers that had at one time jutted out into the river, the ancient warehouses with their strange spicy smells, the ship chandler shops with their heaps of cordage and tackle. From the wooden piers I used to be able to study every type of ocean-going vessel, even great three-masters with their long bowsprits sticking out over the cobbled docks. The Bowery was also sadly changed. These were prohibition days, and the saloons and the life of the old Bowery were gone. Of the artists, I met Bill Zorach and Tom Benton, both of whom I liked immensely. Also I met a set more immediately influenced by Paris, who were extremely cliquey. They imagined that they lived in a superior world of their own, and in that they were very like what is called "The Bloomsbury Highbrows" in London. This New York clique also had the same conviction as their prototypes in London, that everything in art was antique and old-fashioned that was not connected with their generation and themselves. Later on, when I exhibited some of my sculpture at the Art Students' League, my old school, I overheard one student say to another: "The Epsteins are dull. They bore me." And I was astonished to see that all the work of the students was abstract or cubist.

Surrealism had not come in then. Most likely the students are all Abstractionists now. When asked my opinion of the art students' work at the Art Students' League, I congratulated them on working "like Niggers". New York monuments were appalling to me, rivalling those of London in their commonplaceness.

I can recall that while looking at the monument of "Civic Virtue", near the City Hall, one of the few beggars I saw in New York accosted me. This was in pre-slump days. He asked me what I thought of the group, and we talked about it. I felt I was back in old New York again. My companion was a real "bum", genial and in amazing rags. He and I talked of the New York of twenty-five years ago which we knew.

MY EXHIBITION IN NEW YORK, 1927

My exhibition was held in a gallery which, when I first viewed it, made my heart sink. In New York galleries have no top daylight as in London, and this particular gallery presented a tawdry, conventional appearance, curtained walls, plants, and chandeliers. The owner of the gallery also did not recommend himself particularly to me. I found that I was looked upon as just another fortnight's exhibition, in the yearly round of exhibitions, and my tremendous struggle and expense in coming to New York was a matter of just casual interest to him. Moreover, the gallery was occupied at the time by some unfortunate Spanish artist, who, like myself, had trusted his all to this exhibition of his, and it was a failure; no sales, only bills for everything. And meeting this wretch, and listening to his tale of woe was not encouraging. The gallery I discovered was a partnership of three men, one of whom had been a sculptor, and my experience with the three of them was far from pleasant. When I suggested that the walls should be simplified as a setting for sculpture, they were resentful, and in fact bridled at any suggestions I made for showing the sculpture to advantage. Also my discovery that the show was for only a fortnight astonished me. How could one do anything

KATHLEEN, 1921

KATHLEEN, 1929

KATHLEEN, 1933

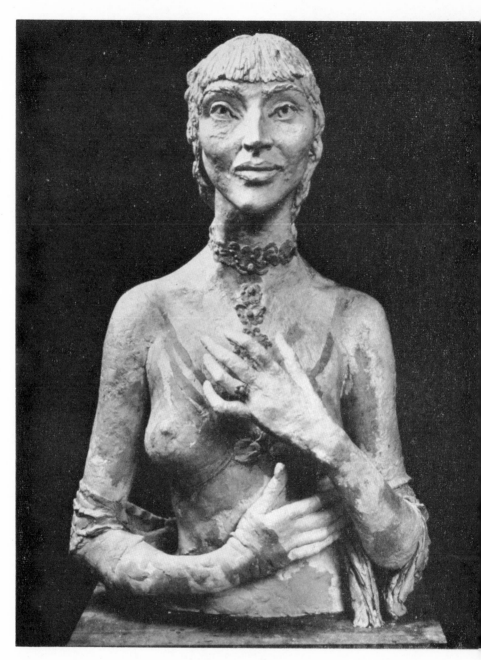

KATHLEEN, 1935

"Madonna and Child": 1927

in a fortnight! Sometimes in a big city it took a fortnight for a show to get going, and in London I was used to at least a month. I had been to terrific expense to get about fifty bronzes to New York, and the large bronze of the "Madonna and Child" was amongst them. With a mid-Victorian gallery, and unsympathetic dealers, I felt, that first night in New York, thoroughly down-hearted. I wished I had never come to waste time and my earnings in a venture that promised so badly. The head of the firm in arranging my show said that a preface to the catalogue was absolutely necessary. For this purpose he wrote one himself which was a strange mixture of illiterate jargon about my aims and achievements. I had, of course, to reject this out of hand, which made him feel none too friendly to me, as he rather fancied himself in the rôle of creative art critic. One partner, an ex-sculptor, was full of schemes by which the gallery could add up expenses to charge me with, and I had my work cut out to evade these impositions. I discovered, moreover, that it was expected that my show after its fortnight's run in New York should go on tour in the States. The prospect of my collection of sculptures going on a tour through literally hundreds of cities and towns did not appeal to me. An American girl had told me of how her work had gone on tour years before, and was still "touring", where she did not know. So I put my foot down on the tour, and to get the gallery to agree to this in writing was "some job", as Americans say. A lawyer and the three partners took a whole morning and well into the afternoon to fix this up; but finally all was settled and the sculpture on a Saturday night was placed round the gallery. The chief partner, who resembled nothing so much as a bar-room tender in appearance and manner, and his assistants, two huge negroes, would lift my bronzes and place them. "Another Beauty!" the chief would say, and with guffaws the burly giants would grab a bronze and place it where I indicated. My dealer had been imbibing dry ginger ale and in this sympathetic atmosphere I began the show. I made the mistake of not going to my private view, or as Americans call it, "preview". Americans want to see *you*. I thought the works were enough.

The exhibition received a great deal of publicity, although I had rejected the special publicity agent the gallery placed at my disposal, at my expense. This particular lady had suggested as a go-off that I should strongly criticise everything in America and so attract attention to my show! I declined her well-meant advice, and relied on the interest of the works themselves. In this poor setting, and with nothing to help them, the show was nevertheless a success, and works were bought, two for public galleries. I made friends with men like Professor John Dewey and Paul Robeson and Carl Van Vechten. The staff of *The New Republic* asked me to lunch and I found an appreciative and intelligent interest in sculpture. I had a hostile reception from what was known as the Mrs. Harry Payne Whitney crew. They ran a journal for themselves, which gave me a notice when the show was practically over, an old trick played here as well as in New York.

I found of course a certain amount of hostility also in the smart Press.

A great friend was Frank Crowninshield, who edited *Vanity Fair*, and took me about to various gatherings. These were meant well, but had the drawback of all those functions. You were expected to get up and give a talk to your audience, and in my case I was generally taken by surprise and had nothing to say; also I intensely dislike being singled out, and so these gatherings were an embarrassment to me. I find it difficult to understand why I should make speeches, although I know that the technique of saying little or nothing is easily learnt. I much preferred Rita Romilly's, where artists and writers gathered, and Paul Robeson sang, and there was no formality of dress or speech. It was here I met a strange character called Bob Chandler, who wished to make me his guest of honour at a luncheon, but I heard that his luncheons were famous for the strength and variety of the drinks, and that Bob himself was invariably seated at the head of the table on a sort of throne, placed well above his guests. This piece of news settled it, and I left the "democratic" Bob severely alone. New York presented some aspects of the "artistic" life which I think are peculiar to itself, and one which is a little disconcerting is that most of those who took an interest in my work invariably were at great pains to advise me what to work on next, and tell me of their great ideas in detail. One such pest would descend on me with irrefutable reasons why I should make "St. Paul" my next great work.

There was a great deal to enjoy, I found. For one thing, my flat overlooked Central Park, and in looking across it in the wintry landscape there was all the beauty of a Hiroshige. At night underneath my windows I could watch the myriad skaters glancing to and fro over the frozen ponds with piercing shouts and gaiety. I enjoyed also eating in restaurants there. Southern food was served by beautiful mulatto girls. At the Metropolitan there were wonderful Rembrandts, and also a fine collection of Cézannes; and as well of an afternoon an orchestra played symphonic music there; a practice later copied in London in our galleries. New York, musically, I should say, had almost too full a fare. The number of artists giving concerts was beyond the ability of any one person to listen to. Theatres were crowded and Broadway of a night was a curious sight, with its bright lights and thousands of sightseers thronging the streets, As a city, New York at night is a fascinating study, with, I should say, its sinister side in the crowded quarters. But perhaps that is common to all large cities. The lighting up of the city towards evening, viewed from my flat, was lovely, and as a spectacle I suppose it is unique. I preferred watching the great sky-scrapers from the outside to travelling inside them, their elevators and countless numbered offices I could never quite master. Actually, in the four months I was in New York I went out very little, and as I had three portraits to do, I was rarely out except at night. I went with Paul Robeson and a party to Harlem, and made the round of negro dance places, but I saw nothing to wonder at beyond the usual stamina of the negro when dancing.

We had to carry our drink with us of course, and the unusual spectacle of ladies carrying bottles under their arms amused me.

I met, through Professor Dewey, Doctor Albert Barnes of Philadelphia, whose wonderful collection of French paintings I went to see. Dr. Barnes has a reputation for boorishness of which, on my visit to see him, I found no trace. He was courtesy itself and showed me over his collection with evident pleasure, going so far as to dismiss his teachers and pupils from the galleries so that I would see the collection in peace. I was told that dictaphones were installed in the walls, so that critics who were facetious or too frank could be instantly reported and told to go. One young Englishman claimed that he was the victim of this detective arrangement.

I believe Dr. Barnes had reason to resent the manner in which his collection of Cézannes and Renoirs were first received by the worthy citizens of Philadelphia, but that is in the long past, and by now Philadelphia is proud to have expensive Cézannes in its midst. Of sculptures in the Barnes collection, I saw none except some African carvings which had come from Paul Guillaume, who had helped Dr. Barnes with his collection of French paintings.

One Sunday morning I was taken to see a collection of old masters. This wonderful assembly of paintings, comprised of Titians, Rubens, and Rembrandts, all fine examples, was owned by a man who had become blind. The old man, taking me by the arm, led me from one to the other of the paintings, talking about them as if he could still see their beauty, as indeed in his mind's eye he did, until we came to the few pieces of sculpture and my host started telling me of a Benvenuto Cellini which should have been on a pedestal, and which I failed to see. Looking about me I espied the Cellini on a table where it had been misplaced. The collection, of course, interested me, and I much enjoyed seeing these wonderful paintings. At the end, though, the collector said, as if congratulating himself: "You see, my taste stopped with 1669, the year of Rembrandt's death." I recall that when leaving him I reflected bitterly on the taste and judgment of this wealthy man who would not purchase a work unless it were three or four hundred years old. Conservatism I found as strongly entrenched in America as it is in England, or in official circles in France.

There was practically the exact equivalent of the Royal Academy in their National Academy of Design, and even in "advanced" groups who took their thinking from Paris or Munich. I saw nothing of a sculpture that would be the equivalent of the *Leaves of Grass*, even in intention. There was a curious harking back to pseudo-classic sculpture, a kind of early Greek stylism; an early Greek made into table ornaments or book-props, or Renaissance motives turned into garden statues or for fountains, or Buddhist placidness on a small decorative scale, a sort of Sunday afternoon Buddhism, I thought, something that was the equivalent in sculpture of Christian Science. I found nothing in sculpture that was native, inspired by the soil, or even the vast commercial enterprises of America. At present, perhaps, the great works like the Boulder Dam or the Panama Canal or the skyscrapers come nearest to an impression of the American soul. Sculpture has to wait.

ISABEL, 1933

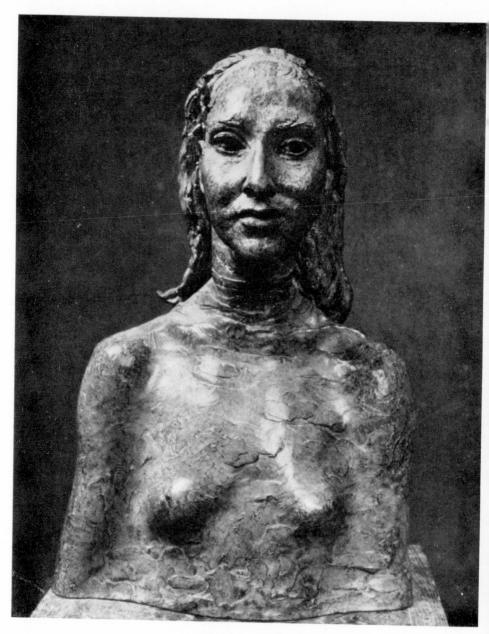

MORNA, 1936

"Madonna and Child": 1927

During my stay I did three portraits, Professor John Dewey, Professor Franz Boas, and Paul Robeson. The John Dewey portrait was a presentation to Columbia University, where it now is. The subscriptions were donated by students and admirers of Dewey who each gave five dollars. As a sitter Dewey was very sympathetic, and Joseph Rattner, a student of his whose idea it was to present the portrait, would come in and talk with him. They kept up a running philosophic conversation, and Rattner contrived at the same time to make coffee for the three of us. I enjoyed making this bust and I recall the event with pleasure. Dewey's son-in-law on seeing the bust said, that I had made him look like a "Vermont horse-dealer". This was not a bad characterisation, as Professor Dewey came from Vermont, and he pleased me with his Yankee drawl and seeming casualness. He was a man absolutely straightforward, simple, and lovable in character. Professor Dewey said of his bust that it pleased him and he "hoped he looked like it".

Professor Boas was also interesting to work from, his face was scarred and criss-crossed with mementoes of many duels of his student days in Heidelberg, but what was still left whole in his face was as spirited as a fighting cock. He seemed to be a man of great courage, both mental and physical.

Paul Robeson sang lullabies to Peggy Jean. I would have liked to have worked longer from him, but I had already booked my passage back, and so the study I did of Robeson remains a sketch. (Lately in London I did a study of his son Pauli, aged eleven. He is as strong as a bull. After the sittings young Pauli would start wrestling, and as this took place to the great danger of the clay model I always edged him out of the studio and locked the door, letting him finish the wrestling outside.) My stay in New York from October 1st, 1927, to January, 1928, was too short to leave me with any settled convictions as to the trend of American Art and Architecture. The amazing skyscrapers looked wonderful, but I recall that an architect showed me his design for a state building which was absolutely Assyrian, and when I suggested this to him he responded by saying that he thought American civilisation was Assyrian.

One of the most amusing episodes in New York was connected with the court trial over the bronze "Bird" by Brancusi. The American authorities had imposed an import duty on the work, judging it as a manufactured implement. The trial took place before three judges, lawyers, and a gathering of witnesses including myself, Frank Crowninshield, Forbes Watson, Henry McBride, and Steichen, the photographer who owned the work. The court-room was high up in a sky-scraper overlooking the Bay, and behind the Judges was draped a huge American flag. On a table in front Brancusi's "Bird" in polished brass rose like a spear. The Government lawyer was evidently at his wits' end to make out a case. Puzzled at the whole proceeding, his method was to bully the witnesses for "The Bird". A statement from a prominent American National Academician, a sculptor, was read, in which he roundly stated that in his opinion this was no work of art or sculpture. I give here a report of the proceedings from the *New York Evening Post* on the following day:

EPSTEIN, IN COURT, HELPS BRANCUSI

Famous Sculptor and Critic tells U.S. Tribunal "The Bird" Worthy, Recognised Art

The moot question of whether Constantin Brancusi, creator of forms of abstract beauty in marble, bronze and wood, is a sculptor or a mechanic, came before the United States Customs Court to-day, when an appeal from the Government's classification of his bronze "The Bird" as not a work of art but a manufacture of metal and as such taxed 40 per cent of its commercial value, was argued for the artist.

Jacob Epstein, famous American sculptor and one of the most embattled of the modernists; Edward Steichen, artist and owner of Exhibit One, "The Bird"; William Henry Fox, director of the Brooklyn Museum of Art; Henry McBride, Forbes Watson and Frank Crowninshield, art critics, all testified that the Rumanian artist is a recognised sculptor and that "The Bird" is a work of art of no utilitarian value.

Presiding Justice Byron S. Waite and Justice George M. Young sat in judgment in the court room on the ninth floor of the Customs Building, at Washington and Christopher Street, and First Assistant Attorney General Marcus Higginbotham, in charge of customs, was the sceptical Government counsel who wanted to know whether Exhibit One was any more artistic than a "polished brass rail harmoniously twisted" and, after all, whether "The Bird" could not just as well be a fish or a tiger.

The disputed Exhibit One rested the while on a table before the Court, seemingly poised for flight straight upwards into space, its polished, curved surface gleaming warmly in the scant sunlight from the windows. Brancusi, its creator, is in Paris, and it stood alone.

Bird, fish or tiger? Justice Waite early in the hearing expressed the opinion that what it was called did not matter, so long as competent authorities said it was a work of art.

Yet the earnest justice could not refrain from asking, with a slight show of incredulity, the various witnesses, as they all said it suggested a bird or had to them the quality of a bird, whether they would "recognise it as a bird if they saw it in a forest and would take a shot at it?"

A number of Brancusi's works, including "The Bird", which he brought to New York for an exhibition last December, were held up by the Customs appraisers, as originally revealed in *The Evening Post*. As works of art, they would not have been subject to duty, but they were held for 40 per cent customs.

"The Bird", which had been purchased in Paris by Mr. Steichen, was invoiced at $600 and was taxed $240, which Brancusi paid under protest. No decision was reached to-day, and the Government will wait to present its case until a deposition can be obtained from Brancusi that the disputed piece was his own work.

All the witnesses carefully explained that in their opinion the name of Exhibit One did not matter to them, that they felt it was a work of art because it satisfied their sense of beauty by reason of its form and balance. Mr. Higginbotham kept demanding scornfully whether any good mechanic could not do as well with a brass pipe.

Epstein, who has just returned from many troubled years in England to hold an exhibition of his own works, triumphantly produced a piece of stone which he assured the Court was an Egyptian sculpture dating back to 3000 B.C. and represented a hawk. He offered it as proof that Brancusi was not strictly modernistic and individual but derived from ancient art.

The sculptor, harmoniously dressed in a suit of warm brown and a lavender shirt, smiled helpfully and expansively as he tried hard to make the Justices and a Government counsel understand that a mechanic can't make a work of art, because as soon as he does so he becomes an artist.

"A VERY GREAT ARTIST"

Questioned first by Brancusi's counsel, who were Charles J. Lane of this city and Maurice J. Speiser of Philadelphia, Epstein said he was a sculptor and had studied and worked at his art for thirty years in New York, London and Paris, and was represented in the Metropolitan Museum here and in English and other foreign galleries.

In his opinion Brancusi was "decidedly" a sculptor, and declared that he was regarded as a very great artist by other artists. Asked to give his opinion of Exhibit One, he said:

"In my opinion, it is a work of art."

Then the Assistant Attorney-General wanted to know where Epstein had studied and what diplomas he held. Epstein said he had studied here and in various Paris schools including the École des Beaux Arts, but was puzzled about the diplomas.

"I don't believe that diplomas are ever given by art schools," he said, hesitantly.

"Whether you know it or not, did you ever receive one?" demanded the literal Mr. Higginbotham.

"I know of no such thing," said the artist.

MR. HIGGINBOTHAM'S BREAK

"What is your line of sculpture?" pursued Mr. Higginbotham.

The question evoked a snigger from the artists and critics in the back of the room. When the Government counsel elucidated by asking him if he did "human figures and that sort of thing", Epstein replied:

"I do everything."

"Have you done anything like Exhibit One?"

"But all sculptors are different. I might not want to."

Justice Waite thought this was quibbling and demanded an answer, which was in the negative.

"Why is this a work of art?" the lawyer continued.

"It pleases my sense of beauty. I find it a beautiful object."

"So if we had a brass rail, highly polished and harmoniously curved, it would also be a work of art?"

"It could become so," said Epstein.

"Then a mechanic could have done this thing?" asked the lawyer triumphantly.

"No; a mechanic could not make a work of art. He could have polished this, but he could not have conceived it."

This answer was greeted by exclamations of approval from the back seats.

"This is bird to you?"

"It is a matter of indifference to me what it represents, but if the artist calls it a bird so would I. In this there are certain elements of a bird. The profile suggests perhaps the breast of a bird."

"It might also suggest the keel of a boat or the crescent of a new moon?" asked Justice Waite.

JACOB AND THE ANGEL, 1941

JACOB AND THE ANGEL, 1941

"*Madonna and Child*": *1927*

"Or a fish or a tiger?" chorused the lawyer.

When the lawyer asked him if Brancusi were not an isolated phenomenon, Epstein asked permission to produce the Egyptian hawk to show a similar lack of realistic detail.

After two more years of litigation, a verdict in favour of "The Bird" was obtained.

I returned to London, found a studio in Kensington, and immediately set to work on "A Pieta" for which I had the materials ready. I would have continued with this but for the commission to work on the groups for the Underground Building in Westminster.

I had had my exhibition of sculpture, I had made three portraits, and I had met friends and enemies. It was a diversion—an interesting *démarche*.

14

UNDERGROUND HEADQUARTERS' BUILDING: GROUPS OF "DAY" AND "NIGHT": 1929

CHARLES HOLDEN, for whom I had worked on the British Medical Association's Building, asked me to do the two groups above the doors of the Underground Headquarters' Buildings, and I proposed groups of "Day" and "Night" as appropriate to a building that housed offices for transport and for speed. Other sculptors (five of them) were to work on figures up above, representing the Winds. When I went down with the architect for the first time to examine the site, I was introduced to the Clerk of the Works as "the sculptor", which seemed to me strange; but outside his hut, Mr. Holden explained that it would not do for me to be known as yet, at any rate not until I had actually set to work. "Dark forces might upset things." I had to be smuggled in.

It was in this atmosphere of mystery that I began a six-months' work, which took me through the entire bitter winter months of 1928, working out of doors and in a draught of wind that whistled on one side down the narrow canyon of the street. I invariably began work with a terrible stomach-ache, brought on by the cold. After I got over this I was all right and remained on the building until nightfall, having my lunch there, out of doors, so as not to lose time.

The carvings were direct in stone, and the building was being put up at the same time. I had to be oblivious to the fact that for some time tons of stone were being hauled up above my head, on a chain, and if this chain broke . . .

The sculptors working on the building were insured, but for less than the navvies who did the hauling and carrying work. I suppose a sculpture's life was not considered worth very much, and injury to him was not looked upon as anything serious. Of course my work astonished the men on the building, and many a facetious remark was passed, in between flirtations with the office girls in the street. I had a shed built around the work, as it got altogether too public for my liking, but I arrived one morning to find my shed broken open. Such was the curiosity that sculpture aroused in London. Peeping journalists bribed the watchman to let them in and have a look at me at work through the slits in the boards, and my actions were described in the Press the following day!

At last, when the two groups were finished, Muirhead Bone, who throughout had taken a great interest in these sculptures, invited the critics to come and see the result. They mounted the ladders on to the scaffolding, shook hands, and congratulated me on my achievement. The next day they let themselves go in the Press and left me with no delusions as to what they really thought. The outcry over the "Night" and "Day" resulted in a Committee of the Transport Company sitting in judgment on the groups, and it was only the intervention of Muirhead Bone that prevented the "Day" from being cut off the building. "Day" represented a Father and Son, and what there was that was obscene in it beats me. Even *The Manchester Guardian*, usually very sensible and even-tempered in matters of Art, saw fit to bowdlerise the photograph they reproduced. A party of hooligans in a car attempted, by throwing glass containers with liquid tar in them to disfigure the group of "Night". At present the groups are left in peace, to gather upon themselves the eternal grime of London.

In connection with the "Day" and "Night" I recall that I was asked by *The Manchester Guardian* to give them a sketch of what my intentions were when carving these two groups. I wrote or dictated an account which failed to satisfy those persons who want you to reveal to them your innermost soul, and I remember how disappointed they were that my "aims" did not seem more idealistic. Immediately, of course, their estimate of the sculpture itself fell. Thus achievement is confused with literary exposition and the inability of the artist to explain himself. The fame and popularity of a painter like George Frederick Watts is undoubtedly due to his marvellous faculty of putting himself across with high philosophic purpose, like his exclamation when asked what his aim was: "The utmost for the highest", and other like phrases. The low estimate to which his paintings have fallen naturally follows the oblivion into which his transcendental aims have sunk. "Good wine needs no bush." To-day there is such a plethora of "bush" that an art resting on its own merits is practically unknown. Of one famous French painter it is known that he subsidises journals expressly published to advertise his own works, although this is cleverly concealed by admitting a few other artists, or preferably articles on ancient works or archæology.*

* See Appendix: Underground Headquarters' Buildings, for letters and articles.

NORMAN, 1937

GENESIS, 1931

15

"Genesis": 1931

I CONCEIVED the "Genesis" after I had made the study for "Visitation", and it is another facet of the same idea. I felt the necessity for giving expression to the profoundly elemental in motherhood, the deep down instinctive female, without the trappings and charm of what is known as feminine; *my* feminine would be the eternal primeval feminine, the mother of the race. The figure from the base upward, beginning just under the knees, seems to rise from the earth itself. From that the broad thighs and buttocks ascend, base solid and permanent for her who is to be the bearer of man. She feels within herself the child moving, her hand instinctively and soothingly placed where it can feel this enclosed new life so closely bound with herself. The expression of the head is one of calm, mindless wonder. This boulder, massive yet delicate, with transparent shadows of the light marble goes deep, deep down in human half-animal consciousness. The forms are realistic, the treatment grave. There is a luminous aura about it as if it partook of light and air. Complete in herself, now that there is that consummated within her, for which she was created. She is serene and majestic, an elemental force of nature. How a figure like this contrasts with our coquetries and fanciful erotic nudes of modern sculpture.* At one blow, whole generations of sculptors and sculpture are shattered and sent flying into the limbo of triviality, and my "Genesis", with her fruitful womb, confronts our enfeebled generation. Within her, Man takes on new hope for the future. The generous earth gives herself up to us, meets our masculine desires, and says: "Rejoice, I am Fruitfulness, I am Plenitude."

* See Appendix: "Genesis": 1931, for articles and letters.

I worked on this figure with no hesitations, and with no preliminary studies, and knew very clearly what I wished to achieve. I attacked the stone with my aim very clearly defined in my mind, and with a sympathetic material. I was not long in evolving the idea. This figure, when shown, aroused a storm of protest, which was as unexpected as it was vehement. Our emasculated period was shocked by a figure without "sex-appeal", without indecencies, and without charm. It was not the eternal feminine of eroticism, and perhaps for that reason aroused the ire of women. Women complained I had insulted their sex; there is something in this complaint. Missing in this statue all the usual appealing, so called "feminine" graces, they would see in it an attempt to undermine their attractiveness, their desire to please and seduce. This is where "the insult" to womanhood came in. They were more alarmed at the symbolic truth of this statue than at the many cruel caricatures perpetrated by a Daumier, a Toulouse Lautrec, or a Grosz, whereas my work is a hymn of praise and rejoicing. The misunderstanding of my motives and the perverse construction placed upon my aims always astonishes me. This statue, when offered on loan to the Tate Gallery, was refused on the grounds that it had caused a "sensation" and, therefore, was unsuitable for the solemn halls of the Gallery.

The "Genesis" was carved in a block of Seravezza marble which I bought in Paris. The block was commenced in my shed in Epping Forest, and was still unfinished when I had to live again in London. I took the unfinished work to my Hyde Park Gate studio where I finished it. I had a foretaste of what was to come, when one day, lifting my head from the work, I saw looking at me, through the window of an adjoining property, two gardeners with their mouths agape, eyes staring, rooted to the spot in astonishment. When I moved they fled.

It is imagined that I do my work in a storm of controversy, somewhat like the atmosphere of a boxing ring, with adherents and enemies shouting encouragement and abuse to each other. The reality is that for long periods, thank God, I work quietly and give no heed to anything else. I do not know or care who is Prime Minister or what the London weather is like. The periods of exhibition are for the most part a nuisance to me. I have one day—or even, I might say, one brief hour of pleasure, when my works are assembled for the first time in the Gallery. With the Press day and the Private View day, and then the subsequent visits of the public, all pleasure goes, and only chagrin and irritation follow. The exhibition becomes my nightmare, and I long for the day when it will close down and I can return to work in peace.

16

PAINTINGS OF EPPING FOREST AND OLD
TESTAMENT DRAWINGS: 1933

URING the summer of 1933 I painted nearly a hundred water-colours of Epping Forest, where I rented a cottage. I would go out with my daughter and we did not have to walk far before seeing something worth painting. As usual with me, what I started as a mere diversion became in the end a passion, and I could think of nothing else but painting. I arose to paint, and painted until sundown, and when later I exhibited these paintings in a London Gallery, it was a source of annoyance to some critics that I had painted so many. This to the critic is really a sign of bad taste. Why not paint only two or three paintings a year? Why are you so prolific? You increase and multiply. What commercialism! To the sterile and unproductive person a hundred paintings all done in a couple of months is disgusting, a kind of littering.

Nevertheless I was very pleased with the result, and the paintings looked well. Later I was to repeat this frenzy of painting, only with flowers. I had been asked to paint some blooms by a firm of Dutch dealers in old masters. I said I would paint twenty, and in the end I painted sixty. Not content with this, I went on painting, giving up sculpture for the time being, and painted three hundred more. I lived and painted flowers. My rooms were piled with flowers, and this was a wonderful and colourful period. I had these flower paint-ings mounted and framed by a firm of dealers, who let it be known that I had painted flowers, and so when my exhibition of flowers was ready, at least five other flower exhibitions started at the same time. London became a veritable flower garden.

I was, of course, told that the shoemaker should stick to his last.

142

Paintings of Epping Forest: 1933

A sculptor is supposed to be a dull dog any way, so why should he not break out in colour sometimes, and in my case I'd as soon be hanged for a sheep as a lamb. Blake says: "The Gateway of Excess leads to the Palace of Wisdom."

In 1931 I made a series of drawings for the Old Testament. I became so absorbed in the text and in the countless images evoked by my readings, a whole new world passed in vision before me. I lost no time in putting this upon paper. When I exhibited them it seemed that I had again committed some kind of blasphemy, and countless jibes were forthcoming. There is an element in all countries which would suppress the free artist, kill original thoughts, and bind the minds of men in chains. In England, happily, this retrograde element does not make much headway. Our totalitarians are still in the minority. Daumier was imprisoned for his political cartoons, Courbet fined heavily for his partisanship in the Commune; and in many countries artists and writers who are suspect are banned or exiled. To-day, no artist must imagine that he's back in the happy-go-lucky days, when he was looked upon as a rather irresponsible fellow, and allowed to go his way. Oh, no! The artist to-day is part of the culture—Kultur it is rather, part of the consciousness of the nation, with a responsible mission towards the race. Whatever he paints or sculptures cannot be separated from the body-politic. He is to be called to account. A bureau, a commissar, or gauleiter must look after his activities, and after a day's work he had best review what he has done and see that it is in line (*gleichschaltung*) with the right political and social ideology.

Sculpture in the future may well be made under the supervision of guards with rifles and machine guns.

POSTSCRIPT

I remember that soon after I first wrote the above I came across an article in a Spanish paper, *A.B.C.*, November 22nd, 1939, praising the Franco system of compelling political prisoners to work for the state as part of the national industry—in reality, a system of organised slavery.

This is the sentence which most impressed me: "A great number

of shops have been established in the jails and as a model can be
pointed out that of Alcala de Henares, with carpentry and print-
ing shops, and the sculpturing of religious images which are really
beautiful."

17

A T the stone-yard I see a tremendous block of marble about to be sliced up and used for interior decoration. When I see these great monoliths lying ready for the butcher's hands, as it were, I instantly have sentimental feelings of pity that the fate of a noble block of stone should be so ignominious. Knowing that this stone could contain a wonderful statue moves me to purchase it and rescue it, even though at the moment I have no definite idea for it. Never mind—that will come. Merely looking at the block and studying it will give me many ideas. This Subiaco block of marble, when I carved it, I found the toughest, most difficult piece of stone I had ever tackled. All the tools I had broke on it, and it was only after trying out endless "points", as they are called, with different toolmakers that I finally hit upon a "point" that resisted, and began to make an impression on the stone. I wished to make an "Ecce Homo", a symbol of man, bound, crowned with thorns and facing with a relentless and over-mastering gaze of pity and prescience our unhappy world. Because of the hardness of the material I treated the work in a large way, with a juxtaposition of flat planes, always with a view to retaining the impression of the original block. Matthew Smith on seeing the statue in my studio said: "You have made a heavy stone seem heavier"—a profound comment. The plastic aim was always of paramount importance and the "preaching" side secondary, or rather the idea, the subject, was so clear and simple to me, that, once having decided on it, I gave myself up wholly to a realisation of lines and planes, what our critics are fond of calling "the formal relations". I have not attempted to describe this statue as I think it describes itself. I will let the beholder do that. I look at the work and feel that it confronts time and eternity.

I exhibited this statue before it was quite finished. I had worked at it at different periods whenever I could, and I still have it in my studio and return to it from time to time. It is the largest statue I have made, and was one of the most vehemently attacked. *The Catholic Times* opened the attack with this:

Mr. Epstein has chosen the opening of Lent, when Christians commemorate the death and sufferings of our Saviour, to make known to the world his conception of Christ. We have looked, painful as the experience was, but we have not seen the man, or even a man. We see only a distorted reminiscence of a man: the debased, sensuous, flat features of an Asiatic monstrosity. We protest against the insult offered to Christ by this work of an artist who has genius and skill, but who has not considered that experiments are made only on vile bodies.

As an art-lover, I deeply appreciate beauty, but "Behold the Man" is not beautiful: it is ugly and vile.

Other opinions expressed to *The Daily Mirror* were:

Mr. G. K. Chesterton: "It is an outrage, and I admire *The Daily Mirror* for refusing to publish a picture of the statue. It is one of the greatest insults to religion I have ever seen, and will offend the religious feelings of the whole community."

Lady Snowden: "I congratulate you. To publish such an atrocity would have offended thousands. Your newspaper is to be admired, for taking such a step."

Miss Mary Borden, author of the noted *Mary of Nazareth*: "I am an admirer of Mr. Epstein, but in this case I think he has done something outrageous. I feel, after looking at the picture, that he knows nothing about the man he has called Christ and portrayed. I believe he has not troubled to find out about Him, or His character, or His personality. If he had, then he might have been inspired by hate, but I don't think that is so. I think it is an abstraction of his own, and unfortunately it is of a Man who is adored generally by the world."

Colonel Hamilton, an official of the Salvation Army, expressed a similar view, and said he congratulated the editor on refusing to publish such a picture. "It is grotesque," he added, ". . . nothing more than sacrilege. Words almost fail me."

The price Mr. Jacob Epstein is asking for his carving is 3000 guineas!

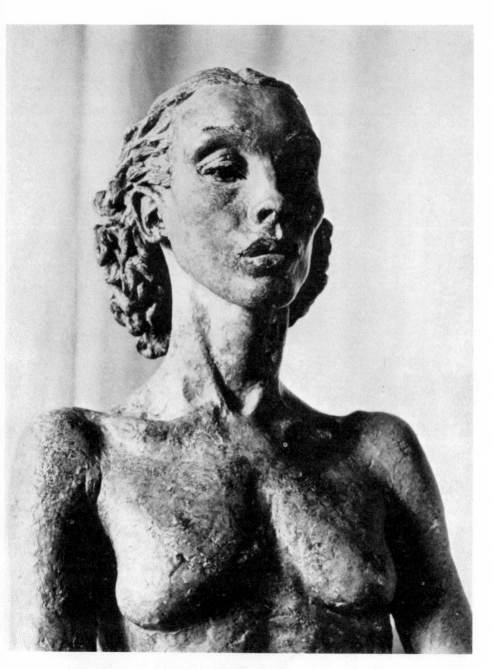

POLA, 1937

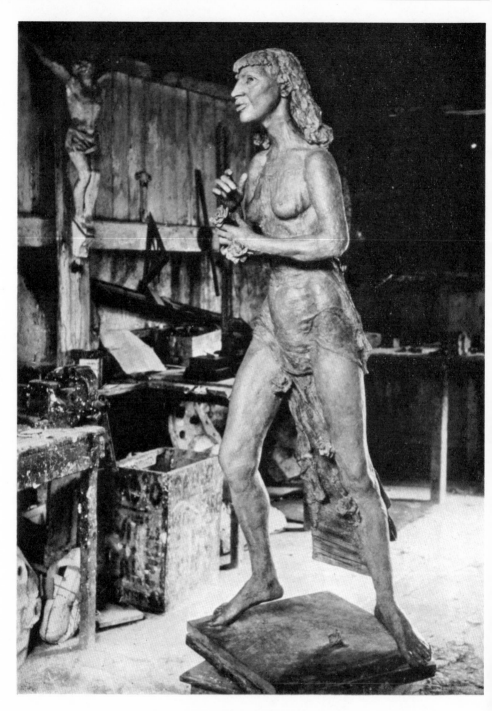

GIRL WITH THE GARDENIAS, 1941

"Behold the Man!": 1935

T. W. Earp, in *The Daily Telegraph*, off-set outbursts like this with a well-reasoned article:

Sculpture in England owes Mr. Epstein a considerable debt of gratitude. He found it an exhausted art, devoted to academic exercise, conscientious portraiture, and a small—almost codified—range of subjects. Sometimes the commemoration of a national occasion or figure gave an impulse to invention, though such distinction was not frequent in the public monuments executed at the beginning of the century. The beau-ideal and a convention of the heroic, which had become sadly mechanical, still held the field. But Mr. Epstein gave the art a new lease of life. He brought to it an enthusiasm and an impetuous imagination which broke its rigid mould. He enlarged its scope and originated a spirit of experiment which to-day is showing the liveliest results.

With astonishing virtuosity, and frequently with something more, he still keeps abreast of his disciples. He has put sculpture back into the news and aroused a public interest in his own work that may occasionally be embarrassing. At his exhibition at the Leicester Galleries controversy rages as usual, this time over the large figure of Christ entitled "Behold the Man". It should be noted, however, that no photograph can give a fair conception of a figure so essentially sculpturesque, that in the limits of a gallery room it is not seen under fair conditions, and that the subject is one on whose treatment preconceived judgments may have an unfair weight.

A particular kind of formal realism has so long been exercised on religious themes in art that it may be forgotten that "Behold the Man!" has the authority of tradition behind it. The great mass of derivations from the Gothic convention tends to obscure an unprejudiced view of this work, which goes back to the Romanesque for its affinities, both in symbolism and actual workmanship. It stands square and gestureless, keeping closely in shape to the elongated cube of Subiaco marble from which it is constructed. But an impressive energy radiates from the self-contained rhythm of its volume, while its austere pattern, and the rudimentary indication of facial features, possess greater emotional content than would a nearer approach to physical verisimilitude.

For that we must turn to Mr. Epstein's portrait busts. In them no general idea calls for expression, no conception reaching beyond the bounds of time and space; the artist's attention must be concentrated on actuality, the individual and the particular. This intensive contraction oɪ the imagination Mr. Epstein always achieves in a manner that silences even his more obstinate critics. The present series of busts shows with what fine humility he serves the suggestions, æsthetic or psychological, with which his sitters provide him, the twinkle lurking within the hirsute

147

luxuriance of Mr. Shaw's philosophic mask, or the frankness and simplicity in such a human symbol of elemental nature as the "Man of Aran". There is a similar revelation of character in all these portraits, in the men more accentuated and more complicated intellectually, and in the women mingled with a gracious element of repose and charm, though still radiant with vitality. And the actual modelling—a baroque that is never empty ornament, but always dynamically significant of character—is that of a master, a superb union of strength and sensitiveness.

T. W. EARP.

Here are two further notices. The first is from *The Manchester Guardian* of March 7th, 1935:

EPSTEIN'S NEW SCULPTURES

"BEHOLD THE MAN!"

In his colossal figure, "Behold the Man!" at his exhibition in the Leicester Galleries, Mr. Jacob Epstein returns again to the idea of Christ. Ten years ago he carved a standing figure of Christ with the nail-marks in his hands after the Resurrection. He also made a great bronze of the Virgin and the child Christ. The present sculpture stands eleven feet high, carved of Subiaco marble. It is too large for the gallery, but this cramped-ness intensifies the sense of crushing agony bearing upon the squat endur-ing figure crowned with thorns. The gigantic head, the bracing of the chest, the square rock-like shape of the whole with its shallow modelling suggests a caryatid of suffering.

The sculptor never explains his sculptures. Whatever they have to say is there in the language of his art. Did he intend to convey the idea of the unending sorrows of the Master whose teachings were denied by the world everyday and of that cumulative denial crushing down upon him? Some saw in his former figure, Christ crucified every day. As in all his work, racial feeling is somehow there, and one is aware of a further conception of the race of Christ suffering through the centuries and terribly in our day. It is the most impressive of Mr. Epstein's great stone figures, and seems a culmination of his carvings on architecture on the Underground building and his other large relief carvings. There is something of the keystone in the squared, compact shape of the figure, narrowing from its tremendous head.

The rest of the exhibition consists of busts and heads done in the last few years. The visitor turns from the stark, enigmatic stone figure, think-ing of its kinship with the rock carvings at Easter Island, to busts that are almost dainty in the frolicsome handling of hair and beard, as in the Bernard Shaw, or realistic to the last degree, as in the masterly head of

"Behold the Man!": *1935*

Lord Beaverbrook. One imagines that Mr. Shaw must have rallied Mr. Epstein a good deal during the sittings to have so much pugnacious mischief and gaiety in this brilliant presentment. "Hiram Halle" is one of those apparently simple, straightforward renderings of a strongly featured man that is somehow a monumental thing. The bust of Dr. Weizmann, with its fine balance of qualities, is another important work.

Mr. Epstein's manhandling of his material seems too robust for success in women portraits. Nevertheless, out of his method of smears and applied pieces, dents and spots, emerge portraits of extraordinary freshness and youth. "Belle Cramer", "Louise", and "Rani Rama" are vital and haunting works. The exhibition shows Epstein at the height of his strange and sensitive powers.   JAMES BONE.

This was published in *The Spectator* of March 15th, 1935:

EPSTEIN AND RELIGIOUS ART

No society is likely to produce a strong and steady stream of religious art unless religion plays an active part in the life of the society itself. At the present day, therefore, when religion is no longer a dominant factor in life, it would be foolish to expect any outburst of religious art directed towards the satisfaction of a general, popular demand. On the other hand, there is no reason why individual works of art expressing religious ideas should not be produced even in an atmosphere of general indifference to religion such as exists to-day. This has often happened in the past; at the time of the early Renaissance, when science was replacing religion, it was possible for Masaccio to paint pictures almost unrivalled for intensity of religious feeling, and at the end of the Eighteenth Century, the general indifference around him did not prevent Blake from expressing his personal religious views in poetry or engraving.

But though it is possible for religious art to be produced in non-religious periods, it will be different in kind from that produced when religion is itself in the ascendant. Blake is different from a Gothic sculptor in that he is aware of the opposition to what he wishes to express. He is therefore a self-conscious artist and his art a minority art, whereas the sculptors of Chartres were, from the point of view of their religion, unself-conscious and satisfying the demands of a majority.

The situation today is closer to that of the late Eighteenth Century than to that of the Middle Ages. Religion is a minority interest and any religious art must be a minority art, but if we are to have any religious art at all to-day, it looks as though Mr. Epstein is on the right track towards creating it.

Epstein: An Autobiography

His new statue, "Behold the Man!", on view at the Leicester Galleries, is unquestionably a work of religious art, but it represents an approach to the problem new at any rate in England. The great difficulty which has faced religious artists in Europe for about a century is that our natural tradition for expressing religious feeling is utterly used up and dead. During the Nineteenth Century a series of attempts were made to revive the tradition by going back to what were imagined to be the true sources of the religious style. The Gothic revivalists turned back to the architecture of their own middle ages; the Pre-Raphaelites to the early Italians and to mediæval artists; in the more recent times frantic attempts have been made to put life into religious scenes by giving them modern setting and dresses.

Mr. Epstein has approached the problem differently. *His* interest in the arts of the savage races was started, we may imagine, by realising that they offered a new way of looking at the material world, that they were based on formal principles wholly different from those of European art. But this more or less technical interest in savage art seems to have led Mr. Epstein to feel further that these artists also offered a new way of making statements about the supernatural. True, the religious and superstitious ideas which they sought to express were remote from those of Christianity, but at any rate they both existed on the same supernatural plane, and it would be worth trying whether their methods could not be adapted to the needs of European art.

This seems to be what Mr. Epstein has tried to do in "Behold the Man!" He has vivified European religious art by an infusion of dark blood, itself not pure but drawn from the African, the Aztec and many other races. The first result of his experiment is not perhaps in every way a success, but before judging it we must estimate the difficulties in the artist's way. There was much sentimentality and clap-trap to be cleared away from the idea of religious art, and there was the problem of applying savage principles to a Christian theme. Mr. Epstein was, therefore, forced to concentrate on the absolute essentials of his problem, and this may account for the almost too great simplicity of expression, which we can imagine being elaborated in later works of the same kind. In a sense, however, this extreme simplicity makes the statue the more suitable to be placed in a church, where it would be seen from a distance and would make its appeal instantly. Those priests who have said that they would be glad to see the statue in their own church might well find, that apart from delivering a few severe shocks, it would admirably fulfil its function as an image.

ANTHONY BLUNT.

AFRICAN MOTHER AND CHILD, 1940

THE SLAVE HOLD, 1941

"Behold the Man!": 1935

It must be remembered that a statue like "Behold the Man!" is not shown in a public gallery, nor set out in the street, but exhibited in a private gallery into which no one is compelled to go, and be either "affronted or insulted", and where the Gallery, moreover, make a charge for admission. I have carefully refrained from advocating religious or idealistic propaganda of any sort, and have always put out my sculpture as sculpture. I am not connected with a school or movement or cult, and the charge of self-advertisement is clearly ridiculous, as I am one of hundreds, nay thousands of artists, who exhibit every year. The charges of blasphemy make one think of the days of witchcraft and the *auto-da-fé*. Actually my religious statues have had strong support from the clergy. I make no complaint about the attacks on the statues, and wish here only to record favourable with unfavourable views. I do not see myself as a martyr, but what has always astonished me was the bitterness of the attacks on my statues. Their cause I am unable to fathom. In some cases, like those of art critics, I can very well understand the motives, the long-cherished hatred of a powerful rival to artists of their own set, the desire to monopolise and cut out one who threatens their supremacy by his merely existing, working, and exhibiting. It is the almost insane hatred of the average man and woman that is baffling.

18

"CONSUMMATUM EST": 1937

THE unworked alabaster block lies in my studio for a year. While I work at other things I look at it from time to time. The block lies prone in its length, and I consider whether I should raise it, but decide to leave it where it is. I can conceive any number of works in it. I can conceive a single figure or a group of figures. I have been listening to Bach's *B minor Mass*. In the section, Crucifixus, I have a feeling of tremendous quiet, of awe. The music comes from a great distance and in this mood I conceive my "Consummatum Est". I see the figure complete as a whole. I see immediately the upturned hands, with the wounds in the feet, stark, crude, with the stigmata. I even imagine the setting for the finished figure, a dim crypt, with a subdued light on the semi-transparent alabaster.

I now begin on the stone and draw out where the head will come, the lengthened arms, and the draperies and feet, jutting further out. I start carving tentatively, carefully on the head, having chosen the lighter coloured part of the block for this. I work downwards until roughly the whole figure is shaped. I concentrate on the hands and give them definite form and expression. In carving I rarely have recourse to a model, and depend for the form on my experience and knowledge. I block out the containing masses, leaving the details until later; I always try to get the whole feeling and expression of the work, with regard to the material I am working in. This is important. There are sculptors who treat a figure in stone in exactly the same manner as they do a work in clay. With an isolated piece of stone they should regard the sculpture as primarily a block, and do no violence to it as stone. There must be no exact imitation of nature to make one believe that one is seeing a translation of nature into another material.

"Consummatum Est": 1937

Imitation is no aim of sculpture proper, and a true piece of sculpture will always be the material worked into a shape. This shape is the important thing, not whether the eye is fooled by representation, as at Madame Tussaud's wax-works.

As I worked upon this figure in alabaster, I asked myself continually whether I am getting the feeling, the emotion from the work I intended. I do not ask this question consciously. It is subconscious. Many imagine that the artist, having his working hours like any other craftsman, thinks only when in front of his work about its practical problems of shaping and chiselling, but this is not so. The work a sculptor is engaged on is continually in his mind. He sees it with his mind's eye, and quite clearly, so that at any moment of the day or night, or even in lying down to sleep, the vision of the work in progress is there for analysis, as an inescapable presence. I would say that on a work like this, one lives in it until it is finally finished and one has gone on to some other work which usurps its place in one's thoughts. It is a question whether one is more thrilled at beginning a work than in finishing it. I think beginning is the more exciting. The finished work—well, there it is, All one's ardours and hesitations are over, the problem is solved. The sculptor with his vision, planning working, laying loving hands upon the willing and love-returning stone, the creation of a work, the form embodying the idea, strange copulation of spirit and matter, the intellect dominating hammer and chisel—the conception that at last becomes a piece of sculpture. This seems to me fit work for a man. "Consummatum Est"—It is finished. Instead of writing about it, and people standing about talking, arguing, disputing over the prone Son of Man, with protesting palms upturned, there should be music, the solemn Mass of Bach.

What will be the eventual fate of this work? It came from me and returns to me in a world where it is not wanted. I imagine a waste world; argosies from the air have bombed the humans out of existence, and perished themselves, so that no human thing is left alive. The feet are weary from having trod the earth in vain, the hands with their wounds turned to the sky, the face calm with all the suffering drained away. Like the enigmatic stones of a far island that face the sea, my stone will face the sky and give no answer. Meanwhile to my great disgust it has been bought by a showman and put on show in fair grounds.

153

Epstein: An Autobiography

I exhibited the "Consummatum Est" at the Leicester Galleries. When the statue was in place I studied the effect of the work in its new setting. After all, a work such as this is done in the studio with perhaps a totally different lighting, and every sculptor knows how peculiar his work can look under other conditions. I was pleased with the work and the solitude of the Gallery, and I felt the satisfaction that all artists, I suppose, feel for a few fleeting moments. Surrounding the large work were bronzes, which were, I thought, amongst my best. There was the "Pola", the "Nerenska", the "Kathleen", the "Young Communist", the "Berenice", and the "Morna"; all works, I thought, living and solid, and well able to stand the malicious scrutiny of my critics. Years before, when preparing an exhibition, I always imagined it as a feast that I had spread out for enjoyment; with the years and experience I have come to have a different feeling from this generous one, for one's attitude is apt to get warped and somewhat waspish and self-protective. An exhibition is another exposure of oneself to the slings and arrows; and mixed with the pleasure of seeing two or three years' work assembled together is the feeling that on the morrow the critics—the enemy—will invade with their cynicism, their jealousy, their rancour, and their impotence, your sanctuary.

Opinion about the "Consummatum Est" was strongly divided. As usual there were bitter attacks from the clergy, and more particularly from Roman Catholic journalists. As everyone had an opinion, the newspapers gave expression to all, in one case sending out their Sports Editor to write upon it. In reviewing the printed criticism I am hard put to it to find serious attacks; there is much that is virulent and embittered, and much that is downright silly. The defence is in all cases far more considered, even better written, and actually were a plebiscite to be taken of these controversies, I am not sure but that the consensus of opinion would be for the statues rather than against. Appreciation is not always vocal, whereas the incensed visitor to the Gallery is shocked into immediately writing to *The Times* or *The Daily Mirror*; and an M.P. must hold up the business of the nation while he asks questions to relieve his outraged artistic feelings.

As usual the row starts with someone entirely ignorant of the science of sculpture, in this case Sir Charles Allom, an architect

154

DIERDRE, 1941

CHIA PIA, 1942

and contractor, who acquired a great deal of publicity by exclaiming:

A disgusting travesty. An outrage on Christian ideals.

How could it be possible for Christ to be the clumsy, heavy, bloated figure which Epstein has depicted?

Look at those dreadful feet. They are not the feet of the active man Christ must have been. He lived the simplest life: He must have been a man of remarkable physical and nervous energy, seldom resting, everlastingly doing.

Epstein's presentation of Him is physically quite inconsistent with what we know of Christ. Artistically it is false too.

Christ, you know, spent His life curing cripples. If He had seen Himself as Epstein has seen Him, He would have realised that there was not one piece of Himself that was not crippled.

One cannot conceive of such a spirit inhabiting the gross, ugly, bloated form which Epstein has given Him.

The Roman Catholic *Universe* (November 5th, 1937) followed with this:

What is all this about Mr. Epstein or Mr. Einstein or whoever it is? I know one invented Relativity and the other Rima, only I never remember which is which. Probably because I can't make head or tail of either.

But to whichever gentleman it is who says time doesn't exist, I would put one question. Has he ever done it? Because, if so, he'd find out something. I don't mean I've done time in the prison way, of course; but there was the army, and doesn't time just count! And it's no use your proving that you are the Emperor Napoleon and really in the last century when the provost-sergeant has it in his head that you're a defaulter with the next eighty days to do.

The new statue-thing I don't understand either. From the pictures it only looks to me like a child's first attempt in plasticine, the sort of unfortunate child who later gets looked at by a doctor and sent to a home. But of course I'm not an art critic; nor do I believe it's going to have the faintest effect on religion one way or the other. For I'm old enough to remember other "modernisms" that passed. There was what I fancy we called "New Art", and it was really photo-frames of a sort of tarnished imitation-silver that you put on the top of the piano. Well, that was ugly enough, but it never affected religion much.

There was Aubrey Beardsley, and he did rather queer pictures that looked vaguely unpleasant. They were the absolute last word in their day, and people said they were going to revolutionise civilisation. And other people said they were too, too utterly wicked for anything. Well, I saw some last week in a second-hand shop just marked "quaint"; they may have been thirty years old. But the Madonnas and Crucifixions of the masters have lasted some centuries; and you can't buy them for eighteen-pence! I don't know that the Catholic Church need worry too much about this new statue-thing.

With this from *The Sunday Dispatch* I will finish with the simpler fry:

By John Macadam (Sports Editor), October 31st 1937

Who am I to wonder about Epstein and his Christ? And yet who am I not? My business is with footballers and boxers and jockeys— not with art.

Only, what has this piece of sculpture to do with art? And what has it to do with Christ; at least with the Christ I have in my mind? What skill has Epstein plied on that marble with his chisel that I could not have plied?

Questioning. . . . That's what it does to you. It is unavoidable.

Look at it. This Christ has been taken down from the Cross. He is laid out in a vast shapeless shroud that allows only His feet to protrude . . . great flat feet with square toes upturned; on the soles and through to the tops, the nail marks.

A Parson

As I stood looking at it, a parson took his place beside me. He pondered for a moment and I could feel him looking at me as if to test my reactions.

"Are you a religious man?" he asked, and I said, "Not particularly," and quoting from Omar as well as I could remember, added that I should "come out by that same door as in I went."

He looked back at the recumbent figure and said: "It baffles me too."

I looked again at the face. Couldn't I have done that? Couldn't I have chiselled—supposing I had the little ability I have with a chisel that I have with a typewriter—those plain lines, that domed, sloping-away head, the curved ridge of a nose?

Couldn't I?

Whatever mystery the piece has as a whole, there is no mystery about the sculpting of it. There is no subtle line to sway an emotion, no delicate nuance in marble to point a moral.

Is It Ugly?

Only this shapeless mass boldly chiselled in ugliness. And yet . . . is that right? I have been looking at it for half an hour now, and it does not startle me as it did when I came on it first.

"*Consummatum Est*": *1937*

Is this ugly, or is my conventional conception of Christ, derived through Watts and the Italians, merely chocolate-box?

Or, if it *is* ugly, isn't that what Epstein means it to be; symbolic of the ugliness of suffering?

Suppose I could have chiselled these lines, there is the certainty in my mind that I could not have made their squat shapelessness cry out as Epstein does.

Those Hands

The beautifully modelled arms with nail-torn palms turned up supplicate. It is these hands that dwell with me now that I am away from the piece.

The face is a dead face, and the thick gross body is a dead body. But the arms and hands seem to live on; seem to say: "Is it nothing to you, all ye that pass by?"

But, for the rest, what?

Is this the body of a Christ who rose from the grave? Does it look as if it could ever move again? To me, it does not. I am given the picture of a hopeless, despairing man done cruelly to death by those whom He loved; showing them the wounds they have made. For what? I didn't know, nor did the parson by my side.

Nor did many of the spectators, mostly women; particularly the pretty one who consented to be photographed in an attitude of Adoration . . .

Still, it had something, for the chattering with which they made their way round the busts in the outside rooms was hushed to a reverent whisper as they approached the figure in the inner place. There was no laughter or giggling; only a sort of wonder.

Wondering Pity

Myself, I was filled, after a time, with a wondering pity—much the same kind of emotion as I experienced the first time I saw Primo Carnera lumbering around the ring in the Albert Hall. I should say the same kind of pity any of you would feel for a grotesque.

It is not a figure of hope, or promise of things to come in the Hereafter. It is a pitiful outsize in Death.

Whether these things I have thought come from this Christ or whether they come from me I do not know. I am still left with the memory of that shapeless husk and the wondering feeling that I could have done it myself. Or you.

Now the heavyweight critic of *The Times* has a go. As usual he is a quibbler for formula and with clever insinuation would convince his readers that it is a mistake that I should be alive at all. He implies that, with all my skill and labour, I do not understand the tragic significance of the words "It is Finished" as well as he does! And in his final "wrong thing done very well indeed", he destroys himself with his own cleverness, but I think he should be quoted in full to give one the really fine flavour of one of our more pretentious critics.

As is usual when he shows his work both Mr. Jacob Epstein the great artist and Mr. Jacob Epstein the Great Artist are represented in his present exhibition at the Leicester Galleries. How far the latter is at the expense of the former must be left to his own judgment. All the necessary criticism of "Consummatum Est" is contained in the title. That is to say, Mr. Epstein has used many hundredweights of alabaster to say a great deal less than is contained in two words, or, if you prefer the English, "It is Finished", three. In emotional comparison it is as if one said "Bo!" in a thunderstorm. But one either feels the tragic finality of the words "It is Finished" or does not, and therefore argument is useless. Mantegna's "Dead Christ", which might seem to bear upon the question, bears heavily the wrong way for Mr. Epstein, because it makes no attempt to embody the emotional content of the words.

In comparison with the artistic stupidity implied in its conception all the other criticisms which are likely to be passed on the work—whether the feet are or are not too big, whether the supinated forearms are or are not anatomically correct, and whether or not the incised treatment of the features is right—are artistically irrelevant. In matters of composition—the parallel disposition of the limbs and the enclosure of the work in an imaginary rectangle—and of execution—the degree of anatomical realisation attempted, surface finish, and so forth—"Consummatum Est" has great merits. It is the wrong thing done very well indeed.

As a portrait sculptor in bronze, Mr. Epstein, the great artist, goes on advancing—particularly in the formal control of his gifts of character and expression. "Kathleen", with its spiral disposition of the arms and decorative relief to the surfaces, is about as happy a composition as he has yet produced, and both it and "Rosemary" have an unexpected elegance. Between the male and the female portraits of Mr. Epstein there is an interesting comparison. Probably the male portraits, with their greater artistic detachment and concentration upon character and the formal and technical problems of the task, will rank highest to posterity, but the emotional emphasis on eyes and mouths peculiar to the artist when he is modelling women makes them more exciting at the moment. They contain more of those extra-artistic impulses of the artist which are summed up in the word "personality". None of the male portraits in this exhibition quite reaches the level of "Einstein", but "Professor Franz Boas", "Sir Alec Martin", "Sir Frank Fletcher", and "J. B. Priestley" are all portraits of astonishing vitality—and it is vitality that distinguishes Mr. Epstein from any other living sculptor.

The peculiarities of this technique of criticism will be apparent. To start with, there is praise, what seems to be a generous appreciation, then a "still, small Voice" intervenes, and by the time the critic is through with you, no shred is left, you are stripped bare of all honour and are only a poor wight to be pitied. In this case, to make an appearance of exhibiting an unprejudiced mind, the jam is put on at the end. Certainly, were I as good as these critics say, I could not possibly be as bad as they make out. How monotonous the attack becomes! If it is a "Consummatum Est", then it is as if one said "Bo!" in a thunderstorm. If it is an "Adam", then instead of a Whitmanic epic it is as if one had written a sonnet. Always a belittling, a whittling down to the trivial, to the impertinent. If the statue is in marble then a "beautiful block of marble" is ruined; a large bronze, the wasted labour is deplored. I remember how astonished I was to read, after one of these criticisms of the "Genesis" by the same critic, praise of a most clumsy piece of sculpture by a painter of his clique. It was described as "this beautiful bronze". I then realised that the dailies and weeklies were almost completely dominated by these types of prejudiced critics, determined at all costs to boost themselves and theirs only. Their distortions are often so ludicrous as not to be worth answering, as when in comparing the treatment of the hair in my busts and heads it was pointed out that a certain French sculptor's treatment was in all cases sensitive and mine coarse; the truth being that that particular sculptor was invariably insensitive. In any case, why the inevitable comparison with me; why not compare the work of their French and English sculptors with the past, Egypt, Donatello Verrocchio? That is where they should look for comparisons.

This article appeared in *The News Chronicle* of October 28th, 1937:

By William McCance

Whenever Jacob Epstein produces a major piece of sculpture there comes from all sides a flood of abuse; and some of it, were it directed

159

against anyone other than this very tolerant artist, would be considered libellous in any court of law.

I should like to state as clearly as I can where his carvings stand in relation to art, if not in relation to the panic-stricken, emotional reaction of that section of the loud-voiced public which is heard more often than met or seen.

The general confusion arises from the fact that whereas in music, literature and the drama it is recognised that there are different kinds, each with its own qualities, there is no such recognition of different kinds of sculpture.

To the man-in-the-street it is either good or bad, according to whichever mouthpiece provides his ready-made æsthetic fare in the daily Press.

As there were in the old days of the Scottish clans three distinct types of pipe music called the small music, the middle music and the big music, represented respectively by marches, dance music, and the pibroch, so in painting and sculpture there is a similar classification. And these three categories of art may be placed in the following order:

(*a*) Reportage
(*b*) Interpretation
(*c*) Creation

Reporting in painting or in sculpture consists of making a faithful and accurate copy of the particular subject.

It requires a certain degree of expert craftsmanship, but little creative ability—none, in fact. A number of lurid touches may be added here and there to attain effectiveness, in much the same way as a good reporter of police court proceedings may embellish his write-up to make it more readable.

Reporting in painting or sculpture may be called Small Art, and, of its kind, may be good or bad.

The second class of art, Interpretation, demands, for its success, that the artist have some unique quality of personality, which comes through the work and gives to it a greater intensity.

He interprets the subject in such a way that the spectator gets from it something fresh and new that hitherto has been hidden from him.

The subject, after flowing through the artist, is made more vivid. There is a little creation here; but very little. The artist is giving to the spectator the benefit of his more interesting reaction of the subject-matter.

This kind of art might be called the Middle Art, and has its good and bad examples. Epstein's modelled heads are among the best examples of interpretive art.

160

"Consummatum est": 1937

In order to understand Big, or Major Art, it may be best to quote from Nietzsche: "The artist has the ability *not* to react to immediate stimuli."

In the major work of art, the subject or idea, when first perceived or conceived, is allowed to sink down into the deeper levels of the artist's creative sources, where it is shaped and reshaped, and imbued with vitality and organic unity, not only through his present life experience, but also through the long-lived memories of that little part of him which has endured from all time through his ancestry—that little speck within him which links him with Adam and the beginning of all things.

In so far as it reaches to these early sources can the major work of art be said to be Primitive.

It is almost a biological act. Every major work of art embodies these creative birth-pangs, and for this reason it is at times lacking in the pleasant suavity of the two lesser forms of art.

For the same reason the grammar used in its expression is so free from fashionable colloquialism and its technique must needs be so stark in its logic that those who accept only the immediate and conventional values of our present mad civilisation are bound to be shocked by it.

In the two lesser forms of art, Reportage and Interpretation for instance, it may be legitimate for the sculptor to make his stone look like human flesh or, for that matter, butter; but when a sculptor is creating a major work he must allow the stone the logic of its own hard nature.

His idea must be expressed in stone, as stone: remaining all the time stone, but stone with a new vitality and power added to it. Not all major art is successful. There are many failures, for the task is greater.

In a democracy of free peoples there are four possible attitudes to a work of this kind. You do not understand it, but like it all the same. You do not understand it, and do not like it. You understand it and like it. Or you understand it, and do not like it. And that is all that can be said. There is no need for hysteria.

This latest work by Epstein, "Consummatum Est", satisfies the laws of a major work of art. It is logically conceived and rendered in stone. It is no mere reporting or transcribing of naturalistic shapes. It is an act of creation.

It is not an immediate and facile reaction to the subject. It has power, vitality and organic unity. In my opinion it comes off.

Leave Epstein alone and your children will bless you in days to come. Strangle him by abuse and receive the immediate blessings of Dr. Goebbels and his band of tenth-rate reporters in paint and plaster who are leading a nation to cultural suicide.

Epstein: An Autobiography

On the last day of the showing I went into the Gallery, after I had thought everyone had left, and the exhibition was supposed to be closed down. I entered the Gallery to look upon my work with solitude and silence, and I then noticed a man in a corner who came forward and spoke to me of the sculpture as if he sensed me to be the sculptor. He spoke well and eloquently. He was a foreigner, and when I questioned him, he told me he was a German, a Jew, an engineer. What impressed me was his evident desire to remain anonymous. A Jew out of Germany. A man of culture and of understanding who did not wish me to make anything of him personally! We parted and that is my last impression at the end of the Exhibition of "Consummatum Est".*

* See Appendix for other articles on "Consummatum Est".

GENERAL SIR ALAN CUNNINGHAM, 1943

ERNEST BEVIN, 1943

19

DRAWINGS FOR *FLEURS DU MAL*: 1938

I MUST say at once that my drawings for Baudelaire I consider, at the same time, amongst my best work and my greatest failure when exhibited, from the point of view of any intelligent appreciation. I had made the drawings for an edition of the *Fleurs du Mal* to be published in America by the Limited Editions Club. I believe only six or seven drawings were wanted, but when I started reading the text with a view to illustrating it, I found the subject so absorbing I made sixty drawings. I believe Mr. Macy, who originally asked me to make the drawings, was somewhat taken aback at this over-measure, and I realised that I had taken the commission all too seriously. The drawings now are scattered, some have been bought, others sent to America, and I regret they have not been kept as a collection or published entire.

I cannot imagine why these drawings, so brooded on and worked over, were received, I will not say with contempt, though that was also their portion, but with an indifference and a coldness I do not understand. They were, in the ugly parlance of to-day, "a flop". To my astonishment a poet, who I had imagined was practically unknown in England and whom I had scarcely ever heard mentioned, was, according to the critics, almost a household word

Strange discovery, indeed! The connoisseurs without exception found that I had no "understanding of the poet", and that the drawings were "no more illustrations of *Les Fleurs du Mal* than they were of Bunyan's *Pilgrim's Progress*". It seemed to me that my blasphemy was considered as great, in this case, as in that of the Old Testament drawings. This reverence for Baudelaire was really most

163

touching, and to the lover of the French Dante, a source of great gratification.

The drawings of the same format, when hung in the Gallery, seemed to me like a decoration which could be carried out on a large scale with magnificent effect. In these drawings I had tried to represent the spiritual, religious, and ecstatic sense of the poems with their tragic and sombre shades, avoiding for the most part those cheap sensual interpretations in illustrations so commonly found in volumes of the *Fleurs du Mal.* I wrote a preface for the catalogue which I will quote as appropriate to the story of the drawings.

HOMAGE À BAUDELAIRE

Solely to satisfy a craving of my own, I have made these drawings for *Les Fleurs du Mal* of Baudelaire. This Bible of the modern man has long called to me, and brooding upon the powerful and subtle images evoked by long reading, a world comes forth filled with splendid and maleficent entities.

I am aware that these are not the first drawings for *Les Fleurs du Mal*, but I have felt that the erotic and sensuous side has hitherto been unduly stressed and that drawings of seductive mulattos, exotic negresses, and nostalgic eldorados do not altogether sum up Baudelaire. This forestalls, perhaps, the charge that I have neglected to illustrate such poems as "L'invitation au Voyage" or "Le Beau Navire".

For long I have been haunted by the images of revolt, anguish, and despair—disgust with the world and self, expressed in *Les Fleurs du Mal.*

To evoke upon paper this profoundly felt and pitiful drama was an aim that called for imaginative and courageous treatment. Here is an adventure wholly of the soul. Man caught in the snare of sinful existence seeks to escape "La conscience dans le Mal".

My technique, my plan of pencil drawings, with a result somewhat like that of lithography, is justified by the austere and measured form of the poems.

Out of sixty drawings I sold fifteen, a very poor result, and after a fortnight I withdrew the drawings, as I found the Gallery Directors out of sympathy with them and really rather ashamed of them. In such an atmosphere of hostility I thought it best to shut down and withdraw.

In exhibiting, one must at times accept defeat, and go on and not brood too much on failure.

Drawings for Fleurs du Mal: *1938*

The Daily Mail Art Critic wrote as follows:

Horror and near-obscenity, with no æsthetic value that I can perceive, stamp Epstein's new drawings on view at the Tooth Gallery from to-day.

They are pencil illustrations for Baudelaire's *Fleurs du Mal*, a collection of poems which, when published in 1857, brought their author to the dock on a charge of offending against public morals.

Baudelaire is one of the cursed princes of literature. His association with a perverse coloured woman, his mighty mind obsessed by diseased sensuousness, his drift in currents of vice and weakness, despite advantages of birth, and his recourse to opium and drink which brought on paralysis and early death—these form a tragic sequence rarely paralleled in the annals of genius.

But genius of the purest water redeems his abasement like repentance the sinner.

The *Fleurs du Mal*—flowers of evil, indeed—are a garden of verbal beauty astonishing in its tropical luxuriance. The grandeur of its accumulated growth fills the beholder with heart-wrung respect and holy pity.

Its flaming wealth of colour, black and red, overawe like a vision of Satanic fate clasping a magnificent but defenceless soul.

What has Epstein done with all this?

He has retained the morbidity, the shameless lasciviousness, and made them even more tangible.

Visual images immobilise literary imagery and break the solemn cadence of inspired verse, which gradually effaces even the clearest descriptive passages.

And Epstein has produced no beauty of form and composition analogous to Baudelaire's rhythmic language and able to off-set the gruesomeness or indecency of the themes.

Take the lines:

> *Les yeux fixes sur moi, comme un tigre dompté,*
> *D'un air vague et rêveur elle essayait des poses,*
> *Et la candeur unie à la lubricité*
> *Donnait un charme neuf à ses metamorphoses . . .*

The voluptuous temptress, as figured by Epstein in the guise of a naked malformed contortionist practising a particularly graceless twist of the torso. Imagine Epstein's notoriously ugly statues of "Night" and "Genesis" grotesquely playing the rôle of Potiphar's wife, and you have his attempt at invoking Baudelaire's muse.

The entire series—with misshapen females, sometimes decapitated, always repellent; lewd navvies fresh from or leaving for the torturer's rack; and disgusting embryos—is an insult to good taste—and to Baudelaire.

One sympathises with Epstein's view that "drawings of seductive mulattos, exotic Negresses and nostalgic Eldorados do not altogether sum up Baudelaire". Unfortunately his transposition is even worse.

It confirms my belief that great poetry is best left unillustrated.

PIERRE JEANNERAT.

The Observer headed its article:

COCKROACHES OR FLOWERS

BAUDELAIRE PLUS EPSTEIN

By *Jan Gordon*

For certain kinds of effects colour may be felt as an intruder, and, like Picasso in his big decoration "Guernica", Epstein, in his illustrations of *Les Fleurs du Mal* at Tooth's Gallery, has restricted his medium to what might be almost called pencil "painting" to keep in harmony with the "austere and measured form of the poems".

When a man with the artistic intelligence of an Epstein, says "this bible of modern man has long called to me, and brooding upon the powerful and subtle images evoked by long reading, a world comes forth filled with splendid and maleficent entities", we should pause before making a hasty criticism. Nevertheless, just as when a musician turns a poem into song, so when a painter turns a poem into image there is always grave danger that the poet gets overlaid. Clearly the marriage between the bitter, short-lived nostalgic Baudelaire—passionate and disgusted revolté though he was—and the stone-hewing, muscular sculptor, highly capable of mould-ing his own life into something like the shape he intended it to be, was bound to result in a strange progeny.

Epstein also says "I made these drawings solely to satisfy a craving of my own", but the result is so dynamically forcible to crudity that he is in danger of obliterating much of what Baudelaire may mean to us. After all, Baudelaire did entitle his poems *Les Fleurs du Mal*, and that is implicit in the quality of the poems; had he called them "Les Cafards du Mal", Epstein's drawings would have been more wholly appropriate.

In fact, one might counsel those who prefer Baudelaire to Epstein to keep away, but those who prefer Epstein to Baudelaire to go at any cost.

There is little to choose for viciousness of statement between the reviews above and that below. In the best *New Statesman* manner is the following:

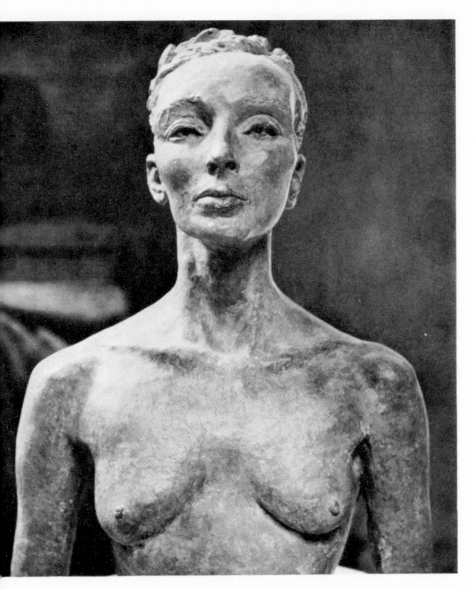

THE PRINCESS DE BRAGANZA, 1944

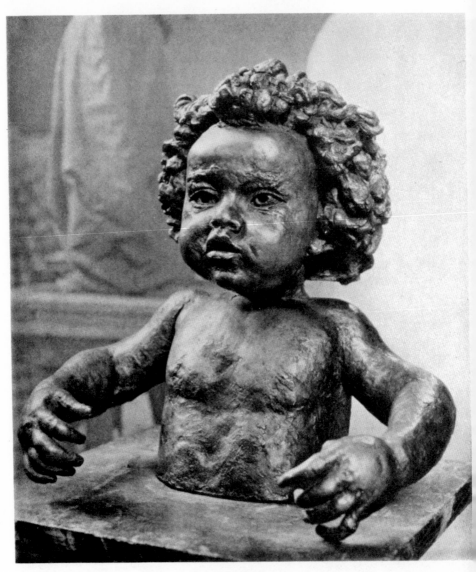

IAN, 1942

Drawings for Fleurs du Mal: 1938

Now I must place a word about the drawings at Tooth's. "Solely to satisfy a craving of my own", Mr. Epstein explains, "I have made these drawings for Les Fleurs du Mal of Baudelaire." Nobody will question his right to satisfy so private a need, but was it necessary to expose the results to the public gaze? Mr. Epstein's virtues have always been vigour and expressiveness, and in his better works these have gone far to compensate for the absence of distinction and sensibility. But Baudelaire is a great classical poet, at once marmoreal and exquisitely fine. The Racine of the Romantic Movement. Illustrations by Flaxman for Defoe, by Marie Laurencin for Whitman, by Kokoschka for Pope, could not be more unsuitable than those Mr. Epstein has made for Baudelaire. And not only are they impertinent, they must be classed among the emptiest works that he has ever exhibited. He has sought to express revolt, anguish and despair —emotions that the present condition of man must excite in every artist —but compared with Picasso's Guernica drawings, these are hardly more significant than graffiti. One does not need to be a Blimp in order to feel that ugliness is not enough. The greater one's devotion to Baudelaire, the less one can enjoy these unlucky illustrations. Upstairs in the same gallery there is a roomful of Paul Nash paintings, most of them not new, but a nice enough sight for one's sore eyes.

From vulgar abuse to the would-be humours of the above is a short step. What is odd is that the critic, knowing full well that his eyes are going to be sorely tried by my drawings, should go out of his way to afflict himself with these horrors, as the exhibit of Mr. Nash's work was in a quite different part of the house. The high-brow critic is often annoyed to find himself in the same boat as the low-brow critic with regard to me. How irritating to find yourself bedfellow with the gutter journalist in questions of art! The high-brow critic gets round this by asserting that his low-brow twin dislikes me for the "wrong reasons". The truth is that, of course, I stand in the light of some little bantam-weight sculptor of their own, whose sole distinction is an endless capacity for borrowing and watering down Picasso, Maillol, or Despiau.

After the foregoing three reviews, readers might turn with relief to an article from The Birmingham Mail by L. B. Powell:

It is the Baudelaire of a very human compassion that Epstein sees in these drawings for Les Fleurs du Mal.

These verses of an unforgettably poignant beauty are for him "this Bible of the modern man", long brooding upon which, he writes in the foreword of the catalogue, "brings forth a world filled with splendid and maleficent entities".

Some of the entities are like the gargoyles at Winchcombe, to take the best near examples of Gothic fantasy which Epstein's drawings resemble in their fertility of invention, and occasionally in manner.

And there is a curious reflection for you: the Gothic gargoyle was an adventure of the soul—a phrase which Epstein uses in description of his work. Adventures of the soul are not, unfortunately, popular nowadays. In any case, they are likely too soon to be confronted by the modern Inquisition of totalitarianism.

ESSENTIAL HUMANISM

More than a Gothic reminder, however, is to be seen in these absorbing drawings. In manner and emotional significance they are widely varied. Here and there they have a mournfulness and a profundity of serious expression which irresistibly recall the mysticism of Da Vinci.

If, on the whole, they should be found strange and difficult to understand, that must be because the all-embracing humanism of which they are an expression, like the verses that inspire them, is in itself a quality in eclipse to-day, in the visual arts perhaps rather more than most things.

"For long," writes Epstein, "I have been haunted by the images of revolt, anguish and despair—disgust with the world and self expressed in *Les Fleurs du Mal.*" But let it not be imagined that the drawings are piquant titbits offered to the public appetite, omnivorous for the confessions of the great. Nor are they tracts for the times, except in the sense that all Art is a tract for the times.

The fact is that they exemplify the real and the rare artistic capacity for making a personal statement to which a universal significance is added. Art, or what passes for it, is everything nowadays, from the exercise of an arid intellectualism to the erotic perversities of surrealism. But it still remains for Epstein to beat the abstractionists and the surrealists at their own game by giving us an art in which the intellectual expression is made properly the vehicle of the emotion intended to be conveyed. To put it another way, he comes at natural forms through a creative intelligence which, knowing the values of symbolism and its limits, can invest the forms with the meaning that is achieved only through the language of art.

GREATER SUBTLETY

These drawings reveal a decided advance in the command of the subtleties of linear forms of expression as compared with the Old Testament drawings of a few years ago. Here and there, perhaps, greater use of the effect of chiaroscuro would not come amiss, the dramatic purport being what it is. But on technical grounds it is illuminating to observe the freedom and resourcefulness in which rhythmic patterns are discovered to fit the emotional theme. They vary from such relatively simple devices as the "Danse Macabre" drawing, where a recumbent skeleton-like figure is seen against a background in which a fountain plays, to the elaborate synthesis of elliptical forms in one of the drawings to "Une Gravure Fantastique".

The directness of inspiration from the text is evident in most examples, and is matched, in a unique degree, by ease and grace of accomplishment. *Les Fleurs du Mal* is a theme felt acutely enough and of the artist's joy in creation there is no doubt.

20

"ADAM": 1938–1939

MY LARGE carving I did at this period was worked in a block of alabaster that had been for several years in my studio. The conception, fairly clear in my mind in its general outlines, developed a law of its own as it proceeded, and I managed to get a tremendous movement within the compass of a not very wide, upright stone. The movement lies not in flung-out forms, but in an inner energy, comparable to a dynamo where a tremendous energy is generated. Into no other work had I merged myself so much, yet an Australian said to me: "It is as if a people had done this work and not just an individual." I feel also that generations spoke through me, and the inner urge that took shape here was the universal one.

For some time, owing to my having portraits to do, I was retarded in finishing it. Then having a couple of months of freedom, I made a great spurt, working on it relentlessly, day after day, and I had it in a fit state to exhibit when my long-promised exhibition at the Leicester Gallery took place.

I am not particularly secretive about my work, but I find that if I show a work of mine to friends in the process of carving, they are inclined to try and stay my hand by exclaiming: "Oh, leave it like that. It is so interesting in that state."

A carving is interesting from the moment you begin it, and in that lies the danger of showing an unfinished work; so I make it a rule not to show my carvings. I am therefore accused of being secretive. In this case, I only let my Gallery Directors know at first that I was at work upon an "Adam", and with this they had to be content. When I did let them see the carving, they said nothing and left my studio. The next day they wrote to me saying that they could not see

ADAM, 1939

LA SERVANTE AU GRAND CŒUR, 1938
An illustration for Charles Baudelaire's *Les Fleurs du Mal*

their way to showing the statue. I was astounded, and did not try to persuade them. Their fears seemed groundless to me, and I recalled with amusement that this Gallery had, a short time before this, shown a series of French coloured engravings that were decidedly "near the bone", in fact did not leave anything ambiguous as far as frankness went.

As I had other work to show, bronzes and a series of drawings of children, I was anxious about the success of my exhibition, and let it be known that I would not withdraw my "Adam" and exhibit the rest. Thereupon the Directors paid another visit to my studio, finally to make up their minds. I left them alone with "Adam" for three hours, after which, with many qualms and forebodings, they agreed to show the carving.

All this I took in a rather bantering spirit, as I could not for the life of me see anything to be afraid of. The result justified my anticipations. The exaggerated fears of the Directors were superfluous, interest in the work was shown by the attendance, and apart from the usual intentional misunderstandings of a section of the Press, and the deliberate personal insults of the so-called "Left Intelligentsia", the work was well received. Perhaps I have at last educated the public, if not to complete understanding, to, at any rate, a more tolerant attitude.

Foaming at the mouth and foul abuse were for once absent. The only drawback in this exhibition was that a collection of child studies, on which I had set much store, was completely overlooked. So much for the interest in beautiful sculpture and drawings that a great many persons profess. They exclaim: "Why does not Epstein do something beautiful? Why always monsters?" You exhibit a collection of drawings of children and bronzes into which you have put your matured talent, and the gaze of all these people is spell-bound upon "the Monster", and they fail utterly to see the small works for which they have always clamoured. Go into any Gallery in London—the British Museum, the National Gallery, the Tate Gallery, or South Kensington Museum—and you will find them empty. You can enjoy works without any crowding. Perhaps you will see a solitary wastrel trying to snatch a few minutes' sleep upon a bench. When I first lived in London I had a studio near the British Museum, and for a period visited it daily. I can say that never once did I meet a sculptor there.

In fact, I discovered that sculptors would be rather ashamed to be seen in the British Museum, as painters would not care to be caught in the National Gallery. Their notion is that they would be thought to be cribbing something, borrowing something, and of course that would never do. Artists have a feeling that if they studied ancient work they would be thought less original, liable to be influenced. English Art students do not mind being influenced by some third-rate teacher in an Art School, but at the idea of being influenced by the great works in the Museum by a Raphael, a Mantegna, or a Veronese, I can almost hear them exclaim: "God save us! Never!"

Despite the scepticism and fears of the Directors of the Leicester Gallery, the "Adam" was well received. Some of the criticism was naturally hostile, but no more so than usual. When a purchaser came along, the Gallery was astounded, and also the newspapers, who showed their hostility by leading articles commenting on the purchase. One paper wondered why a "statue completely out of joint", as it called it, should be bought, and another commented on the purchase price, which was rumoured as seven thousand pounds, and expressed its amazement and almost horror that a work of sculpture should fetch so high a price. This paper, which naturally reports deals in business amounting to hundreds of thousands, nay millions of pounds, with no comment, raised its eyebrows in astonishment that I could "easily" earn seven thousand pounds. One thinks of what is spent on armaments, warships, aeroplanes, gas, and engines of destruction of all kinds in the world, the industries of death. Think of the manner in which millions of money are made on the Stock Exchange, by looking at the ticker-in offices, with the help of managers, vast staffs, and with no surprising comment by leader critics; yet the fact that a sculptor, single-handed, could with all his out-of-pocket expenses, over-head charges for studio, sustenance for himself and his family, and the labour of about fifteen months, earn the magnificent sum of seven thousand pounds, passes their belief. Of this sum received, one quarter was deducted for the Gallery, another quarter or more went to the Income Tax, and to sum up, and to make the whole thing more grotesque, the actual price of the work was not one-quarter of the published sum.

The vast sums expended on death and destruction, or for millions of foolish and banal activities, are taken for granted.

"*Adam*": *1938-1939*

To end this chronicle to my own satisfaction for once, I will leave out the mud-slinging articles and comments, and publish two reviews: one by L. B. Powell in *The Birmingham Mail* of June 9th, 1939, and the other by William McCance in *Picture Post* of June 24th, 1939 (printed in the Appendix).

This is Mr. Powell's:

Crowded private view days are not the best occasions for seeing great works of art, but they cannot be improved upon for hearing what people say regarding them. I shall remember yesterday's private view at the Leicester Galleries, London, of Epstein's "Adam", his latest, and in every way his most imposing addition to the series of big-scale carvings which are unequalled in the free sculpture of our time, for a chance conversation with a visitor from New York.

"To me," she said, with that charming diffidence which seems characteristic of cultured New Yorkers, "'Adam' is as if it were not made by a man, but by mankind."

Now there is a phrase which any professional writer upon art must envy. Powerful impressions are not often sorted out with such clarity, or with such complete embodying of a world of thought in a few words, and I am sure nothing better than this can be said about "Adam".

With equal confidence it can be said that no one who sees only a photographic reproduction of this piece of monumental sculpture in alabaster (I call it "free" because it is unrelated to any architectural requirements) can feel about it in the same way. The experience is one to be gained only in the presence of the thing itself: and there, it is to be feared, the melancholy end to all philosophic or other speculation upon the emotions expressed in any manifestation of the creative artistic impulse would be to say one either is, or is not, born to the way of grasping its meaning.

EARTH BOUND

But this is a sort of doctrine of determinism, applied perhaps much too readily to what is very far from being ineluctable or unchangeable. We may reject an idea outright, think it wholly disposed of, and yet unconsciously be profoundly influenced by it. I take the American visitor's words to mean what Epstein himself hoped and knew he would mean in this elemental depiction of man, earth-bound but reaching upwards because man knows no other destiny, and can put himself, when all his frailty is reckoned, to no better purpose.

Not, it is important to observe if and when you are lucky enough to stand before the carving itself, reaching upwards with the hands, which

173

are raised only to the level of the chest and there significantly left; but reaching mentally with all his faculties on the stretch, with the mind symbolised by the head thrown back until its line is horizontal and the eyes escape detection in their skyward stare.

The whole attitude of the figure is this gesture of reaching, and they will escape the deep extra-physical meaning of "Adam" who point out that the features of the face cannot be seen without the aid of a ladder. This objection, one very likely to be heard, springs from the same fallacy as some of the objections to "Genesis", and accordingly, "Let's see if we recognise the woman" becomes "Do we know anybody like this man?"—as if sculpture, when it is the image of thought, should be judged by its resemblance to people we meet in the street.

And yet, standing before "Adam" long enough, it is presently made obvious that we do know him very well indeed. We meet him in fact, every day, for he is none other than our next-door neighbour. He has been our neighbour since man began, and likely as not, he perceives in our own lineaments just the same points of identification.

NON-ACCEPTANCE

Therefore I would say, to blazes with the idea of recognising him as a detachable entity. He is not a man, but mankind, and a point about this universal analogy is surely that genius is so far removed from abnormality that it is always pregnant with meaning for men everywhere. To which it may be added that the culture of any period or of any people is to be measured by the readiness with which it accepts those who are subsequently regarded by general consent as geniuses. My American commentator desired to know if Epstein had been accepted in England, to which I felt obliged to reply that he had not.

I believe this in spite of the fact that an exhibition of flower paintings by him, or of Old Testament drawings, or portraits of children, will sell out in a few days; and of the fact that the bronze portraits are fairly well bought, or of the knowledge that "Night" and "Day" have not yet been pulled down to make room for a group by a Royal Academician showing a dance of sugar-plum fairies.

I believe it because acceptance, in the sense in which we are thinking, would imply widespread admission of the influence of the artist as a teacher of truths that are essentially religious in nature: between which and being a teacher of religion a world of difference exists.

Yes, but with "Adam" in mind, what sort of truths? I can best attempt an answer by saying that if the carving has any influence at all upon thought and feeling, it must surely be to send us away humbled. Not,

174

RAGAMUFFIN, 1940

PEGGY JEAN, 1919

PEGGY JEAN ASLEEP, 1920

LEDA, 1940

please, in Uriah Heep's understanding of the word, but essentially, the taking on of humility.

And there's the rub. When the American visitor remarked that we have lost the faculty of looking at things simply, she was implying also that we have become so knowledgeable as to resist, with a good deal of indignation, the underlying expectation of the creative genius that we should look upon his work as if it were something done for the very first time. The suggestion even that it is part of the artist's business to teach us humility accounts for the continued strangeness, the remoteness of Epstein, and the repulsion which many feel towards his work. We swing easily to the opposite view: it has become barbarous to suppose that we retain any relic of primitive man. What with one thing and another—the methods and materials of modern war for example, we are confident that we have civilised the brute out of existence and do not feel flattered when Epstein or anybody else has the effrontery to hint that we are still groping, as he groped, towards some irresistible light.

Not to put too fine a point on it, it seems to me Epstein is rejected because, after all, he is inferring that the blasphemy may be in hearts other than his own. Of "Adam" it is certainly true, as of most other art, that we find in it what we bring to it.

L. B. POWELL.*

21

STUDIES OF CHILDREN

I HAVE always been attracted by children as models for plastic work. I feel that the life of children has hardly been touched upon in sculpture, and this representation is avoided perhaps because of the difficulties that confront an artist who sets out to present a child. For one thing the child cannot sit still, and to compel a child to be quiet is at once to destroy the spontaneity and charm which lie in its frank and natural expressions. Yet I have attempted time after time this most difficult subject for sculpture. In Joan Greenwood, there is the precocious child with elfin smile, and also in portraits of Peggy Jean. I made many studies—Peggy Jean "Laughing Studies" and Peggy Jean "Sleeping Studies". Later I have indulged my fancy for this expression in sculpture by studies of coloured children, and the studies of Jackie and others in bronze, and drawings, of which I have made a whole series of endless moods and variety of movement. Here again I have not restrained myself, but freely given what I have observed and felt, and I know that I have by no means exhausted the subject. The Florentines had a special love of children. From Donatello's mad incarnations of robust vitality, to graceful Verrocchio's, to the waywardness of a Desiderio Da Settignano.

To work from a child the sculptor has to have endless patience. He must wait and observe, and observe and wait. The small forms, so seemingly simple, are in reality so subtle, and the hunting of the form is an occupation that is at once tantalising and fascinating. At the end of an hour or two the nerves of an artist are torn to shreds, and neurasthenia and eye-strain might well result from a too prolonged preoccupation with this form of sculptural expression.

176

Studies of Children

This "Babe" confronts time and his destiny with round, creased arms and hands held out before him, as if in self-protection. He boldly and trustingly looks out upon a world newly born to his vision. This is a man-child, and his sturdy frame is like that of an Egyptian King in its compact lines. Every form full, complete, and with a sense of new, fresh power. This man-child confronts a world which we older ones know only too well, and our grey, haggard glance must light up at this fresh revelation—an undying flame of life embodied again.

THE STUDIES OF PEGGY JEAN

To have a child to work from was delightful. The little Peggy Jean was a real source of inspiration. I never tired of watching her, and to watch her was, for me, to work from her. To make studies in clay of all her moods; and when she tired and fell asleep, there was something new to do, charming and complete. To work from a child seemed to me the only work worth doing, and I was prepared to go on for the rest of my life looking at Peggy Jean, and making new studies of her. I exhibited these later in one of my exhibitions, and the reactions of some persons were far from amusing. Of the "Peggy Jean Asleep", one kind soul said: "How cruel of Mr. Epstein to compel a child to pose like that." Others said: "She is not at all a pretty child," as if that was the sole business of the artist to find a "pretty" child to work from.

I regret that I have not done more children, and I plan some day to do only children. I think I should be quite content with that, and not bother about the grown-ups at all. I would love to fill my studio with studies of children. Children just born. Children growing up. Children nude. Children in fantastic costumes *en prince*, with pets of all kinds, and toys. Dark children, Piccaninnies, Chinese, Mongolian-eyed children.

This is a fancy, a dream of mine, but naturally I must sometimes turn to and earn a living like other persons, and not indulge too much in strange and unrealisable longings and desires.

Epstein: An Autobiography

I begin the drawings of Jackie, and at first my drawings are somewhat sketchy, loose, although from the beginning I know what I want to render. It is the life, free, careless, and apprehensive at the same time, of the little boy with his lively intelligence and quick ways, especially his eyes, and also his expressive hands in their infinite and unconscious gestures, that I wish to capture. I find that I must have great patience, as there is no such thing as posing, and I have to watch for the return of a gesture and the movement of the head. The same movement of the arms or hands never seems to recur, and I often rise after an hour or two, enervated and discouraged, with nothing to show but an abandoned beginning. Gradually I seem to gain in swiftness and assurance, and the drawings become more satisfactory. I reject a dozen drawings, and one seems to me to have got something of the little fellow's peculiarity. I have him read to and that fixes his attention. The stories with pictures hold him, especially drawings of animals. Rabier's graphic accounts, above all and stories about snakes fascinate him. At the adventures of the monkey, the rabbit, the hedgehog, and the ducks, he roars with delight, and I then work with devoted fury and attention. In time I see hundreds of things to do, all different, and the drawings are like preludes and fugues, or to put it better, variations on a theme—the theme of young child life. An endless series of variations. I can see no monotony in my studies of this boy, although that is the easiest and readiest criticism. To-day, variety means something different from what it once did. To me, the changes of expression in a child's head, the change of the direction of the pupil of the eye, the contraction and expansion of the eye, the change in nostrils and cheeks, give great variety, such variety that it would take a highly sensitive and skilful observer to record. A technique must be at one's command, transcending mere stylism. The aim must be achieved, whatever the means. As I say, I work with fury and appetite, and before the miracle of the child's moods, I am almost nonplussed; but a partial achievement spurs me on, and with the multiplicity of drawings I feel the abundant harvest has made my efforts well worth while. I look upon this body of drawings of a child as a legacy well worth achieving. In reviewing them now, I see a development in technique,

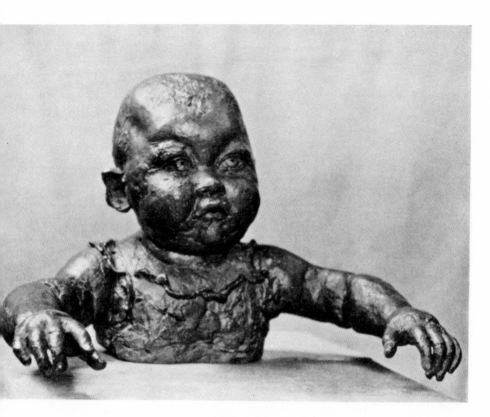

JACKIE, 1935

JACKIE, 1939

and a final mastery, also great variety of line, and rendering of form, through light and shade. I compare these drawings with any others I have made, and am pleased at their lightness and solidity. I feel really sorry that I have sold a number, as I would have liked to have kept them intact as a collection. My drawings of Jackie present a period of my life, and mark out, through drawings, a plastic expression I am proud of. To have captured the fugitive and endless expressions and changes of movement of a child has been a rare experience.

22

THE BRITISH MUSEUM AND GREEK SCULPTURE

SOME few years after the First World War, in visiting the British Museum, I noticed that some of the Greek Marbles were being restored. This reprehensible practice I had thought long gone out. Later, one day, to my horror, I noticed that the Demeter Statue had been tampered with, a plaster nose had been added, and other additions had been made to shoulders and neck. Also the head had received a savage scraping. I had observed with apprehension how workmen of the Museum were severely manhandling the Marbles with some kind of sand and scrubbing brushes. This restoration of so beautiful a work as the Demeter made me feel that I had reached the end of my endurance, so I wrote a letter which was published on May 2nd, 1921, to *The Times* as follows:

SIR,

All those who care for antique sculpture view with astonishment and dismay the present policy followed by the British Museum authorities in restoring the Marbles, that is, working them up with new plaster noses, etc.

I have remarked with growing alarm marble after marble so treated during the last year. I felt the futility of protesting, and so held my peace, but now that the incredible crime of "restoring" the head of the Demeter of Cnidus has at last been committed, the atrocity calls for immediate protest.

No doubt the Museum authorities do not really like the Marbles in their possession, but why they should translate the masterpieces into something more nearly approaching the Albert Moore ideal of Greek, passes my understanding. The Demeter has not only been improved with a new plaster nose, but to bring the rest of the head into consistency with the nose, the whole face has been scraped and cleaned, thus destroying the mellow golden patine of centuries. Other important pieces "improved" are the marble boy extracting a thorn from his foot, and the very fine priestess from Cnidus, so altered as to give an entirely different effect from that it originally had. How long are these vandals to have in their "care" the golden treasury of sculpture which at least they might leave untouched.

Yours respectfully,

JACOB EPSTEIN.

For my letter I was severely taken to task. Professor Gardiner wrote a letter in defence of the Museum authorities and said it was only a matter of difference of opinion between two schools of thought, in fact, merely a academic question. Any damage to the statues was scouted, and the discussion ended by *The Times* itself awarding the Museum officials 100 per cent marks, the maximum, for their custodianship, I suppose.

Two years later Dr. Bernard Smith hit upon the idea of squirting on to the Demeter's head raspberry juice from a syringe. This again called the attention of the British Museum officials to the restorations, and this amazing incident was instrumental in finally convincing them of the wisdom of removing the false nose. However, all this was only a prelude to something far graver which happened in 1939, and of which the last has not yet been heard. That is the cleaning and restoring of the Elgin Marbles. So far, any damage done has remained a mystery, but a speaker in the House at the time, referring to his report from the British Museum authorities, said:

The Marbles are in process of transference to the new Gallery, but none of those so far transferred have suffered in any way by the removal. So far as cleaning is concerned, I am informed by the Trustees of the British Museum that there has been some unauthorised cleaning of some of the Marbles, but that it is not yet possible to determine precisely what the effect has been. I am assured, however, that the effects are imperceptible to anyone but an expert, and I think it follows that the intrinsic beauty of the Marbles has not been impaired.

(Extract from *The Times*, May 20th, 1939, from a speech by Captain Crookshank, Financial Secretary to the Treasury.)

The resignation of two officials and the dismissal of the Head Cleaner from the Museum Staff pointed to some very grave condition of the Elgin Mables. See, for instance, the admissions of the

Epstein: An Autobiography

Head Cleaner in *The Daily Express*. Mr. Arthur Holcombe, the Head Cleaner of the British Museum, in an interview said:

I was told to begin cleaning the Elgin Marbles two years ago. As head man I was put in charge of six Museum Labourers. We were given a solution of soap and water and ammonia. First we brushed the dirt off the Marbles with a soft brush. Then we applied the solution with the same brush. After that we sponged them dry, then wiped them over with distilled water.

That was all we were told to do. To get off some of the dirtier spots I rubbed the Marbles with a blunt copper tool. Some of them were as black with dirt as that grate, said Mr. Holcombe, pointing to his grate.

As far as I know, all that had been done for years to clean them was to blow them with bellows.

The other men borrowed my copper tools and rubbed the Marbles with them as I did. I knew it would not do them any harm, because the copper is softer than the stone. I have used the same tools for cleaning the Marbles at the Museum under four Directors.

One or two of the slabs of the frieze came up rather white, and I am afraid they caused the trouble. But anybody who knows anything about marble knows that if you treat two slabs in exactly the same manner it is possible that they will come up a different colour.

All the time that we were working, Officials of the Museum were passing through the room. We had been at it fifteen months, when I was told there was a complaint.

The six men and I were called before the Committee of Trustees and the Director of the Museum. We went in separately and they asked us all kinds of questions about how we had been cleaning the Marbles.

(*May 19th*, 1939.)

I have repeatedly pointed out the danger to our national heritage from officials who have no expert or technical knowledge of sculpture, and I have insisted that sculptors—men who are brought up with sculpture—should be on the board of Trustees. My advice was ignored and one would imagine from the attitude of the official bodies that I was, ironically enough, the enemy of the antique work, instead of, as it happens, its most sincere protector. In a controversy carried on in *The Times*, Sir George Hill, a former Director of the British Museum, seemed bent, as you will see from letters here given, on proving that my eye-sight deceived me and that I, the sculptor Epstein, mistook a plaster cast for a marble! To such miser-

ESTHER, 1944

KITTY, 1944

able shifts do the Museum officials descend in their efforts to discredit criticism of their stupidities.

On May 19th I wrote to *The Times* as follows:

SIR,

In your issue of May 2nd 1921, I protested against the cleaning and restoring of the Greek Marbles at the British Museum, particularly the Demeter of Cnidus. My protest went unheeded, and I was jeered at for concerning myself with what I was told was no business of mine. Eighteen years have passed, and now the cleaning and restoration of the Elgin Marbles are causing uneasiness, and questions are asked as to whether the famous Marbles have been damaged in the process. The British Museum authorities have admitted that the change in the Marbles is only to be distinguished by the practised eye "of an expert", wherever that resides! An interview published in the Press with the Head Cleaner of the Marbles has elicited the information that a copper tool "softer than marble" (how incredible) was used. Why a cleaner and six hefty men should be allowed for fifteen months to tamper with the Elgin Marbles, as revealed by the head cleaner, passes the comprehension of a sculptor. When will the British Museum authorities understand that they are only the custodians and never the creators of these masterpieces?

Faithfully yours,

JACOB EPSTEIN.

Sir George Hill answered this letter by writing to *The Times*:

SIR,

In his letter to you of to-day's date Mr. Jacob Epstein refers to his letter of May 2nd, 1921, in which he complained of the "cleaning" and restoring of the Greek Marbles at the British Museum, particularly the Demeter of Cnidus. He now complains that his protest went unheeded; but he must have missed the statement of your issue on May 3rd and Professor Gardiner's letter of May 4th. Had he read these he would have understood that the Demeter had not been cleaned in the drastic way which he alleged. The "restoration" was confined to the experimental addition of the nose in plaster which could be easily, and was indeed immediately afterwards, removed.

A point that was not made in those communications, however, may be mentioned here. The Demeter has never had a "mellow golden patine" within living memory. (My own memories of her go back to the eighties.) But the plaster cast which, for safety's sake, filled her place during the War was of a nice yellow colour. Mr. Epstein must have become accustomed to the cast, which less expert critics than himself may well have taken for an original.

I may be allowed to add that no such thing as "restoration" of the Parthenon Marbles has been or will be undertaken as long as the authorities of the British Museum have them in their keeping; and no "cleaning" other than simple washing with neutral soap and distilled water is authorised in the Museum. I am, Sir, your obedient servant,

GEORGE HILL.

(*May 20th*, 1939.)

I answered this letter of Sir George Hill's by writing to *The Times* on May 22nd, 1939, as follows:

SIR,

With regard to the Elgin Marbles and the Demeter of Cnidus, Sir George Hill in his letter in your issue of to-day imagines that I took no cognisance of the letters and statements following my letter of May 2nd, 1921. He mentions Professor Percy Gardiner's letter of May 4th, 1921, in which, as I recall, the Professor indulged himself in what was to my mind merely a scholastic discussion and ignored the vital issues at stake.

All these letters and statements, as I pointed out in my letter in your last issue, were directed towards one purpose, which was to point out how wrong I was in criticising the British Museum authorities, and I summed them all up there by saying simply, "My protest went unheeded." The proof of this statement is that there is now a very grave question about the cleaning of the Elgin Marbles.

Sir George Hill was Keeper at the British Museum during the years 1921–30 and he will doubtless be able to recall that, far from the Demeter's restorations being removed immediately, they were only removed in February, 1923, about two years later, when Dr. Bernard Smith, exasperated beyond endurance by the obduracy of the Museum authorities, had squirted coloured juice on the head of the Demeter, thereby forcing the Museum to take action.

Sir George is at circumstantial pains to prove that I was unacquainted with the original marble and that, as he so disingenuously suggests, I may have mistaken a plaster cast shown during the War for the Demeter. My memory of the Demeter goes back to 1904, not very much later than Sir George's. I am not mistaken when I assert that the head of the Demeter of Cnidus was drastically treated in 1921.

It is not only a question of "a yellow golden patine" but of what is far more important, the scraping of the surfaces, and the effect of that scraping on the planes of the marble. I have myself seen the workmen at the Museum at work on the Marbles and have been horrified by the methods employed.

Sir George ignores the statement of the chief cleaner, Mr. Arthur Holcombe, three days ago in the Press, that he had been in the habit at the Museum, under all of the last four Directors, of cleaning all of the marbles with a "blunt copper tool" and that he started on the Elgin Marbles about two years ago and used this tool.

"Copper is softer than stone", he says. The absurdity of "the softer than marble theory" is manifest. Has Sir George never heard of the bronze toe of the statue of St. Peter in Rome kissed away by the worshippers' soft lips?

"Putting me in my place" seems to be of greater importance to the Museum officials than the proper care of the Greek Marbles.

The whole thing boils down not to an academic discussion on cleaning and patination, but to the grave question as to whether the Elgin Marbles and the other Greek Marbles are to be kept intact, or to be in jeopardy of being periodically treated and perhaps, in the end, being permanently ruined by the Museum officials, through their lack of sculptural science.

The public is dissatisfied with the present state of affairs and clearly uneasy about the present condition of the Elgin Marbles, and must consider the answer for the Treasury in Parliament by Captain Crookshank to a question about them as both equivocal and misleading. It is an admission of damage, with an attempt to minimise the responsibility of the Trustees of the British Museum.

Faithfully yours,

Jacob Epstein.

Sir George Hill again answered my letter by writing to *The Times* on May 25th, 1939, as follows:

Sir,

I have no wish to continue with Mr. Epstein a correspondence which appears to be taking a personal turn, and I should be the last to wish to "put him in his place", as to which we have all of us made up our minds by this time.

But I repeat that the only method of cleaning the Marbles authorised by the Trustees was and is washing with soap and water. It would be valuable to know what exactly were the methods which Mr. Epstein says he saw used to his horror, and whether they were being applied to marble or to plaster.

Epstein: An Autobiography

I must admit Mr. Epstein's correction as to the length of the period during which Demeter wore her false nose; I will not therefore quarrel with his assumption that there is not much difference in the length of our familiarity with the Marbles (to be exact it is a matter of twenty years). We must, I fear, agree to differ on his statement that the head was "scraped" in 1921.

The public may well feel uneasy, owing to the agitation which, as Mr. Epstein's own experience will remind him, can be only too easily worked up artificially. But how far they can trust those who seek to instruct them in the public Press may be inferred from the fact that they have been asked (though not, of course, by Mr. Epstein) to believe that the group of "Cecrops and his daughter" has been a victim of such drastic "cleaning" that it now seems "little better than withered stone". Since the original is still in its place on the Parthenon and it is represented in the British Museum only by a plaster cast, it is hardly reasonable to hold the Trustees responsible for its present condition.

I am, Sir,

Your obedient servant,

GEORGE HILL.

In this connection, and to prove how little the officials at a Museum may know about their own subject, I give the incident of a Sumerian statue I own. A friend of mine, very interested in this statue, said that he would like to bring along the head of the Sumerian department to see it. Coming to my studio, this gentleman, immediately on entering the room, with hardly a glance, declared the statue not Sumerian. On asking him his reasons for this view, he answered that the position of the hands and feet was wrong. This astonished me, as the hands and feet were exactly in the position of all Gudeas of that period. I pointed this out to my expert, and he then determined evidently to put me in my place and declared the statue a forgery. So much for Museum experts. Should you find some work a masterpiece perhaps of ancient Art, and let it be known to the Museum, even before they see it they will declare it to be a fake. Their lack of enterprise is only equalled by their snobbishness, and one would imagine from their attitude that they had created the works. They show them off as if they were their private property.

The two beautiful works now in the Boston Museum, The Chios Head and the other half of the Venus Throne in Rome (Terme Museum), were both in England about 1907 and were offered to the

GIRL FROM BAKU, 1945

LUCIFER, 1945

The British Museum

British Museum by Mr. John Marshall and Mr. Warren, who invited the Museum officials down to see them, about an hour's journey from London. The officials replied that they would look at them if the works were brought to them. Boston got there first, of course.

23

AFRICAN AND POLYNESIAN CARVINGS, AND MASK OF NEFERTITI

WHEN I was in Paris in 1912, I saw an advertisement in a colonial paper asking for African carvings in hard wood. Calling at the address in Montmartre I met Paul Guillaume for the first time, in a small attic room. He started the vogue in African work. Of course, it was the artists who first saw the sculptural qualities of African work, and they were followed by the dealer who saw money in it. Picasso, Matisse, and Vlaminck collected African, and I myself bought pieces at prices I could afford. "Art Snobs" quickly took it up. The prices rose so that soon there was keen bidding at the Hotel Drouot and Sotheby's for African and Polynesian. Later in New York, at the Museum of Modern Art, a large exhibition was held. I was amused that Lord Duveen should ask me to exhibit ten pieces there out of my collection. The idea of Lord Duveen taking an interest in an Art so alien was ludicrous, and just another example of the facile and unthought-out opinion of the opportunists of Art. There is a profound and genuine reason for a sculptor's interest in African Art, for new methods and problems are presented in it different from those of European Art. African work opens up to us a world hitherto unknown, and exhibits characteristics that are far removed from our traditional European rendering of form in Greek, in Gothic, or in Renaissance traditions. The African are almost entirely wood carvings, and the wood block is the basis. Single figures and masks predominate; the group is rare, although some exist. As fetishes their importance is religious or, at any rate, magical. They were used to impress, terrify and impart to the beholders a state of mind bordering on, or actually, hallucinatory.

188

African and Polynesian Carvings

Unless one understands this purpose in the masks they can only be regarded as grotesque and fantastic. In fact that is how they are looked upon by most of us. At one time they were also thought to be devoid of skill, crude, and incapably savage. We now know better, and no more cogent example could be presented of how accepted notions in matters of Art can be changed, and even completely revised.

In the reaction against European sculpture, the newly enlightened are inclined to declare European, Greek, and Egyptian sculpture insipid and meaningless. This is a great error. It is as if someone became greatly enamoured of exotic foods and turned aside from all normal nourishment with disastrous results to their digestion. African works lend themselves to analysis of their plasticity, and several writers have attempted such analysis. I have in my possession the great work called "Brummer Head" which I had seen in Joseph Brummer's shop in Paris many years before in 1913. On that occasion when I asked the price of it, this astute dealer told me there was no price to it and removed the work from view. The piece was later sold and disappeared. In 1935, when all Paris was seeking it, the owner having just died, I came on it by chance in a dealer's basement. I was looking at some indifferent pieces, when, opening a cupboard, I saw it hidden away as if it were not meant to be seen. I immediately negotiated for it, and secured it, much to the surprise and chagrin of the Paris dealers. This remarkable Pahouin head has qualities which transcend the most mysterious Egyptian work. It is an evocation of a spirit that penetrates into another world, a world of ghosts and occult forces, and could only be produced where spiritism still holds sway. On the plastic side also, the head is very remarkable, with its surrounding prongs of hair off-setting the large roundness of the forehead, a perfect example of free wood-carving. I also have the head known as the "Grand Bieri Head", also Pahouin, which once belonged to Paul Guillaume and which has very impressive qualities. In the De Miré Sale of 1932, a superb collection was dispersed at the Hotel Drouot. This was undoubtedly the finest collection of African Art outside a museum, and the great standing figure from Gabun River equals anything that has come out of Africa. This piece, with its natural poise and striking head, is very remarkable. It has the astounding attitude of being held spell-bound by sorcery. It still retains the metal discs used for eyes, bringing light into the dark head. Often the figures are clothed in brass ornaments which enhance by variation of material the effect of the sculpture. The masks exhibit a great variety of form, changing in character according to the use for which they were made. Some are terrible in their expression of horror, others are solemn and in-drawn, and there are others still that are pensive, mysterious, and brooding. Often they carry fetish emblems on top, birds or animals, alligators or insects. We, of course, see them now as isolated pieces on pedestals, but if we can imagine them as originally used in their sacred or tribal dances, worn by the fetish men moving through the crowds of onlookers, brought to the highest pitch of excitement by drums and chanting, their effect must have been tremendous. Now we can study at leisure their formal relations and coldly calculate how the parts are correlated, and examine the laws of rhythm and form they embody. I believe there is an attempt in Africa, under sympathetic government teachers, to revive the art of wood-carving and clay-modelling. I have seen some examples of this work and they are disappointing. The life has gone out of them; the impulse is not a living one. A European outlook has been substituted for the native African, and however hard the young artist tries to embody his own naïve feelings, he is no longer a "believer", and the result is only more or less trained craftsmanship. Perhaps in the future a new African genius will arise. He will not be the African of the past. The whole future of Africa, especially of its native peoples, is so obscure that it is no use prophesying. Of the past Africa we have these carvings. I have, because of my appreciation of and my enthusiasm for African work, been accused—as if it were a crime—of being largely influenced by it. *That is not so.*

My sculpture (apart from a short period in 1912–1913 when cubism was in the air, and abstraction an interesting experiment) has remained in the European tradition of my early training. Most advanced painters and sculptors have been influenced by primitive work. They include Matisse, Gauguin, Picasso, Modigliani, Brancusi, Henry Moore, Lipschitz, and many lesser artists. When I say that my work is not African, I do not rebut what I would be ashamed to admit, but simply state a fact. Brancusi, some of whose early work was influenced by African Art, now declares categorically that one must not be influenced by African, and he even went so far as to destroy work of his that he thought had African influence in it.

These two frail, ghost-like figures rise somewhat obliquely, moving away from each other. They are spirits not of earth. The earth part of them has been drained out. They are Mother and Son, ancestral ghosts, or Husband and Wife. The female is the taller of the two. Their feet slant downwards. The inexpressible melancholy of their heads is matched by the delicate hands, fingers like the tracery of veins on leaves . . . a breath . . . a frailty unparalleled. Their four limbs are like water plants rising out of liquid pedestals. They have lain a long time at the bottom of a lake in New Guinea. I saw them for the first time in Paris. The enchantment of the Group is beyond description, and I so desired them that I mortgaged my future earnings for a long time to be able to obtain them. Their discreet and sympathetic presence lifts me into a world ethereal as the last quartets of Beethoven . . . a sighing wind-blown regret. A message is sent out as ineffable as autumn mist arising from damp woodlands, plaintive, like a single-noted melody played in the obscurity of a forest. This is a piece of sculpture which seems to reject the very quality by which sculpture exists, solidity of form.

A primitive sculpture is supposed to be rude, savage, the product of uncultured and uncivilised peoples. I find, on the contrary, restraint in craftsmanship, delicacy, and sensitiveness, a regard for the material, and none of the stupid vulgarity, pomposity, and crudeness so evident in sculpture to-day, and most especially in the sculpture at the Paris Exhibition in 1937. Compare the blatant nudes to be seen everywhere at that Exhibition with these two beings, evocations one might call them, and the difference is at once apparent, and it is easily understood why the intelligent modern sculptor turns with relief to them—a haven of culture in a world of pretence and pornography. Primitive work when it expresses the principle of sex, does it in a manner which cannot be offensive. First, because it is frankly sexual and, moreover, is part of an attitude which can only be termed ritualistic. Those African statues which are double-sexed are undoubtedly ritual works, embodying the sexual principle in life, and are in no way offensive.

In Indian work of this nature there is a deeply religious element, sometimes amounting to a fury of passion which is elemental in its power. Shiva dances, creating the world and destroying it, his large rhythms conjure up vast æons of time, and his movements have a relentless and magical power of incantation. A small Group at the British Museum is the most tragic summing up of the death in love motive I have ever seen, and it epitomises, as no other work, the fatal element in human passion. Our European allegories are banal and pointless by comparison with these profound works, devoid of the trappings of symbolism, concentrating on the essential, the essentially plastic.

The modern sculptor without religion, without direction, tradition, and stability, is at a terrible disadvantage compared with the sculptors of previous periods. He has to invent even his subject matter, and he has at last been driven into the cul-de-sac of "pure form", where he is either making works which are totally meaningless or repeating endlessly the same set of forms with slight variations.

THE MASK OF NEFERTITI

From an English collection, where it had lain unrecognised since 1904, I obtained the mask of the Egyptian Queen. This life-sized mask is undoubtedly the original of the bust in the Berlin Museum. I have not seen the Berlin stone bust, but judging from photographs and a cast I have of it, this mask is more sensitive, and if anything more aristocratic than the bust. The calm-faced Queen, with her cold, mysterious glance. This mask is a real presence, a person out of the past, almost alive, with extraordinary beauty of modelling from the lower eyelid, along the cheek, to the mouth with the closed, full lips. It is one of the most wonderful works in the world, this mask. Whether it is a life-mask, worked over, or whether it is the work wholly of a sculptor, it is difficult to determine. It has some of the elements of a life-mask, but the formalism of the brow and the open eyes suggest modelling. Here is the Queen who, with Akhenaton, attempted to establish a new order in a land ruled by conservative priesthood, abolishing the old gods, and substituting the life-giving

Sun instead; who detested war and all violence, and whose city was a city of beauty, flowers, and prayers. There seems to radiate from this mask a perfume of loveliness as if the delicate flesh were a flower itself, giving out perfume only just perceptible.

I turn this mask into a different light, and now it is a weary dead face, pleased to be dead, anticipating that mask in Cairo, where the Queen is emaciated, tragic—the thin neck hardly able to uphold the shrunken and sorrowful head. Here, removed from the strife of the living, is the silent witness to a destiny noble and pathetic The Sculptor becomes the priest of sorrow and beauty.

24

JOURNALISTS AND PUBLICITY

WORD or two about the journalists and critics might not be amiss, as I have had more than enough of both.

I have rarely had a visit from newspaper men or women that did not cause me chagrin and annoyance. The woman journalist is the worst. She will telephone a pleading request to be allowed to come and see and write about sculpture. She arrives, usually a badly educated woman with a provincial accent, evidently the office girl promoted by favour, and, concealing her intentions, spends her time, in observations, asking questions that are beside the point and taking only mental notes of one's appearance, age, clothing, and surroundings; and then, when she leaves, she rehashes her acid observations, merely personalities with no understanding of anything but gossip, and dishes this mixture up in the papers the following morning. With these false pretences of interest in sculpture she decides she has got a "good gossipy story". The old-time journalist who wrote down what you said in shorthand has long ago gone out, unfortunately, and only a kind of "Tom the Peeper" is sent out to get a good "peppy" story. I have sometimes taxed journalists with this disregard of what was actually said to them by me, and I was told confidentially that they were sorry, but that their orders were to get an impression, "never mind what the blighter says".

Moreover, as the journalist is usually totally incapable of comprehending or taking in what you have really said, your words are translated into a journalese account that has entirely changed their real meaning, and you read some ridiculous, garbled jargon the next day, which is supposed to have been said by you, and goes under your name. Art Critics, of course, never want to know what an Artist

THE SCULPTOR WITH "LAZARUS", 1948

H.R.H. The Duchess of Kent examines "Lazarus" at the opening of the Open Air Sculpture Exhibition, Battersea Park, 1951

thinks. They know what *they* want to think. As they are to-day, very often, practising artists themselves, or well-to-do amateurs, there is the element of rivalry and jealousy to reckon with. If I seem to be flogging a dead donkey, it is because I have all my life suffered from these gentry. One fondly imagines that they will die off. They do sometimes, but where they fell out and disappeared, I have found new spawn rising up from the same muddy depths the old ones were bred in, with the same horrid characteristics, jealous, carping, biting, and snarling, and always the hatred that attempts to belittle works whose superiority makes their own failures seem worse.

I have found them in London. When I went to New York they were there, and they exist in Paris, and in all capitals. Once when I was with Modigliani, he was greeted by two chic young gentlemen. I asked who they were; he answered: "Snobs d'Art." He always hit the nail right on the head. "We working artists," he said, "suffer from 'Les Snobs d'Art'."

In the *New Age* appeared the following anti-Semitic article. If one refers to the date, February, 1924, it will be seen that hatred of and propaganda against the Jews in Art is of no recent growth. I, for the life of me, cannot see why my bronzes in this exhibition were peculiarly Jewish, any more than the works of Rembrandt, and he is certainly not condemned for his Jewish subject matter. I remember that Modigliani was intensely proud of his Jewish origin, and would contend with absurd vehemence that Rembrandt was Jewish. He gave as his reason that Rembrandt must have been Jewish on account of his profound humanity. In this article in the *New Age*, where even the Child's Studies of Peggy Jean "are touched with horror", Aryanism has run amok. This review, so venomous, so vile, was signed with a pseudonym—Rusticus. Obviously a forerunner of Herr Streicher. I print this piece of Aryanism for what it is worth. I will add that with the growth of Nazism and Fascism, both Italian and English, I was favoured by articles in *Der Stürmer*, and similar periodicals in Germany and Austria; not to speak of attacks in our own Fascist Press, and the painting of the Hudson Memorial in Hyde Park with Swastikas. When invited to show at the Venice Biennial by the Italian Government, receiving a personal invitation from Count Volpi, my works on arrival at the British Pavilion were held up, as Mussolini, in imitation of Hitler, had brought in his Aryan decrees;

Epstein: An Autobiography

but the twenty-two works were, nevertheless, eventually shown, owing to the strong representations made by the British Committee. Here is the *New Age* article of February 14th, 1924:

"There is no race in the world more enigmatic, more fatal, and therefore more interesting than the Jews."—Dr. Oscar Levy.

On leaving the exhibition we remarked to the attendant that a world peopled by such inhabitants as the artist depicted would be a nightmare. "But different peoples have different ideas of art," was the reply. "For instance, you might not like Chinese art, but still it is art."

He apparently recognised that Epstein was not of the Aryan race, for this significant fact burns itself on the consciousness of every European who enters that room. Surrounded by Epstein's sculptures, the Aryan is in face of an alien genius.

Puzzled, vaguely uneasy, you wander round closely inspecting each head in turn. Wonderfully moulded, they are the work of a genius. They grip you. They will not let you go. But a sickening disgust gradually conquers you. The intensity of repulsion aroused by them cannot be explained merely on the ground of their Semitic cast—their high cheek bones, their half-shut eyes, their prominent noses and their full open lips. There is something more. They are instinct with evil.

On closer analysis, it is found that there is a wide gulf between the men and women represented by Epstein. The women appear to be of a lower race. They are types without individuality. Full of primitive sensuality and suffering, his women are like animals—coarse, heavy, and anguished. The intellectual development of the forehead is overbalanced by the heavy jaw and sensual mouth. The spirituality, which is the distinguishing characteristic of the best types of Aryan women, is unrepresented. So detestable has Epstein found the Aryan type that we turn from his insipid frigid creatures, "An English girl" and "Selina", with distaste. At least his Semitic creations are full of vitality and power.

Mr. Orage contended that the Jew forms a link between the black and white races. This theory would explain how Epstein could so sympathetically depict a young Senegalese girl. Although she possesses the usual heavy features of the negress, the sculptor has endowed her with a gentle smile which makes us feel the human predominates over the animal.

The men's heads are highly individualised. But they represent the power of intellect divorced from character. Here is old Pinager with knotted hands, terribly alive in spite of his amusing attitude. Dr. Adolph S. Oko, with intellectual head and cold, sneering, irresistible smile; the Duke of Marlborough cased in aristocratic pride; the Napoleonic study of a man;

and the marvellously vivid head of R. B. Cunninghame Graham. Into these sculptures Epstein has poured his genius. But they are incarnations of evil.

We recall the poise and balance of the Greek gods and feel that we are surrounded in their stead by Circean beasts. Where is man's power to erect himself above himself? How loathsome is the species when deprived of nobility and dignity! Even the charming studies of "Peggy Jean", the baby laughing, grave, asleep, are touched with horror when we contemplate the adults by whom she is surrounded and whom she will grow up to resemble.

It is significant that Jacob Epstein should choose to display his undoubted genius in the portrayal of such savage types. His models, according to the photographs published in the daily Press, are ordinary good-looking people. But he has read into them certain bestial characteristics. Why has he done so?

We believe that in the artistic genius the soul of the race speaks. The individual is here the instrument impelled by a power far greater than himself. And we believe that in his gallery of sculptures, Jacob Epstein has expressed the subconscious racial Hebraic life—utterly and entirely alien to the Aryan life which reached its artistic apotheosis in Greek sculpture, and Christian painting and poetry.

In the Grecian marbles, the human spirit sought expression for the ideal. Before even their mutilated remains we are uplifted and chastened —we glimpse Olympia beyond and above our petty selves and share the larger life of common aspiration. But before Epstein's works we are humiliated and cast down. It seems scarcely worth while to belong to such a bestialised or evil humanity. He narrows us down to tribal conceptions— to animal women serving the lust of their patriarchal owners, cunning and cruel. The centuries are obliterated. European civilisation has vanished. Balance, self-poise, control, proportion—the gifts of ages—have been swept away. He transports us anew to the twilight of early Jewry, where power is the motive force of man, and woman is but an instrument of sensuality."

This astonishing tirade might have been written in Nazi Germany. I remember when in New York one evening, at a party to which a friend had taken me, I met the genial Pascin, very depressed, and recall with what pleasure he greeted me. At that time in New York he was attacked by anti-Semitic art critics, and as he had had great popularity there, this weighed upon him. Shortly after that he committed suicide in Paris. The average unfavourable criticism of my sculpture or drawings I had never put down to anti-Semitism, and I have never joined in all-Jewish exhibitions of art. Artists are of all races and climes, and to band together in racial groups is ridiculous. I am most often annoyed rather than flattered to be told that I am the best or foremost Jewish artist. Surely to be an artist is enough. Who thinks of whether Yehudi Menuhin is Jewish when you hear him playing the violin? Or whether Einstein is Semitic in science? Einstein said to me when I worked from him that it was only the Nazis who had made him conscious of his Jewish origin. This pernicious racialism in art should be forever banished.

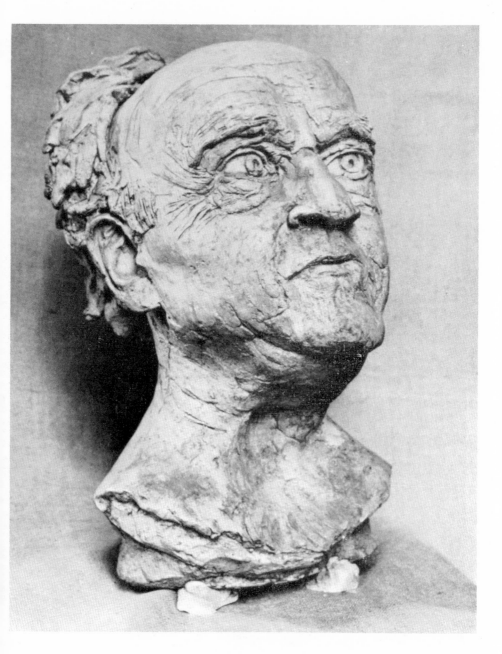

ERNEST BLOCH, 1949

PANDIT JAWAHARLAL NEHRU, 1949

25

DOG EATS DOG

A NEW and strange phenomenon has of late years come into being, the artist turned critic and publicist. At one time it would not have been considered "professional conduct" for an artist to express publicly his opinion concerning another artist, at any rate a derogatory opinion, that would have been considered at least ungentlemanly. But now the artist, under the excuse that he has a public service to perform, vents in print his feelings as to his fellow artist. To begin with, he obtains a post as contributor to a journal and then in his "capacity as publicist" proceeds to lay down the law.

This, of course, gives this particular type the reputation for cleverness and judgment which the merely working artist can never obtain. In time the voluble one is elected to committees, trusteeships, and may even become the curator of a gallery. A good example of this type of critic-artist is furnished in the following article by Roger Fry in the *Dial*, June 24th, 1920, a man who wrote, lectured, painted, and even sculptured. A complete failure from my point of view in the practice of art, an imitator of whatever style was fashionable in Paris, and an enemy, so it appears to me, of every artist who loomed larger than himself and his circle, his point of view was poured out in cleverly written articles for the "intellectual" weeklies.

Naturally I have suffered from this form of hostility. In the course if a long article on one of my exhibitions of sculpture, he starts off in this manner:

Such, then, being the main uses of sculpture, most of us naturally look upon it as entirely remote from any personal emotion or interest other than that general all-pervading feeling of boredom with which it is so thoroughly imbued. We are brought up to a pious belief that sculpture is

199

an altogether noble and reputable affair. We know the names of the great sculptors of all ages, and yet sculpture has always bored us—till now—and now comes Mr. Epstein. As we passed round the Leicester Gallery where his work has been on exhibition, each bronze head gave us a new and distinct sensation, a thrill of wonder, surprise, recognition, and, as a result of so pleasant a shock, admiration and gratitude. What miraculous gift was this which could make bronze reveal to us definite, singular, vivid human beings—human beings more definite, more emphatically personal, more incisive in the accent of their individuality, more invasive, at a first glance, of our own consciousness than the individuals of actual life?

Mr. Epstein started from the first with remarkable gifts, but in his early work he was an experimentalist in styles.

Now at last he found himself; he has developed a method and a manner of seeing which look as though they were definitive. One imagines that he can go on indefinitely along these lines, increasing the intimacy of his reading of character, the psychological intensity of the mood, the incisiveness and brio of the execution. He is surely to be congratulated on having found his own indisputably original and unique artistic personality. There is no doubt about it; it sticks out authentically from all the works, however varied the subjects may be. However completely he seems to abandon himself to the personality he is interpreting, it is Epstein's personality that really startles, interests, and intrigues us. That is the way of the great masters, or at least of most of them; and indeed, when we realise the astonishing assurance, the indisputable completeness and efficacy of these works, the brilliant resourcefulness and certainty of the technique, we must call Epstein a master. His technical resourcefulness is extraordinary. Decidedly Mr. Epstein is a master.

Reading this and wondering what would come next, as I knew this gentleman to be really no admirer of mine, I went further and came upon this really astonishing bit:

But a master of what? murmurs a still, small voice within me which all the turbulence and impressiveness of these works does not entirely silence. A master of what? Of the craft of sculpture, undoubtedly; of vigorous characterisation, certainly after a fashion, but even here I should have to make reservations. Even if we are to regard sculpture as a peculiarly effective form of representation—more than making up for the lack of colour by the palpability of its form—even so, one can imagine a finer, more penetrating, less clamant kind of interpretation of character. One might tire, perhaps, of the element not only of caricature—since all interpretation of character partakes of the nature of caricature—but of its direction. One might soon long for something which, even at the cost of being less immediately impressive, wooed one to a gentler, more intimate contemplation—something in which the finer shades were not so immediately blotted out by the big sweep of the most striking, first-seen peculiarities. One would prefer to live with something less vehement in its attack, rather more persuasive.

But this digression has not stopped the inner voice. It persists: Is he a master of sculpture? And, alas! I am bound to say to the best of my belief, No. If I examine my own sensations and emotions, I am bound to confess that they seem to be of quite a different nature when I look at good sculpture from what I feel in front of Mr. Epstein's bronzes. There is an undoubted pleasure in seeing any work accomplished with such confidence and assurance, such certainty and precision of touch; there is a powerful stimulus in the presence of such vividly dramatised personalities, but the peculiar emotions which great sculpture gives seems to me quite different. They come from the recognition of inevitable harmonic sequences of planes, of a complete equilibrium established through the interplay of diverse movements, and a perfect subordination of surface and handling to the full apprehension of these and similar qualities. It may be, of course, that I am so carried away, so disturbed if you like, by all those other qualities of drama and actuality which Mr. Epstein's work displays that I cannot feel this purely formal stimulus to the imagination which is what I seek for in sculpture. But there is the fact, as I see it. These busts are for me brilliant but rather crude representations in the round. If these are sculpture, then I want another word for what M. Maillol and Mr. Dobson practise, let alone Luca della Robbia and the Sumerians.

Fortunately for Mr. Epstein, there are a great many people whose imaginations are excited by really capable dramatic representation, and there are very few people who happen to like sculpture in my sense. The majority are quite right to acclaim him as a master, since the gift necessary for such work is a very rare one and he has used it and developed it pertinaciously, and since it does give genuine pleasure. It is a triumphant expression of genuine feelings about people's character as expressed in their features, and if it does not evince any peculiar and exhilarating sense of formal harmony, so much the worse for the few people who happen to have a passion of such an odd kind.

So that the flattering edifice built up in the beginning is torn down and this mass of self-contradictions passes as a more than fair criticism of the living sculptor, even pretending to humility, which accompanied by a sly, cunning smile clearly says: "How cleverly I have demolished him."

Epstein: An Autobiography

Another writer, a painter, Mr. Paul Nash, after my "Genesis" had been shown, let himself go on what he was pleased to call "A psychological Post Mortem" (*Week-end Review*, April 18th, 1931).

I had included extracts from his article here, but Mr. Nash refused permission to reprint them and I will content myself with saying that the gist of Mr. Nash's criticism was that I intentionally set out to shock the public, in his own phrase, "To shock and wound the minds of men." Leaving out the question as to whether or not this is a legitimate aim for an artist, certainly a quite disputable point, I answered Mr. Nash in a letter in the same journal which I give herewith.

(*Week-end Review*, April 25th, 1931.)

Sir,

I suppose I ought to be extremely flattered at the length of Mr. Nash's so-called "Post-Mortem" on "Genesis" and myself but, apart from the many amusing quips and divagations, I am struck by the ready accusation, for it amounts to that in my mind, that I am out "to shock", and further on this is varied as follows: "to shock, to challenge, even to hurt the minds of men". I might assert, with as much authority, that Mr. Nash paints anæmic pictures in order not to shock or hurt people's feelings.

Mr. Nash, by his accusation of my intention to shock, allies himself with that large body of journalists and critics who declare that I work with my tongue in my cheek. His saying that my concern is not only with "pure form", whatever that may be, proves that Mr. Nash is not above borrowing an idea from that school of æsthetes and critics commonly supposed to reside in the neighbourhood of Gordon Square: the "through the teeth school."

Mr. Nash deplores the fact that when a work of mine is in question the critics and purists are shoved aside, if not positively trampled on.

Actually the critics in the case of "Genesis" came out in force and had their say in full, and all agreed with the gossip writers, comic men and indignant letter-writers that "Genesis" was "shocking". How does Mr. Nash explain this?

Personally I would see nothing to deplore were the critics shoved aside or self-muzzled. We all know art critics are recruited either from the ranks of journalists or are disappointed failures as artists. Is there any danger of Mr. Nash "passing over"?

Truly yours,
Jacob Epstein.

ESTHER, 1949

KITTY, 1949

Dog Eats Dog

When this letter appeared the critic commenced to whine and claimed that I had hit him below the belt. I might only add that Paul Nash allied himself with the surrealists, who, of course, never have the intention to shock anybody.

A third scribbler, this time a sculptor, Eric Gill, wrote in a Catholic propaganda journal thus: (I begin also in the middle of the article, as to quote it in its entirety would be boring.) To give a notion of his pert style, he starts off with:

"A thing well made", what pregnant words! Let us take them in order. A *thing*: this is the essence of the matter. Here we are confronted by the intellect and the object of the intelligence is Truth. A thing—what thing? That is the point. Is the thing really there, and, if so, is it what it purports to be? A kettle, a statue—what are such things? Let the philosopher answer, but let the artist *know*. And, in moments of doubt, let the artist *think* a bit. It is manifestly of the first importance that one should know precisely *what* one is making—the more so because it is impossible to make well what is only vaguely known. And the lack of precise knowledge is the buyer's difficulty also. He doesn't know precisely what he wants—how *can* he be happy when he gets it? But this business of precise knowledge is the main trouble of our time. It's not only the arts that suffer; though they, being in a manner the fruits, are what we shall be known by. Everything suffers and the arts last of all—last, therefore last to bother about, and we're not bothering—we're only stating our position—which is this: Look after Goodness and Truth, and Beauty will take care of itself.

Beauty! Who said the arts had anything to do with Beauty? Well, you knew that without our saying so—what you didn't know was that it would bloomin' well take care of itself. So we are looking after goodness and truth, and we took truth first because, in the nature of things, it comes first.

We ask again: a kettle, a statue—what are such things? If you knew precisely what a kettle is, you wouldn't be put off with the wretched make-shifts they give you for sixpence-ha'penny in the shops. If you knew precisely what a statue is, you wouldn't criticise the maker of such things from twenty different contradictory points of view at once.

When he actually gets to grips with the subject (in this case the Hudson Memorial) he comes out with this fine mouthful:

All the controversy, then, about the Hudson Memorial, and what not, is so much fiddling while we leave the main business unremedied. The Hudson Memorial is what one would expect it to be. Shall I have the effrontery to add another criticism to the already too many? I say it is what one would expect it to be, considering how it was done. Consider. You have a writer—peculiar sort of writer, wrote some marvellous but very odd romances and some books of observation on Nature—good books, very, no one doubts that. But he's not exactly a popular hero—most people won't have heard of him before they read about his monument and few will read his books even then. There is a committee to decide about the monument—very mixed committee, mixed in mind. There's no harm in a mixed committee if the mixing is merely due to the variety of trades or professions followed by its members (one king, one bishop, one hairdresser, one journalist . . . but all of one faith), but there's every harm if the mixing is due to the variety of misbeliefs held by its members (one agnostic, one C. of E., one Jew . . . but all of middle-class). What *can* such a committee agree about but what the most forceful "high brow" among them can persuade?

What happens next? There's an architect. Oh, my Lord! What's an architect for? Why, to defend his customers from the rapacity of the commercial building contractor and to supply what such a person is naturally somewhat lacking in, a sense of beauty in design. Well, they choose an architect—a very good architect, very good choice—no more Albert Memorials in Hyde Park—back number that! Strong, silent men's turn. And there's a sculptor—must have sculpture. ("I do love Sculpture; It has such beautiful lines." Lady's very own words—truth!) So they choose a sculptor. Oh my . . . ! What shall I say about Epstein?

Well, Epstein is a very gifted man and has done some monstrous fine portraits, but stone-carving doesn't happen to be what he's best at—the stuff isn't flexible enough for him; he can't control it as he can clay. Result unfair to Epstein—unfair to architect, but committee gets what it deserves —a mix up. For the rest, his work is what you'd expect—dull, mechanical, lifeless—making the sculpture look as though Epstein had gnawed it with his teeth.

How's that for doggerel to cover up something else let loose?

26

I LISTEN TO MUSIC

WE crowd into the hall to listen to Beethoven's *Mass in D*, as in other periods worshippers devoutly made their way into cathedrals to attend Holy Mass. With equal piety we crowd the seats of the tawdry concert hall, an expectant audience, the orchestra, and tier on tier, the chorus. Toscanini appears, a small man full of nervous energy urging himself forward without any self-consciousness, as if intent on some very particular business. He mounts the rostrum, surveys his orchestra and battalions of singers, then, in the hush, raises his hands and begins the orchestral introduction. Powerful massive chords lead to the majestic choral outburst of the "Kyrie Eleison" and then on to the triumphant "Gloria in Excelsis Deo". With dramatic suddenness comes the contrasting "Et in terra pax." The music now is hushed and filled with divine peace. Soon, to the words "Pater omnipotens", there comes the magnificent outburst of chorus with orchestra and organ. The slow prayer, "Qui tollis peccata mundi", rising and falling, male and female voices alternating, pleading, and supplicating, die mysteriously away. Then distant drums announcing the "Quoniam Tu Solus Sanctus" growing in glory, ending with the majestic fugue. I watch the conductor, who seems now to be possessed with dynamic energy and controls the music like plastic material. A wonderful sculptor I think, moulding and conjuring the material in its varied and intricate shapes, lengthening out, scooping with tremendous curves, evening out great planes, broad sides of sound, compelling the advance and retreat with beckonings of the left hand, his expression determined, with dark eyes glowing with the profound emotion of the work. The "Credo" begins. A song of divine praise, until the sudden change of key and mood with the words "descendit de cœlis". The hushed mystery of the section "et incarnatus est" is sung by the solo quartet. The throbbing passionate statement of the tenor declaims "Et Homo Factus Est" rising to a culminating ecstasy. The solemn tragedy of the Crucifixion, the dramatic resurrection at the end with the great fugue "Et Vitam Venturi". The beautiful "Sanctus", then a long pause, "Osanna in Excelsis". The "Praeludium" and the "Benedictus" follow. The "Agnus Dei" begins with a solemn prayer from the bass voice answered by a chorus of male voices, and this final movement is pierced through and through by a poignant female cry, as if it were the voice of Eve, as in Michelangelo's "Last Judgment", where Eve lifts her hands to the enthroned figure pleading for her children. Throughout the work I am reminded of those great masses in the "Last Judgment" groups, clusters of figures, now clear, now shadowy, a surging humanity lifting its hands in supplication with wailing cries amidst trumpets of doom. This dramatic agony compressed into sound tears the very heart out of the body. The commonplace surroundings disappear, we are whirled into space by an almost physical assault upon our emotions, and are left helpless, exhausted by this great musical experience. The work comes to a close with humanity's prayer for peace rising triumphant above the sullen retreating drums. The conductor leans back holding on to the rail, as if to save himself from falling; his dark eyes are sunk into his pale drawn face. We turn from the hall and pour into the humdrum streets of a London Sunday afternoon.

BEETHOVEN'S LAST QUARTETS

In these quartets one witnesses a terrible struggle of the deaf man with fate itself. This music is the expression of one who wills himself beyond life and death and attains to a spirit world. He seems to choose the quartet form on account of its peculiar suitability for intimate expression, a last statement of personal thought and philosophy. How urgently the strings speak to us, how lucidly they sing. The idea of flight from a mortal to an immortal world is most completely summed up in Opus 127 in E flat major. The opening statement of heroic faith quickly dissolves into wistful melancholy, which turns, in the *Adagio* movement, to profoundest mourning. With incredible sweetness the music seems to brood over lost human joys. At times the sorrow is lightened by reminiscent gaiety. With the *Scherzo* the spirit has escaped from our world of human experience and is tossed hither and thither, fugitive and despairing. The scattered fragments of melody seem to be waiting for the master-will to weld them together before the spirit can take flight and soar into its kingdom of musical ecstasy and fulfilment. The *Finale* rushes inevitably to its end like a river to the sea. The doubt and hesitation of the *Presto* are dispersed. At one point the strings seem to transport us to a heavenly grove of nightingales. All is resolved in mysterious and mystical joy.

In the B flat major quartet, Opus 130, the first movement expresses the heart-broken utterance of a mind completely isolated from the world. The melancholy is unrelieved. The *Presto* has a ghoulish quality despite its vigour. At one point the violins wail with macabre gaiety. This mocking dance is like that scene in the Dybbuk played by the Habima where the bride, as if in a trance, is forced to dance with insane and deformed beggars. The *Andante* opens with a sorrowful statement by the violins. The grim dance is over, but the lonely soul is still tormented by the mocking spirits of doubt and despair and the main theme pleads continuously for deliverance. Abruptly the *Allegro* brings an entire change of movement. Beethoven seems to look back to past happiness and the music is gracious with a wistful gaiety. The famous *Cavatina* is described by Beethoven when he said : "Never did music of mine make so deep an impression on me, even the remembrance of the emotion it aroused always costs me a tear." This is the Gethsemane of music, the tragic and shadowy hour before the end In this wonderful melodious section the profound sorrow seems to bring its own noble consolation. It does not prepare us for the harrowing and nervous intensity of the *Grosse Fugue* which is the actual finale of this quartet. This is probably the most tortured music ever written, and the strictness of the fugal form seems deliberately chosen to enhance the despair and struggle it expresses. The final summing-up can be put in Beethoven's own words : "I will seize fate by the throat. It shall never wholly overcome me."

In the C sharp minor quartet, Opus 131, the composer develops the quartet forms in the most original way.*

---

* The later quartets could be compared to the later works of Rembrandt. When abandoning the tight forms of the earlier and middle period, Rembrandt became

Epstein: An Autobiography

The seven sections are as closely related as a sonnet sequence, and one feels conscious throughout this work of the musician's delight in his own consummate handling of the form, the ever-gushing spring of new ideas and musical invention. The opening fugue develops with an impelling intensity. One feels it should be headed "De Profundis Clamavi", so like is it to a sorrowful prayer filled, at once, with despair and faith. An irrepressible liveliness inspires the next movement which leads to the beautifully lyrical variations, and so straight on to an exuberant *Presto* with its changing rhythms and insistently recurring opening theme. The ninth section seems to be a lyrical counter-point of the prayer-like spirit of the opening, which suddenly gives way to the impetus of the *Finale* filled with challenge and assertion.

The longest of the five quartets is in A minor, Opus 132. The hushed introduction seems to prepare us for a kingdom not of this world. The first movement alternates between resolution to attain that state and a yearning regret for lost joys. What a contradiction between form and content fills the next section, the movement of which is lively and dancing but permeated with melancholy, like a spirit dancing in fog-bound desolation "without a habitation or a name". On this shadow world the "Heilige Dankgesang" dawns like a transfiguration and the liberated spirit contemplates and communes with the Divine being. Then, as if for respite, knowing the human spirit cannot dwell forever on such heights, Beethoven almost playfully introduces a little movement of child-like gaiety. A poignant recitative with the urgency of a human voice takes us straight into the *Finale*, which rushes exultantly to its triumphant end.

The last quartet, in F major, Opus 135, is shorter than the preceding ones, and it seems a cursory but complete summing-up of the various states of mind previously dwelt upon. The first movement is more profound and expressive, even more dramatic in content, as in the etching of the three crosses, when from the first state Rembrandt proceeds to blot out and eliminate, until in the third state only the great central figure with a terrible downpouring shaft of light enhancing it is left. All else recedes into a tragic abyss of gloom; or a parallel could be even more aptly drawn between these last quartets and the last works of Donatello, the small bronze bas-relief at South Kensington of the Pietà, filled from end to end with a passionate grief, and the reliefs on the pulpits of San Lorenzo where every scene depicted is filled with a passionate fury. In these powerful reliefs Donatello and Beethoven are akin, alike in the impetuous movement, the wild fury and harsh demoniacal emotions depicted.

full of wistful regret, with short phrases alternating between doubt and resolution. The *Vivace* is yet another of the trance-like spirit dances approaching, receding, at some points pausing breathlessly, then back to the enforced and mocking dance. It is almost as if, looking back at life, Beethoven saw humanity whirling round in circles, fearful of stopping lest death overtake them, but achieving nothing and making no progress. Then comes one of the most beautiful of all the slow movements which seems clearly to say: "O sorrow I have lived and wrestled with you so long and suddenly seeing the beauty of your face, I embrace you." But it was not in Beethoven's nature to end on a note of resignation. Summoning his forces he seems to challenge his own spirit with a searching, questioning phrase repeated several times, rising to a shrill intensity, then fading away. The answer comes bravely enough with a somewhat forced resolution, repeated with almost harsh aggression. Melancholy creeps back and the spirit sinks to the depths, only to be challenged again by the repeated question. The final answer is given first with an eerie gaiety by the high strings over pizzicato accompaniment, and then with the last summoning up of triumphant resolution by the whole quartet.*

How can one write of the later quartets of Beethoven without seeming to gild fine gold? Yet to leave unsaid what I owe to listening to these works would leave unacknowledged a great debt of gratitude. There is nothing else in all the wide realm of art that one can quite compare with these works. With awe one listens to the great Masses of Bach and Beethoven, and the music of Palestrina is like heaven's own choirs. Mozart's miraculous works we love and treasure. But here in these quartets Beethoven seems to have written for himself alone. They are hardly meant to have listeners. They are like a soliloquy of one who, having experienced all sorrow, communes with his own soul in a final and withdrawn, unique language. In no confessional has so heartbroken an utterance taken place, no prisoner in the condemned cell felt a reality more poignant, and this confession is communicated to us with a vividness and clarity, a mastery of form, which leaves one astounded that a human being could achieve, in affliction and despair, work of this order.

* The same ironic commentary on life is shown in Rembrandt's last self-portrait, with its tortured and almost maniacal laugh.

I have often, when showing my larger works, wished that for once only a quartet would play while the work was shown, or even a recording of the great B minor Mass by Bach or Beethoven's in D major. The lack of opportunity and doubt as to how this would be received have prevented me from carrying this out. And yet I know that this combination of music and sculpture would be a wonderful experience.

LADY MADELEINE LYTTON, 1949

DR. VAUGHAN WILLIAMS, O.M., 1950

27

THE POSITION OF THE ARTIST NOW,
AND SCULPTORS OF TO-DAY

FOR those artists who feel the urge to creative work, the position
to-day is hazardous and beset with difficulties.

We imagine that we have at last emerged into a period of
enlightenment; that no longer can a Cézanne be misunderstood and
neglected, or a Van Gogh or a Modigliani be unable to earn a living
during his lifetime. This is far from true. The creative artist of to-day
is in exactly the same position as his predecessors. He has against him
a formidable array of enemy forces, who attack him directly and
obliquely. To start with, those who handle his work, the dealers.
They are not content to be mere dealers. They wish to be, and often
are, the dictators of the artist's production. They admonish the artist
as to what the public will like or dislike, and they can also keep the
artist in poverty, so that he is easier to control. The commonest
grouse of the dealer is that the artist is a self-willed person, who does
not know on which side his bread is buttered. I myself have often
been asked to furnish the dealer with what he considers the most sale-
able of all work, the small female nude, which can ornament a
mantelpiece or a smoking-room table. I have never succumbed to
this demand, and it has even set me against this form of sculpture.
The really popular works of Maillol are those little nudes, of which I
have seen a hundred copies at one time cast by a dealer in Paris, all
ready for the market.

A landscape artist I know, whose spring and summer landscapes
sold well, was advised to go on doing spring and summer landscapes by his dealer, who looked with disfavour on his attempts to
paint autumn and winter landscapes. Again, those subjects which the

dealer finds tragic or sinister, he often thinks unsuitable for the public.

When I had done a series of drawings for Baudelaire's *Les Fleurs du Mal*, to my astonishment the card of invitation appeared to read Fleurs du Mai. Later, as the exhibition was held in December, another dealer remarked jocosely of these drawings which were necessarily macabre in many cases: "Hardly Christmas cards, eh?"

The dealer demands of newcomers 33⅓ per cent of the price of any work sold, and only artists with big reputations can reduce this to 25 per cent.

In Paris the conditions are even worse, where 50 per cent or even more is demanded from newcomers.

The Art Racket rarely is in favour of the artist. A favourite trick is to take great care that the work does not sell, and this can be easily managed, as exhibitions must necessarily be in the hands of the dealers. I once tried this out on a dealer who had a work of mine for sale, sent in by the owner. She was then told that there were no claimants for it. I had sent a friend who admired the work and who was genuinely interested in it. He could not get any information as to the price by calling or writing. So far as any effort was made to connect him with the object, he was as far off at the end as at the beginning. Naturally the work fell into the dealer's hands. It was my first carved work in marble, and he put a big price on it. In Gauguin's letters Gauguin complains of a celebrated dealer who handled his work while he was in the Marquesas, and who kept on writing to him that there was no demand nor even an enquiry about his paintings. Gauguin, in his letters, expresses a natural astonishment at this and asks his friends to find out if his paintings are really being shown at all. That this dealer had a great quantity of Gauguin's work later, after his death, was altogether natural and satisfactory to the dealer.

The majority of the dealers will not, of course, settle with the artists until they are paid. This seems fair, but as things are, dealers often give very long credits for works sold, to please their clients, and while they can afford this, the artist waits and waits, hoping for payments.

There is a peculiar attitude about the purchasing of works of art, and I have heard an average collector say that he expected two years' credit if he bought anything. This man probably never realised that he was keeping the artist waiting for two years.

The reader may be inclined to ask why artists do not band together and run a shop for their own benefit. The answer to this is the difficulty in reckoning with the human element in managers. There is hardly any manager on earth who will not see where, with artists to deal with, he can easily feather his own nest. Thus the temptation to dishonesty is more than likely to overcome him.

There is something in the Art dealing business, an element of gambling, which can convert an ordinary business man into a potential inmate of a jail sooner than almost any other occupation. Dealers, as a rule, adopt towards the artist an attitude of benevolence, such as the poor-house inmate meets at the hand of the County Council visitor or Charity Organisation inspector. He is just a poor devil who would starve if not for them. Perhaps he would. To bend one's energy to the creation of work, and to make one's living at the same time, is beyond the power of the average artist. It is said that Picasso and Matisse succeeded in doing this. One can only express one's astonishment and admiration for their business acumen.

To-day, of course, there is a large body of artists who have private incomes. These happy artists are amateurs for the most part, who take to abstract and surrealist art. That does not take up much time, and leaves one free for that social intercourse so necessary for the propagation of advanced ideas. Most of these moneyed folk have never been to an Art School in their lives and often began their "careers" somewhat later than professional artists. Often they have started by purchasing a work of one of the most known "advanced" men, and from that to practise is of course easy.

Once when I spoke to one of the leaders of this movement, and mentioned how easy it was to do the kind of stuff a certain artist of the abstract persuasion was turning out, he exclaimed: "Oh, that is just what that artist thinks. He says everyone should work at Art." Of course, there is no training, no drudgery, no learning of a craft. How would that do for surgery, engineering, or any other profession than Art? It is so easy evidently: if you have an idle moment and do not know what to do with yourself, just take to painting or a bit of sculpture. You can just as easily drop it again. I once met an American doctor, a mental specialist, who advised his wealthy patients to paint, and I saw some of their paintings which were done in the Van Gogh manner, evidently by weak-minded people who had reproductions of Van Gogh placed in front of them for imitation. Madness of Van Gogh—imbecility of idle, wealthy persons! The two went together well, the doctor thought.

On another occasion a shell-shocked young man told me that he had been advised to take up sculpture. As if sculpture did not need strong nerves. Sculpture is an exacting and difficult medium, and I have known of sculptors giving it up after a time and taking to painting . . . certainly less hard work, and less expensive. I cannot assert here too strongly that sculpture is a science needing many years of preparation and study, and requiring an equal exercise of the imagination to that needed in any form of creation, poetry, music, or great drama; the same effort and sacrifice and lifetime of devotion. The titled female sculptor is rampant in England, and in America women have taken to sculpture with gusto. As one explained to me, they felt so "creative". Here is a subject for Freud, and I expect he could easily have explained it.

The artist has not only the dealer to contend with. He has also the Art Critic, Art Patron, and Art Director or Keeper of Galleries and Art Institutions of all kinds. To take the Art Critic first. He is often a journalist, who has accidentally taken up the function of critic of exhibitions, or a failed artist, one who found he could make an easier living by writing than by painting. His pen is dipped in gall and venom. He gets back at those artists who have persevered and still keep on working. He has, of course, an inside knowledge, knows how to write as if he could do the thing himself, and achieves sometimes a tremendous reputation as a "Know-all in Art" on just fine writing. There is now a school of such critics in all countries. In the field of Old Masters they are the experts who command thousands of pounds a year for their services to great dealers. With modern work in their hands their pens are also for sale to the dealers.

One one occasion when my friend, Matthew Smith, was holding an exhibition, I remarked on one critic's praise, knowing that that same critic had often written disparagingly of Matthew Smith's work. I said: "How strange this new view is." The dealer merely remarked that with regard to this critic they had "loaded the dice". A critic to whom I had complained that he wrote diametrically opposed articles

GWEN, LADY MELCHETT, 1950

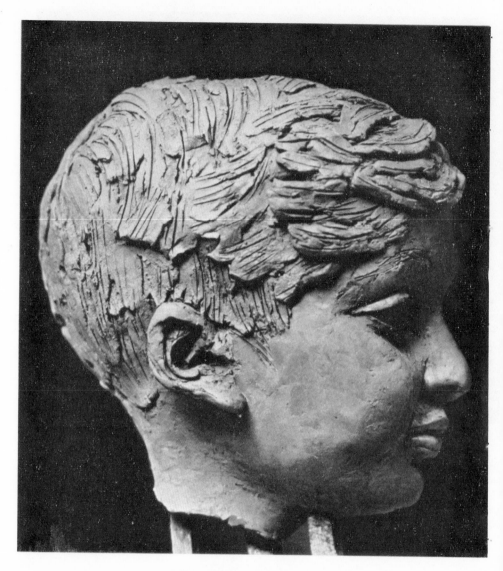

THE LITTLE PRINCE, 1951
(Son of H.H. The Maharaja of Baroda)

in two different papers, said that he had to consider the different publics he was writing for.

Another critic told me that he could be commissioned to write an article on a piece of work of mine only on condition that it was unfavourable to me.

In any other occupation or trade on earth this would be considered libellous or damaging. Not so with the artist. Hit him and hit him hard. If he shows the slightest sign of originality, close the doors of your academies against him. Rob him. Drive him out of his profession.

Taxation is another enemy of the artist which weighs on him. He is taxed on his work, which is his principal, instead of on "purely income". Sculptors work as it were in gold and cannot get it all repaid. The cost of producing a work of sculpture is left out of account when it comes to the price of even the smallest work. If it is in clay, there is first the clay model to be made and then the plaster cast. Then the bronze casting, which is costly. In stone, there is the material to be bought, and the carving takes a long time. Yet artists are considered "lucky beggars". Perhaps they are. They certainly are not wage-slaves. In that they are indeed "lucky" beggars.

The uncertainty in which artists live with regard to their incomes makes them into Micawbers, who are always expecting something to turn up. If they are accused of extravagance, this only argues the inherent hopefulness in the artist's nature. The artist is the world's scapegoat. He has a reputation for profligacy in living. One critic wrote that Gauguin could not possibly make fine works as he had had illegitimate children in Tahiti. Did not Stephen Crane say that if an artist is seen just clinking a glass of beer, it was immediately called from the house-tops: "Look at Jones, the artist, what a drunkard!"

Was not Rembrandt a terrible drunkard? Look at his portraits of himself. It is said that he has condemned himself out of his own self-portraits alone. Degas said that to make a fine work of art was similar to committing a crime. A cryptic saying from a Master; a saying with wide implications. Toulouse Lautrec is an artist with a reputation for debauchery. Yet look at his drawings and paintings, and where do you see the results of debauchery? There is nothing loose, careless, or feeble in them. The drawing is sensitive and tense; the compositions are thought out, the work of a great artist with acute observation. The legend of the debauched artist is just a legend.

When it comes to portraits, sitters are as a rule filled with the desire to be flattered, as they are by the photographer. I have sometimes been compelled to ask a sitter why he chose me to do his portrait. An old lady at the end of a series of sittings said: "And I thought you were going to make me young and beautiful." Of course, I had to reassure her about her beauty (but it was the beauty of old age); as to the youth: "Où sont les neiges d'antan?" Children I love to do, but not at the command of their parents. They likewise want to see them as angels with wings on, and not just lovely and charming, or roguish and capricious.

Of an exhibition of portraits of my daughter, Peggy Jean, two to four years of age, a well-known writer-critic said: "Even the soul of a child is not safe in his hands", and another newspaper man professed to discover that I had done a criminal child. When I made an enquiry as to who could have written this filthy stuff, and why, I was told that it was that newspaper's "crime expert". Dealers, Critics, Patrons, Artists, a host of enemies wait for the man of talent. They are entrenched in Galleries, Newspapers, and Journals, occupying important positions in the World of Art. Administrators of funds, curators of public art galleries, experts of all kinds living upon the activities of the artists.

Cultural propaganda has become important. There are more and more paid positions for the parasites on Art to occupy. If we ever had a Minister of the Fine Arts, the post would go to a gentleman of this kidney. No one would ever imagine a working artist fit for such a responsible position. A position in a museum, say, a museum of antiques such as the British Museum. My advocacy of an expert at the British Museum was met with scorn. Mad to suggest such a thing. Gentlemen who have come from Oxford, having written treatises on Greek sculpture, or on Cézanne, are pitched into such well-paid positions, and given titles of dignity and more often than not, as in the case of the Greek Marbles at the British Museum, do real damage to the works they are supposed to look after. I do not say that a working artist would care for an all-time job of this kind, but for the good of the institutions, such as the British Museum or the Tate Gallery, working painters and sculptors are absolutely necessary on their boards. It is well known that such a public fund as the Chantry Bequest was for years a perquisite of the Royal Academy, and, until Dr. D. S. McColl called attention to the scandal, no works outside that of the Academy artists were ever bought with it. Usually from other funds the purchases for public collections are the works of friends of the Committee, and have no connection with merit. The collections of work in our provincial museums are a disgrace to the cities they are in.

Wealthy corporations, whose aldermen are ignorant of anything outside the city drains, form their Art Committees, and judge what should be bought for the spiritual food of the people.

Usually a visit to the Royal Academy settles that, and the dumpings of this miserable institution are everywhere. "If you do not know an Art, teach it."

At one time the Royal Academy thought they would thwart their enemies by a policy of broadmindedness, in fact, take the "wind out of their critics' sails" by admitting new blood. Artists who are considered unacademic like Augustus John, Walter Sickert, and Stanley Spencer were elected. These artists, individualists with no academic inclinations, found themselves there on sufferance, and in a very short time had their eyes opened as to where they really stood.

Sickert resigned ostensibly on my account. John resigned on account of the rejection of a painting by Wyndham Lewis (returning later, having made his protest), and Stanley Spencer found one fine day that his pictures were rejected by the Hanging Committee, although he had a perfect right to their exhibition.

This Institution enjoys, of course, State support and Royal Patronage. Its annual banquet is graced by every commercial and political and legal luminary in this land. Criticism is savagely resented, and to be hung in the Royal Academy is supposed to be the hall-mark of achievement. I went once to the Royal Academy, since then it has not been necessary to go again, as one Royal Academy is like unto another. Even the old dames photographed going in on Private View day are the same.

The London group contained at one time practically all the genuine painters there were in England, and these included Walter Sickert, Matthew Smith, Gertler, Meninsky, Ginner, Gore, Gilman, Wyndham Lewis, Roberts, Karlowska, and Bevan; also Gaudier and myself as sculptors. New groups spring up now, but they are ephemeral and resemble those primitive creatures that live by parting.

Not that I place great store in groups. I have always felt myself to be alone, and not part of a group, and I do not care for the gregariousness that makes most artists hanker after societies. I believe in individual artists, and the time seems to have gone by when artists, as in mediæval times, could work successfully together on cathedrals.

On a building for which I worked (the St. James's Underground Station) there were six sculptors, and that was not a successful combination. There was little harmony in the result, and one or two sculptors would have done the work much better. The Schools have turned out only some rather poor imitators of the Swedish sculptor Carl Milles, and there are imitators of Maillol or Despiau. Many have taken to imitating Henry Moore, and others misunderstand my work and imitate some technical idiosyncrasies, mostly of my bronzes. Had I been called at any time to teach, I might have had a great influence personally, but it looks as if I have been very deliberately passed over as, on several occasions when a vacancy has occurred at the Slade School, on the death of Havard Thomas for instance, or at the Royal College of Art on other occasions, for one reason or another I have been ignored, and never was there the slightest sign from heads of institutions that they thought I had anything of value to contribute to Art in the teaching of it. Yet I have had academical training and have trained myself in school and museum, and best of all by practice.

SOME MODERN SCULPTORS

With Rodin, whatever his faults, a new era in sculpture began, and though every schoolboy now seems able to pick holes in him, he was a revivifying force, and compelled sculpture into paths which it is still following, or which have developed out of his fecund example. Before Rodin, with Houdon, Rude, Carpeaux, the form, solely realistic and decorative, remained in itself uninteresting. With Rodin, modelling became interesting and individual for its own sake; an element of imagination entered sculpture which included the grotesque. Rodin was a sculptor who, in his search for expression,

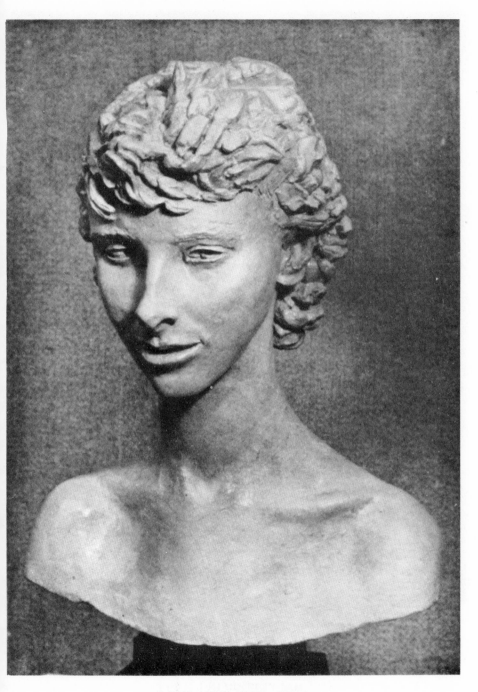

LADY ANNE TREE, 1951

MAI ZETTERLING, 1953

was not afraid to be grotesque and in one or two instances even ridiculous, which of course no living sculptor could ever afford to be. I find Rodin now much underrated, and the wiseacres of to-day will only admit that his drawings have the stuff of immortality in them. This is an absurd judgment, and we need only wait a few years for the pendulum to swing the other way. For one thing, the vast output of Rodin makes his life work difficult to sum up. Where a sculptor of to-day makes one work, Rodin made a hundred, and his own fecundity tires and bewilders us all in such a collection of his works as the Hotel Biron possesses.

I find that a sculptor whose work is much lauded, Despiau, really had his foundation in Rodin. Actually Despiau worked for Rodin, carving marble for him. I could point to a head in the Rodin Musée which contains the whole of Despiau, and to me Despiau's work is monotonous and often insensitive. There is a quality of delicacy in his heads derived from Rodin, and especially recalls the so-called Raphael head in wax. His work is very popular, more especially in America where works of an æsthetic or washed-out character have a great vogue, for example, Whistler, Marie Laurencin, "Abstract Art", Brancusi. His nudes amount to school works which any clever student can produce. When you have seen one Despiau, you have seen all, and to compare this quite talented, but limited, sculptor with Rodin, is nonsense. Rodin did not possess a sense of the architectural, and that is why his Porte D'Enfer is such a failure architecturally. From even a little distance it has all the appearance of an ant-hill in commotion. Rodin concentrated on the individual groups and figures, and the Porte D'Enfer, to be appreciated, must be studied close to, when the tragic and splendid qualities of the groups reveal themselves. When a student in Paris, I was taken to Rodin's studio by a fellow-student, an Englishman, who made himself known to me. He was an elderly man who came into the sculpture class at Julien's, and I noticed his sincere but clumsy attempts to set up a figure. He was Mr. Cayley-Robinson, who was fairly well known as a painter in England, and late in life thought modelling would help him to a better understanding of form.

He asked me one day if I would like to go to Rodin's atelier as he had the *entrée*, and one Saturday afternoon we went together to the rue de l'Université where Rodin had several studios adjoining one

another, given him by the State. I saw there the large Victor Hugo
in marble, still unfinished, and many smaller works in marble and
bronze. One large low table was laden with hundreds of small studies
and sketches brought, I should say, by aspiring sculptors and
"mothers of genius" for Rodin's inspection. How all these people
with their incompetent sketches must have taken up the Master's
time, and how anyone had the impudence to impose on him in this
fashion, is incomprehensible to me. Rodin, himself short, bearded,
with a sort of round flat cap on his head, looked calm and watchful
at the same time. His neck was of enormous thickness and gave his
head a tapering shape upwards. Rodin went about amongst his
guests and he would roll tissue paper around a small bronze head and
show it in that way. His quiet, confident manner I mentally contrast
now with the *cabotin* pose of other artists of great reputation I met
later. I did not speak to Rodin as I had only just arrived in Paris and
knew no French. I was quite content to look at things, and watch
Rodin himself. I never saw him again, although he was several times
in England, and I heard of how, when he was given a reception in
London, Rodin, not used to making speeches, responded very simply,
and with few words. A sculptor called Tweed got up and began a
long discourse commencing: "If Rodin could express himself . . ."
This notion of the inarticulate artist is a common one. People do not
take into account that the artist thinks in form, in his own medium,
as a musician in sounds, and to ask him to explain himself or translate
his work in language is not only unfair, but unnecessary. Surely the
best communication of the sculptor or the painter is through his
work and in no other manner. The fallacy of the critic-artist is
abroad to-day, and present-day artists are pleased to have themselves
explained and even told by writers on Art what their programme of
work should be. Manifestoes are got out in the best futurist, surrealist
manner, imitating political party cries and slogans, and even Groups
give themselves military titles like Unit One or Cell 33.

Bourdelle was another assistant of Rodin. After Rodin's death,
Bourdelle plucked up courage and denounced his old master as "just
a butcher". Bourdelle became a sort of official sculptor of France, and
his large and ambitious, but withal empty, works were everywhere to
be seen. As he was supposed to be an impressive teacher, he gathered
pupils from all lands about him. His work, except in his own small

things, is pseudo-Greek archaic or pseudo-Gothic, and now that he is dead will be completely forgotten.

Of the same order, but far more capable, I would place the work of the Serb, Mestrovic, also a great "stylist". I say stylist in the sense that he could imitate any style or period he set his hand to. Sometimes Assyrian, often early Greek, then Gothic or Rodinesque. He swept England and America off its feet, and was hailed as a heaven-sent genius, aided largely by a picturesque Balkan appearance of beard and hair. For some time the inner emptiness of his heroically gesticulating groups and figures was not discerned, and anyone who dared say he was not another Michelangelo was looked at askance. Since that period the work of Mestrovic has taken a back seat, and even his name, once so well known, would, I think, go unrecognised even amongst sculptors. He fulfilled the bourgeois idea of the sculptor to the utmost limit, both in his work and in his personal pose.

A sculptor totally unknown in England and to the rest of Europe is the American, George Grey Barnard. I knew his work in America and thought his first large work, "The Two Natures", now in the Metropolitan, a very great work in sculpture. It is one of the finest conceptions of our day. He spent a long life devoted to sculpture and was "a law unto himself", going his own way. His statue of Lincoln, which was offered to London in 1917, was most unfairly and bitterly assailed here by a stupid art critic, Sir Claude Phillips. I answered this on October 6th, 1917, defending Barnard's "Lincoln" as a great work, in *The Daily Telegraph*. My letter I give here:

I read with astonishment the pontifical judgments of your Art critic, Sir Claude Phillips, upon the statue of Abraham Lincoln by George Grey Barnard, the American sculptor, based solely upon what he admitted was a very blurred photograph; and he is equally astonishing to me when he is full of respect and solemnity towards his own suggestions of what a monument to Lincoln should be. These two attitudes are by no means uncommon to critics. George Grey Barnard is a very great sculptor, an artist whose achievement is so superb that his statue of Lincoln should be awaited with the eager expectancy due to a new unknown work by a great master. What there may be behind this by no means accidental attack and Press campaign against the Lincoln Statue, I do not know, but undoubtedly Barnard, like all men of genius, and of independent mind, would have

221

ready waiting for him the usual pack, who at the first opportunity would fasten upon him. I raise the only protest I know of against this chorus of calumny, because Barnard has given the world works for which we will always be grateful, and the attack on his statue of Lincoln in England is manifestly unfair and one-sided.

Lincoln's descendants did not like the statue, and this, no doubt, had great weight, for the statue never was accepted for London, but went to Manchester, where it is now in Plattsfield Whitworth Park. Just before the outbreak of war in 1939 I revisited the site. After the lapse of so many years it impressed me more than ever and it was borne in on me how great was London's loss. In its stead a commonplace statue by St. Gaudens was set up in London. Barnard knew of my defence of his statue and wrote to me expressing his pleasure. I was moved to defend Barnard's statue, not only because I considered it a fine work, which should not have had that intrigue launched against it, but also because Barnard had been my teacher in a New York night class for sculpture in the winter of 1901. I remember well his ardour and single-mindedness. Sculpture was his passion, and fortunately he found the support of rich men and also received official commissions. When passing through London in 1926, he asked me to assist him in a great Memorial Arch he was at work on. I listened to him, but in the end decided I would rather do my own work. Later in New York I did not see much of him because of his bad health, but he generously turned over to me a commission which I was unable to accept, as I was returning to England to do some work I had agreed to do. I heard of him going to the Art Students' League and lecturing the students on my pieces in bronze which were there, invoking the name of Donatello. In sculpture, although I had my first lessons from Barnard, we were poles apart in conception and execution. Barnard had a passion for the heroic, derived from an intensive study of Michelangelo, and I believe in all his thoughts and actions he had Michelangelo somewhere in the background. He even boasted of having made more figures and groups of heroic size than the great Florentine himself. To my mind he never achieved the intimate and the personal which so appeals to me. On my return to America I was surprised to find that Barnard's reputation had sunk very low, and mere tyros thought him academic and spoke scornfully of him.

Position of the Artist

Brancusi is perhaps, of all modern sculptors, the man who brought the greatest individual touch into sculpture, and he now has his imitators and followers by the hundred. Indeed his formula—for a formula it became—is used for window decorating, mannequins, and posters. His work was strongly influenced by Negro art, and also by Cycladic sculpture, but in our own period of tortured and realistic work his highly sophisticated art seems fresh and strange—a paradox. Brancusi himself, when I first met him, I found charming and simple in manner and in appearance like a sailor or a farmer. Deeply serious, but with plenty of humour. We sat on a log, the only seat, in his studio in Montparnasse, and he offered his guests sweets out of a paper bag. He was fond of telling funny stories about his sculpture. He had carved a bird and someone asked him why he had not done the feet of the bird. His answer was that "the bird's feet were in water and could not be seen."

Ortiz de Zarate said humorously that whenever Easter came round he was reminded of Brancusi by the eggs. This referred to a good deal of Brancusi's work taking naturally an egg shape.

Twenty years later I again visited Brancusi. Looking about me I could imagine it to be the first visit: the work was the same, Brancusi was the same, somewhat greyer and thinner. Instead of drinking sour milk he now drank hot water: he said that hot water cured one of all ills, even of love. When we were saying good-bye in the courtyard, a French artist passed with the inevitable girl going into their studio. We exchanged glances. Brancusi turned to his studio with its abstract and arid shapes.

In Germany, Lehmbruck did sculpture which has a sensitive, but to my mind, frail or sentimental character of no great interest sculpturally. Kolbe worked cleverly enough in the tradition of Rodin nudes, without adding to them. Barlach worked in wood, and had a wholly Gothic inspiration, but his work has to me the appearance of formula.

A fresh and stimulating note was brought into sculpture by the casting into bronze of Degas's posthumous studies of nude dancers, which I believe Degas had continued to do all his life, but never thought of exhibiting. He let the studies fall into decay. They are in a kind of wax invented by himself. These small works, when shown in London, were derided by sculptors who declared that they were the kind of sketches that they themselves throw away; but I find these bronzes marvellous in their understanding of form and movement; graceful and with original gesture, they combine classic poise and spontaneity.

In Sweden, Carl Milles did a great deal of decorative work, which, while very able technically, seems to me to be academic and derivative, and as a natural result popular. I met Milles in London, and thought him modest and simple, but with no originality. The indifference of London, except for a small purchase for the Tate, led him to seek America, where he found success. He has had an undoubted influence on English architectural sculptors, that is the sculptors whom English architects love to employ, as they subordinate their work to such an extent that it hardly even exists.

In America, as in England, I found most of the younger sculptors influenced by Picasso, Brancusi, and Maillol. Maillol, who was a sculptor influenced by Greek work, is always spoken of as peculiarly modern. I cannot see this, as his work, while often very fine, is to my mind monotonous, and the effect is heavy. More especially the head is treated in a pseudo-Greek manner that is a complete misunderstanding of Greek work. He could never get away from his Greekish nude, which to the modern mind can mean very little.

The cliques of to-day are always asserting the living qualities of Maillol, and give his works titles in their encomiums like "Living Art", or some similar appellation. What there is "Living" or even life-giving about an Art that derives its inspiration so completely from ancient Greece, I fail to see.

In America, Gaston la Chaise's work seemed to me to have a fine quality and with a sculptural understanding of materials. I believe that he died without achieving plans which would have been a solid contribution to sculpture.

Manship struck me as a very superficial, decorative, eclectic borrowing from everywhere. One could imagine that he had a book of Greek designs and on Monday mornings opened it at page one, founded his Monday piece of work on that, and on Tuesday, turned to page two, and so on through the week.

I met Bill Zorach. He seemed to me to have splendid enthusiasm and to be doing work that had fine sculptural qualities. He was then only feeling his way, and I understand that he has since been recognised and given important commissions.

28

MY PLACE IN SCULPTURE

I HAVE often been asked by aspiring sculptors to help them to get on their feet, and not very long after this have had the ironical pleasure of watching them getting large commissions and all sorts of decorative work from sources that would never come near me; nor have the aspirants, when safely in the saddle, taken the same interest in my work that they formerly professed. In other directions this spirit manifests itself thus: a certain author is very eager to write my life, and professes a tremendous admiration for my work. I never answer any fan mail, and after two or three unsuccessful attempts to get me to communicate with him, the author sends me a most abusive letter in which he uses the expression: "Your manners are as atrocious as your marbles." Somewhat revealing!

What amazes me is that from far afield as South Africa, Australia, and Western Canada, I receive letters from well-wishers telling me just where I have not lived up to their ideals in my work. Then there are the would-be *"inspiratrices"* who send me batches of photographs which are indignantly demanded back after a week or two, so giving me much trouble. In many cases sculptors or refugees from the lands of persecution send photographs of their work to solicit my assistance, and I have certainly sworn to their talent time and again. I have yet to receive proof of a new Michelangelo. In some cases hoaxes are attempted, and it always passes my understanding why people should take the trouble to make me believe they will endow me with commissions and make me wealthy. They waste my time and leave a fictitious address, usually an expensive luxury hotel. Perhaps the pleasure of feeling very big and wealthy and in a position to give a commission to an artist, if only a sham one, is sufficient to fill their cup with joy.

Epstein: An Autobiography

From time to time I have received many miniature versions of my larger works from amateurs, who certainly satisfy themselves in this manner, but which I find irritating. What I have dug out of myself with labour they translate into tiny, vague versions, working from newspaper photographs, and in their simplicity imagine I ought to be pleased. These works are always returned to their makers.

It is naturally difficult to assess one's place in the period one lives in, perhaps impossible. It is a process similar to painting one's own portrait, or rather to working on a portrait in the round, a really difficult undertaking. The artist usually dramatises himself, and that is why few self-portraits bear the imprint of truth. My outstanding merit in my own eyes is that I believe myself to be a return in sculpture to the human outlook, without in any way sinking back into the flabby sentimentalising, or the merely decorative, that went before. From the Cubists onwards, sculpture has tended to become more and more abstract, whether the shape it took was that of the clearness and hardness of machinery, or soft and spongy forms, as in Hans Arp, or a combination of both. I fail to see also how the use of novel materials helps, such as glass, tin, strips of lead, stainless steel, and aluminium. The use of these materials might add novel and pleasing effects in connection with architecture, but add nothing to the essential meanings of sculpture, which remain fundamental. The spirit is neglected for detail, for ways and means.

Another addition to sculpture is special lighting, flood lighting, and colouring of sculpture. Fantastic and transient effects can be managed, similar to stage effects, but I look on all this as trivial and not worth serious consideration.

The continual harping on the nude for its own sake has been over-done, and a rest from the nude might do sculpture good. Draped figures, as in Gothic work, might as an alternative to-day seem as novel as the apotheosis of the nude after Gothic. I have not been led astray by experiments in abstraction, or by the new tendency to a tame architectural formula for positive qualities, the deeply intimate and human were always sought by me, and so wrought, that they became classic and enduring. The main charge against my work is that it has no "formal relations"—by "formal relations" the critic meaning that my forms and their juxtaposition were just accidental. This I consider sheer nonsense. Because an artist chooses to put

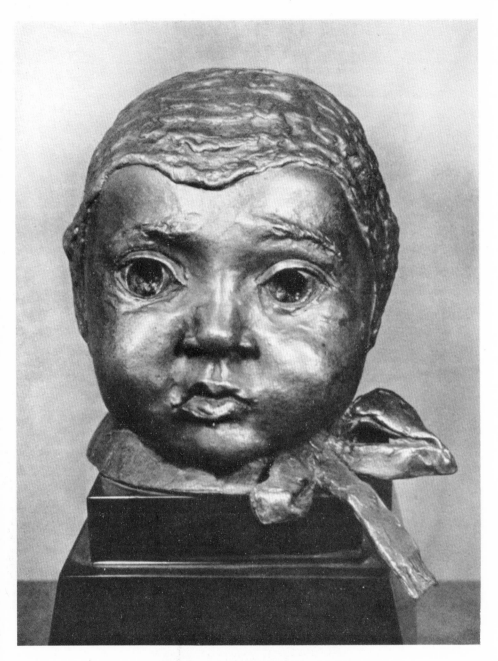

ANNABEL WITH BONNET, 1953

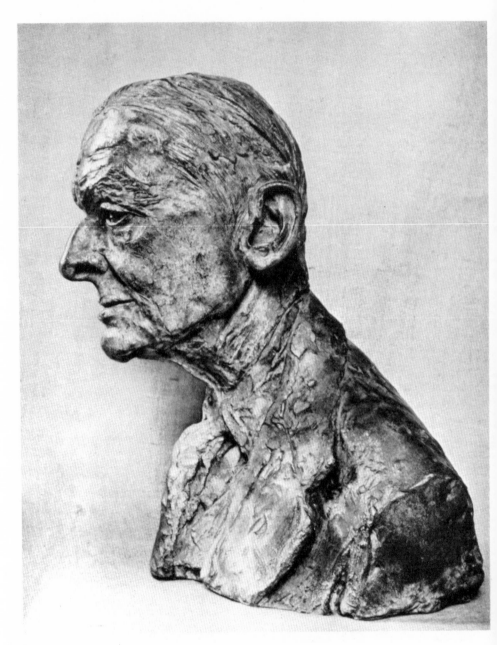

T. S. ELIOT, O.M., 1953

certain abstract forms together does not mean that he has succeeded in creating a better design than mine, whose forms are taken from a study of nature. To construct and relate natural forms may call for a greater sensibility and a more subtle understanding of design than the use of abstract formula.

I can quite justly complain of neglect by architects of my work. Articles in newspapers and critics have instilled fear into them, and I can give specific instances when an architect or an institution has been warned on no account to employ me. All of my larger works will easily fit into any architectural ensemble not totally out of harmony with their character. I would mention in this connection "Consummatum Est" or the "Adam". When my "Madonna and Child" was shown in the new Duveen Gallery at the Tate, it immediately took its place in the architectural setting, and I had the satisfaction of comparing it with other large works, even Rodins, which seemed to have no architectural quality and did not relate themselves in their environment. All my busts and heads take their place in formal wall surroundings.

Most of my larger works remain my property. What is of interest in this connection is that I have proven that I can make more money by painting than by sculpture, as my landscape and flower exhibitions prove. I have none of the pretended illusions that amateurs and those who do not practise an art have about the "sordidness" of money. It takes some courage to remain a sculptor, and Modigliani found that he was forced to take to painting altogether, although I know he had a profound love for sculpture and the practice of it.

Painters (Matisse was one) who occasionally do a piece of sculpture only do so as amateurs for relaxation or out of interest from the safe position of successful painting. The painter Gertler once told me of how he had started a piece of sculpture, and after four or five days' strenuous work, the piece was still unfinished and he gave it up. He argued that in the time he gave to one piece of sculpture he might have made several paintings. One of course ought to live like the Chinese who give years to one piece of work. To do that I suppose one's family should live as Orientals are said to do on a handful of rice a day.

Live and let live. I have always admitted other forms of sculpture than my own and do not reason that if a sculptor does not do as I do he is no sculptor. I have, despite every obstacle of organised hostility on the part of the Press, art critics, art cliques, and personal vendettas, gone my own way and have never truckled to the demands of popularity or pot-boiled. I do not say this with any feeling of self-righteousness, for I have enjoyed myself at work. Sculpture, drawing, and painting I have felt a natural call to do, and I have had the opportunity to create a body of work which, taking all in all, I am not ashamed of.

29

POSTSCRIPT: 1954

IT is fourteen years since this book of recollections was first published and I am asked to bring it up to date and to describe the events which have taken place in this interval. For me, new events mean new sculpture. About 1942 I modelled a life-size figure of a lyric nature which I intended for a garden or woodland setting. It was a new departure and I greatly enjoyed this happy period. I called it "The Girl with the Gardenias" and exhibited it as the central piece at my war-time exhibition at the Leicester Galleries. Strangely enough, in view of the admiration and interest it later called forth at the first Battersea Park outdoor exhibition in 1947 when it was bought for the Aberdeen Art Gallery, this work was ridiculed and minimised by the art critics of the leading papers.

Also during the war when the raids were at their height, I exhibited at the same gallery a series of flower paintings and quoted in the catalogue a couplet from a Shakespeare sonnet: "How with this rage can Beauty hold a plea Whose action is no stronger than a flower?" Yet Beauty held its plea and the whole exhibition was sold out immediately and had a very large attendance.

During the war years the Ministry of Information commissioned me to do portraits of several important war leaders and although the fees offered were nominal I was interested to undertake this work. The first of this series was Sir Alan Cunningham, the victorious commander of the Abyssinian campaign. As he took his place on the stand he came face to face with my portrait of Haile Selassie. "Good heavens!" said the General, "I thought I'd seen the last of him." I remember the General's impassive expression as my plaster moulder, who was in the Home Guard, regaled him with a dramatic description of the epic defence of Putney Bridge by himself and his comrades one Sunday morning. Perhaps the flicker of a smile passed over my sitter's face. Far from being bellicose, I was impressed by the gentle courtesy of a man whose chief ambition at that moment was to grow roses and "cultiver son jardin". I myself was very pleased with this portrait but the most popular of these war-time studies turned out to be the head of Ernest Bevin. At the end of his sittings, however, he looked at it long and seriously and remarked "Epstein, you know I'd have hardly recognised it." Mr. Pandit Nehru was sitting for me after the war; he begged to be shown the plaster model of this head and even descended into the vaults candle in hand to find it, emerging covered with dust and spider-webs, which must greatly have bewildered his plain-clothes man.

Air Marshal, now Lord Portal was one of my distinguished war-time commissions. He could never spare more than his luncheon hours for sittings, but he gladly sacrificed them for this purpose. Promptly at the end of an hour he would leave the studio saying, "Now I must get on with the war!"

The Ministry of Information were naturally eager for me to work from Churchill but the opportunity did not come until after the war when he was living opposite me. He arrived at my studio complete with secretary, and a plain-clothes man who planted himself at the door intending to remain on guard throughout the sitting. I offered this gentleman a chair whereupon Churchill abruptly dismissed him. Lighting his cigar, with his secretary seated behind me ready for dictation, we were all set for a fair start. After an hour this secretary was dismissed and a second appeared for further dictation to the accompaniment of a second cigar. After three somewhat restless sittings Churchill decided to stay at Chartwell where he gave me three further sittings. Unfortunately it was winter and the light far from ideal and I felt that I had made no more than an interesting character study, but still hope to develop it should the opportunity arise. I found Churchill at all times extremely genial and a most hospitable host. He showed me his paintings about which I found him modest to the extreme, laying no claim to professional status. His library as I saw it seemed to consist of books on Napoleon and his celebrated ancestor the first Duke of Marlborough.

I remember this portrait of Churchill followed the completion of

RT. HON. SIR WINSTON CHURCHILL, O.M., 1946

LORD RUSSELL, 1953

the large winged figure in bronze which I called "Lucifer". I had worked on this with great concentration for the greater part of a year and showed it at an exhibition of my work at the Leicester Galleries where it remained unsold. Some time later Professor Lawrence (brother of Lawrence of Arabia and then at Cambridge) wrote to me proposing to purchase the statue from the Seven Pillars of Wisdom Trust and to present it to the Fitzwilliam Museum, Cambridge, confidently believing that this gift would be welcomed by the Syndics of the Museum. To his astonishment the gift was rejected. Vague and unconvincing reasons were given and Professor Lawrence, determined to present the statue to a public gallery, asked my advice. I suggested the V. and A. and the offer was once again rejected, this time on the grounds that this museum did not exhibit work by living artists. He next turned to the Tate Gallery with its large bare sculpture hall. This time the gift of the statue was unanimously rejected by the Board of Trustees, and this, being reported in the Press, brought several requests from leading provincial galleries. I was visited by the Lord Mayor of Birmingham and the Director of the Art Gallery Mr. Trenchard Cox, who asked that Birmingham should be honoured with the gift. I was very moved by their enthusiasm and recommended Professor Lawrence to consent to their request and eventually the statue was unveiled by the Lord Mayor Alderman Bradbeer at a big civic reception. I would like to pay a tribute to, and express my appreciation of, the enthusiasm shown by the provinces for my larger imaginative works compared to the indifference of the London galleries. It was over twenty-five years ago that a major work of mine was purchased by subscription and presented to the Tate Gallery, and my retrospective exhibition at the Tate arranged by the Arts Council, which drew an attendance of 70,000 persons, resulted in a purchase for the Gallery by the Chantry Bequest of a small bust made over forty years ago.

The noble setting for a large stone carving of mine called "Lazarus" made in 1948 was inspired in the happiest possible manner. This work, suggested by the gospel account of Lazarus being raised from the dead, was the outcome of an idea which had haunted me for many years. The carving was exhibited at the Leicester Galleries and received much hostile criticism and was returned unwanted to my studio.

About 1951 I was commissioned by New College, Oxford to do a portrait bust of their Warden, A. Smith. I undertook this with great pleasure as I found him a most sympathetic sitter from every point of view and was reminded when working from him of one of the great humanist scholars of the Renaissance. It must have been during the third sitting after an unusually quiet spell, for he was a great talker, that the Warden suddenly said, contemplating the "Lazarus" —"How wonderful that would look in our cloisters at New College!" The idea took shape and I visited Oxford to view the proposed setting. Beautiful and ideal as the green lawn in the centre of the cloisters is, in consultation with the Warden we decided that in view of the action of the English climate on stone, it would be better to place the carving in New College Chapel. All of the negotiations I left with complete confidence in Warden Smith's hands. Eventually the scheme was accepted by the College authorities and the carving was bought and placed at the west end of New College Chapel. This was one of the happiest issues of my working life.

How often does a sculptor find in these days the ideal setting for his work? I am reminded of Rodin's "Burghers of Calais" so drearily shown that few Londoners or visitors to London ever see it, and it is placed so high that it is impossible to get any adequate idea of its full sculptural qualities. Rodin himself expressed the wish to have these fine heroic figures placed two by two ascending the steps of St. Stephen's. When at last I actually saw the "Lazarus" installed in the Chapel it seemed miraculous to me that the statue should harmonise so completely with the ancient stone walls. The lofty soaring arches seemed to continue the upward thrust of my figure.

The day of the presentation was a very happy one for me and nothing could have exceeded the hospitality of the Warden on that occasion. My affiliations with the University of Oxford were continued by the presentation to me of the treasured degree of D.C.L. which I received from the Vice-Chancellor Sir Maurice Bowra in May 1953. On yet another occasion I was the guest at a dinner at Baliol College on the occasion of the farewell to the retiring Master, the late Lord Lindsay. I was asked to sculpture his head as a farewell gift from the students and it was presented to him at their dinner. As we entered the hall carrying the bronze head there was a deafening clatter of knives being banged on the tables by every student and fellow in the College, the traditional Baliol welcome. After dinner one of the students said how much they would like me to dine in the hall once a week as it seemed the only way of ensuring a satisfying meal!

A famous sitter who posed for me during the post-war period was Pandit Nehru. During a visit by him to this country to attend an Imperial conference he phoned me, although we had never met, expressing a wish to visit me at my studio. Nothing was said about a portrait, but whilst talking to him it occurred to me that we were wasting a rare opportunity, and I asked him immediately to start sitting. He was in session from ten o'clock onwards each day of his visit but he came unfailingly at nine each morning and gave me an hour's sitting. There were only three days of his visit left and naturally I could not make a comprehensive portrait, but a year later, on the Pandit's return, he gave me further sittings and I completed the portrait. At this time, so soon after the assassination of Mahatma Gandhi, Nehru seemed burdened with the cares of office and it was in this mood that I conceived this sombre portrait. I am afraid that his friends might have preferred a more genial and debonair characterisation, but I feel that in the long run my presentation will reveal the more profound and historic aspect of India's first Prime Minister.

About this time I was invited to a party of welcome to the famous composer Ernest Bloch. I seldom accept invitations to parties but I had admired the musical genius of Bloch for some time and was interested to meet the composer in person. A large gathering had assembled to do him honour, but time passed and the principal guest did not materialise. At last, when we had become thoroughly impatient and I was leaving the hall it was announced that Bloch had appeared earlier on, but after a few minutes he had hurried off to a rehearsal of his "Sacred Service" leaving the party to fend for itself. However, when he heard that I had been there to meet him he came to my studio unannounced one Sunday morning as I was leaving for the country. Cancelling my plans I at once put him on the stand and started his portrait. I am told that the whole house resounded with the ensuing conversation, carried on in a resonant mixture of several tongues. Nevertheless the portrait developed rapidly, assisted by Bloch's complete lack of self-consciousness and what might truly be called a dynamic personality. His conversation was a series of eruptions alternating between despair at his chequered career and wild hilarity. He invited us to hear him conduct the rehearsal of his music for a recording. This was a fascinating experience, and later we sat with him listening to the finished record. He was pale and unusually quiet and sat with a smile of complete satisfaction. At the end all he said was, "That is good, that is very good." I couldn't help thinking of Schubert, amongst other unsuccessful composers, who in his lifetime never succeeded in getting a hearing for his great C Major symphony. No wonder Bloch smiled to be able to put on record his own exact version of a major work. I greatly enjoyed these somewhat stormy sessions with Ernest Bloch and greet him from these pages.

Soon after this it was suggested that I should sculpture our great English composer Dr. Vaughan Williams, a personality equally impressive in a very different manner. Here was the master with whom no one would venture to dispute. He reminded me in appearance of some eighteenth-century admiral whose word was law. Notwithstanding, I found him the epitomy of courtesy and consideration and I was impressed by the logic and acuteness of everything he discoursed upon and was made aware of his devotion to an art as demanding as sculpture. It seemed to me characteristic of this great man that at a mature stage in his creative development he decided to study composition with Maurice Ravel in Paris in order to balance his hitherto German training. We were received with charming hospitality by the Master at his country home in Dorking, from where we went at his invitation to hear his annual performance conducting the Bach St. Matthew Passion.

Shortly after this I was commissioned by the Festival of Britain to sculpture a figure for the 1951 exhibition. I conceived the idea of making a figure that should embody youthful courage and resolution, and the result was the over life-size bronze entitled "Youth Advancing". The figure was gilded and placed looking over a sheet of water. I worked very strenuously and earnestly on this work giving up several portrait commissions in order to execute it on time. Imagine my surprise, to put it mildly, to receive with the compliments of the organisers of the exhibition a review of this work referring to it as a mere "pot boiler".

It must have been shortly after this that I was happy to have as a

234

sitter Professor Patrick Blackett, the distinguished scientist and Nobel Prize winner. This head, with its sensitive, profoundly thoughtful expression, together with that of Dr. Vaughan Williams, have proved two of my most widely appreciated male portraits. Somerset Maugham whose portrait I sculptured in 1951 reminded me strongly of some old Roman patrician. In spite of his fastidious and aloof expression he proved a model sitter, was most genial whilst posing and discoursed on contemporary letters most entertainingly. We would leave the studio door open while a friend played Mozart on the piano much to his delight. He once came in for a sitting from an Embassy luncheon accompanied by a tall, stately princess who was, I think, very dismayed at the dusty disorder of my studio and stayed but a very short time.

A recent famous sitter was Bertrand Russell whose fawn-like head I had long wanted to portray. A happy chance brought this about as he had just married an American lady who had commissioned a portrait from me twenty years earlier. Lord Russell, far from being the ponderous philosopher of tradition, was gay and witty as, pipe in hand, he carried on the most sprightly conversation. This portrait was followed by one that I had long wanted to carry out but never found the opportunity to do until last year when a mutual friend brought T. S. Eliot to my studio. I was very impressed by the grave courtesy of his bearing frequently lighted up by a smile at once genial and ironical. Eliot himself seemed most interested in the development of the work and on one occasion he came with me to the foundry where my large "Madonna and Child" was being cast in lead and seemed profoundly impressed. I look back on these sittings with pleasure.

This Madonna and Child, thirteen and a half feet high, was commissioned by the Nuns of the Convent of the Holy Child Jesus to be placed above an arch connecting two fine Palladian style buildings on the north side of Cavendish Square. I gladly seized this opportunity to design and execute a work of this nature with such a great subject and fitting site. The work absorbed me for a period of over six months and then the day arrived for the Mother Superior to come and view it. She came with another Sister and they immediately showed the warmest interest in the work and asked to be allowed to contemplate it quietly and alone for some time. After that they returned several times bringing different nuns on each occasion and eventually the work was cast and the day of its unveiling arrived. It was a May day and fortunately there were brief spells of sunshine for a considerable crowd had gathered and the street had to be cordoned off and the traffic diverted for the opening ceremony performed by Mr. R. A. Butler, the Chancellor of the Exchequer. This ceremony seemed to reach back to the days of the Renaissance when the appearance of a new religious work was the occasion for public rejoicing.

No work of mine has brought so many tributes from so many diverse quarters. One which particularly pleased me by reason of its spontaneity was from a bus driver. Halting his bus as he passed the statue he suddenly saw me standing by and called out across the road, "Hi Governor, you've made a good job of it." A less aesthetic but equally spontaneous comment was overheard when the cockney owner of a bedraggled pony and cart halted beneath the statue and observed wistfully to his mate, "Think of that now. A solid lump of lead." Fortunately the statue is suspended about twenty feet from the ground.

It would be a great mistake were I to give the impression from the foregoing account of celebrated sitters that I only care to work from the great. Perhaps my chief pleasure has been found in working from children of all descriptions. For instance, when I engaged a cook from West Africa I was delighted to see her arrive accompanied by an extremely robust little darkie boy dressed from head to foot in white satin. Victor immediately became my model and a very handsome one at that. It was a very good thing that there was something to compensate for his mother's culinary defects.

On another occasion I was in the Greek Room at the British Museum when I noticed the rapt interest of two small dark-eyed boys who, with their peasant-like mother, were examining the antique works. I asked her if she would bring them to my studio to pose for me and she joyfully assented, much to the glee of the children. I worked from the younger one called Anthony while the older one aged about eight immediately rolled up his sleeves and started making clay vases as if from some age old inheritance. My own grandchildren are frequent and delightful sitters and I constantly see faces in most unexpected places in obscure surroundings which tempt me to work from them. However, at this period of my life, for the first time I have so many large commissions that I am temporarily obliged to put such ideas aside.

I would like to end this chapter by saying something about the monumental work that has absorbed much of my time during the past two and a half years, not only whilst actually in the studio but also during long periods of thought, for a work such as I refer to now is often the result of years of planning, musing upon and developing. It is not only the visual that stimulates an artist's conceptions. Sometimes a poem or a piece of music will evoke a complete image in the most striking fashion. But to return to my latest and largest work which I have just completed. I can only give the brief facts of its origin, its destination and subject matter for at the moment of writing it is in process of being cast in bronze and it has not yet been adequately photographed as a whole.

I was asked by the Fairmount Park Art Association of Philadelphia to make a work with the somewhat baffling title of "Social Consciousness". In 1951 I went to Philadelphia to see the site and was greatly impressed by the fine natural surroundings of rocks and trees and river, and I realised that something on a heroic scale was called for. I planned a group of five figures, two of them thirteen feet in height, flanking a central figure with outstretched arms and upward glance "seated in the adamant of time". The theme of the group of two figures on the right is the Healer succouring the downfallen and that on the left is the eternal Mother supporting future humanity.

It is with great eagerness that I look forward to seeing my Philadelphia group finally placed in its noble setting; but I am already engaged on new projects.

Appendix One

The Evening Standard, June 19th, 1908. The Secretary of the Vigilance Society quoted:

"I have personally, on behalf of the Society, lodged a protest with the Secretary of the British Medical Association," said Mr. W. A. Coote, the secretary of The Vigilance Society. He informed one of our representatives that he is now putting the complaint in a letter of protest to the Committee. "At present the sight is bad enough, but when the hoarding in Agar Street is removed, it will be a scandal. I am at a loss to understand the object of such representations. In no other city in Europe are figures in sculpture of the nature shown on the building in the Strand thrust upon the public gaze.

"If photographs of the statues were sold in the public streets or exposed for sale in any shop, proceedings would at once be taken. We intend, unless the offending figures are removed, to take action and see whether the law is strong enough to deal with such a display. If it is not, the fact will lend additional interest to the proceedings of the Parliamentary Committee which is, at the present time, inquiring into the publication of certain books and pictures, and the holding of certain exhibitions."

The views of Mr. Walter Crane:

I have not seen the statues and do not know who the sculptor is, and I can therefore express no opinion on the artistic merit. So far, however, as the principle involved is concerned, I am entirely in favour of frank sex representation in art. Undisguised portrayal in this respect provides the sculptor with his best opportunities. Michelangelo was seen at his best in the frankly nude, and others whose work is of the highest order did not disguise sex. To be artistic, however, sculpture in this form must be noble. There is ignoble sculpture as well as noble. I do not think it is a question of morality. The exigencies of our northern climate, which necessitate the wearing of so much clothing, are responsible for a great deal of false shame. In India and other warm countries, Nature unadorned gives rise to no such feeling.

The Evening Standard, June 20th, 1908:

Work to be stopped. The sculpture figures to which we have taken objection on the new building of the British Medical Association at the corner of the Strand

"Madonna and Child" in plaster in the Studio, 1952

"Madonna and Child" in Cavendish Square

Mr. R. A. Butler unveils the "Madonna and Child"

WARDEN SMITH OF NEW COLLEGE, 1952

and Agar Street were unreservedly condemned by Mr. Edmund Owen, F.R.C.S., the association's own Chairman of Council, and he intends at once to call a meeting of the Building Committee for the purpose of stopping the removal of any more of the hoarding until the members of the Council have had an opportunity of seeing the figures for themselves, when he hopes they will agree with him that they ought to be very much modified, if not taken away altogether. As a matter of fact, the Council have never had drawings of the statues before them, and the majority of them are unaware of the nature of the figures. Mr. Owen had seen them only in a partially finished state. In view, however, of our protest, he paid a visit to the building to-day, accompanied by one of our representatives. "I have no sympathy with them whatever," he said, after seeing the figures which we have condemned, "and my own opinion is that they ought never to have been put there. I had seen some of them before they were finished, and did not like them from the physical representation point of view. They seemed to be poor figures. But I had no idea they were to be presented in the form that some of them are. I cannot, of course, speak for the Council, but I hope that other members will take the same view as I do when they see the figures. The Council will not meet till July 1st, but I shall call together the Committee immediately connected with the building at once and propose that instructions be given to stop any more of the hoarding being taken down until the Council comes to a decision. I think *The Evening Standard* has taken the right course in calling attention to the matter before the more objectionable statues have been exposed to full public view, and I have no ground for complaint in what has been said."

We welcome this frank statement on the part of one in the position of Mr. Owen. He supports what we have all along contended that no one with a due sense of responsibility who took the trouble to see the figures for himself, could approve of them, and so far our attitude has been justified. As we have already pointed out, only one figure to which the least objection can be taken is at present exposed to the public view. It is one of a group of four on the Strand side of the building. There are, however, four more on the Agar Street elevation, which is still surrounded by a high hoarding. Work is proceeding on other statues, but these are still obscured by the Sculptor's canvas. It is hoped that the Buildings Committee will call for drawings of the unfinished figures. We have purposely refrained from entering into any details with regard to the figures, and even at the risk of being misunderstood we decline to particularise. In the form it appears on the Strand building, the sculpture may have been appropriate in a Medical hall, but it is entirely unsuitable, and not at all artistic or dignified in a busy thoroughfare. The most objectionable representations are still more or less hidden by the hoarding in Agar Street, although two of them are plainly visible from the wards of Charing Cross Hospital and other buildings in the vicinity, and in calling attention to them at this stage one's desire is that they may be modified or removed before they are exposed to full public view. As art, the Strand figures, in their present form, are not beautiful, and one of the figures, at least, has no parallel, so far as we are aware, even in sculpture galleries. What is complained of could not escape the notice of the most casual passer-by, when the hoarding is once removed, and that on a Strand frontage would constitute a gross offence. Moreover, we did not take action until the matter was already becoming a subject of common talk and of vulgar curiosity, whilst the fact of the private, and apparently useless, admonition by the police authorities should suffice to explode the delusion that these figures constitute an innocuous form of art.

The Evening Standard, June 22nd, 1908, announcing that a meeting of the Council would be called for July 1st, went on to quote Mr. H. Percy Adams, of Messrs. Adams and Holden, the architects of the building:

"In my opinion they are magnificent," said Mr. Percy Adams, and he went on to say: "There may be differences of opinion as to the advisability of displaying one or two of them, or any nude figures on a public building in London, but I cannot myself agree with the view that any of them are objectionable. One of the figures to which most objection has been taken is still unfinished." With regard to Mr. Adams' last point, we can only say that the sculptor's canvas has been removed from the statue, and it has as much the appearance of being finished as any of those that are exposed to view. A strong effort is to be made, we understand, to get the Buildings Committee on Wednesday to pass the statues as they stand. It is to be hoped that the members will, before entering on a consideration of the question, see the figures objected to for themselves, and if they do, we have confidence that they will not permit them to go to the public without considerable modification.

The Evening Standard, June 23rd:

Father Vaughan has raised his voice in denouncing the statues which we have condemned, in their present form, on the new building of the British Medical Association at the corner of Agar Street and the Strand.

"As a Christian citizen in a Christian city, I claim the right," he declared, "to say that I object most emphatically to such indecent and inartistic statuary being thrust upon my view in a public thoroughfare, through which I am often compelled by duty to pass.

"To the average man or woman, constructed as they are, these figures will be occasions—I will not say for sin, because I will be told there is no such thing—but of vulgarity and of unwholesome talk, calculated to lead to practices of which there are more than enough in the purlieus of the Strand already. There seems to me to be absolutely no reason for going out of our way to disfigure the façade of our public buildings by such imagery, and it is a disgrace to thrust upon our public highways statuary, talk and discussion which in the lecture room, and for students, may be necessary. Let us teach self-reverence and self-respect, and not convert London into a Fiji Island, where there may be some excuse for want of drapery. Let us not innovate upon our time-honoured practice in this country, and try to out-Continent the Continent in indecent statuary, lest we have cause to regret it in the end.

"In the name of public decency, I beg the Buildings Committee of the British Medical Association not to sanction the uncovering of these statues before the eyes of the public, many of whom, I regretfully say, will not look upon them with the temperament of our artist, but will feast upon them with the hunger of a sensualist. Surely it is our duty not to feed, but to starve, that sort of appetite."

The Evening Standard, June 23rd, 1908: leading article headed "THE STRAND STATUES":

At the best of times, there is great difficulty in defining the limits of art and the boundaries of decency. Here the problem is complicated by our unwillingness to

Strand Statues: 1908–1937

describe the statues in detail. So far we cannot go. Nor the public see for themselves. It is inadvisable that they should, and we trust they will never get the chance. The letter which appears in *The Times* from C. J. Holmes, the Slade Professor of Fine Arts, shows how little assistance can be expected from artists. If this were a question of art, we should regard Professor Holmes's letter as an important contribution to the controversy, though he does not refrain from talking of ill-informed but none the less violent attack. With the artistic value of the figures, however, we have nothing to do. They may or may not have been conceived in the grave, heroic mood of the pre-Pheidian Greeks.

What we have said, and what we maintain, is that they are unfitted for the embellishment of a building in the Strand or any other street. The Police, however, did realise the unsuitability of the statues directly they had an opportunity of seeing them. They were so impressed by their unsuitability, that they immediately considered whether their powers were sufficient to enable them to order a removal of the nuisance. Unfortunately, they found they could not step in. Public opinion and the good sense of the management of the Institution must effect what the Police cannot. We appeal to the British Medical Association not to be misled by talk of art, which is a side issue, but to use their judgment as men of the world.

We can even understand the chagrin of the sculptor and architect on hearing it pointed out to them that their work was not of a fit and proper kind. The desire for symbolism has led men astray before, and will lead them astray again. Modern realism is calculated to assist the aberration. They are certainly not the right kind of symbolism for a public building. We go further; we say that if the hoarding were removed, the public would very quickly arrive at the opinion we ourselves have formed, and that is, that the removal of the statues would be demanded. Is it not better to remove them or modify them now, without more pother?

Letter to *The Times*:

SIR,

The action of the British Medical Association in setting up a building which is actually beautiful in the Strand, and adorning it with decorative sculpture that is even good enough to attract attention, is, it appears, calling forth one of those periodical outbursts of rage against the nude in sculpture, which lovers of art have to endure from time to time.

These periodical outbursts tempt the small minority who love art in this country to blaspheme; but perhaps you will grant me the hospitality of a few of your valuable lines to invite them to possess their souls in patience. The people in this country, as all the world knows, are an astounding but incompletely fused mixture of all sorts of races. Some learned persons tell us that ultimately the bulk of these races may be classified down to two main constituent groups—the descendants of an ancient group of arctic peoples, and the descendants of an ancient group of Mediterranean peoples. It is the strong, big, law-and-order-loving arctic lot that make all this bother. The small, artistic, go-as-you-please wanderers up from the warm lands are the sufferers. Those gaunt, red, cold folk have, deep down inside them, the memory of the glacial epoch, when they clothed themselves in skins and hunted the reindeer not far away from the edge of enormous glaciers. The poor

241

things, in this miserable English climate, have not in a mere ten to twenty thousand years had time to get warm through. It will take countless more of our ordinary English summers to drive the arctic shivers out of their subconscious selves. Naturally, when they see the representation of a nude figure it puts their teeth on edge, and they hold out and hurl against it such handy anathemas as come easiest on their tongues—immoral and the like. Sculptured nudes have an exactly contrary effect on the "small dark man". They stir in him the pleasant memory of ancestors who knew what it was to live in a decent climate, where it was not necessary to wear "flannel next to the skin". Let the happy English substratum of art lovers, instead of railing at their fellow-countrymen with the pleistocene constitutions, pray earnestly for much hot weather. If we could have even a couple of months only, the protest of the "large, red" gentry would grow feeble, and the B.M.A. would find that, after the "large red" fashion, the building and site decoration would be forgotten by its present foes, who are by nature an unobservant lot, and only rail at what is new, because for the moment it happens to attract the attention of their normally unseeing eyes.

I am, Sir,

Yours faithfully,

MARTIN CONWAY.

The Times, June 25th, 1908:

A correspondent of *The Times* yesterday paid a visit to the new premises of the British Medical Association in the Strand, for the purpose of inspecting the statues of Mr. Epstein, which have been already executed and are in process of erection upon the two fronts of the building. These statues have given rise in certain quarters to some adverse criticism, in answer to which a letter from Professor Holmes, Slade Professor of Fine Arts at Oxford, appeared in *The Times* of yesterday. It has been suggested that the statues are objectionable from the point of view of public morality. The artistic aspect of the question is one which the art critics may be left to decide between themselves, but the moral aspect is one of more general interest, and it was with a view to ascertaining how far there is any basis of fact for the criticisms passed upon the statues from this point of view that our correspondent paid his visit. It may be well to explain at the outset that there are eighteen statues representing various phases of human life, and certain symbolical figures.

Our correspondent reports that, accompanied by a friend, he first examined the figures from the street. The statues are at a height of forty feet to fifty feet from the ground and cannot be seen adequately except at some distance from the building. A hoarding at present prevents any complete view of some of the statues. The only figures to which, in the opinion of our correspondent and his companion any exception could conceivably be taken are three or four nude male figues, which, however, are neither indecent nor even remotely suggestive.

The statue of "Maternity" represents a woman in pregnancy. This figure is turned towards the wall, and is so high up on the building that the particular feature to which exception is taken can scarcely be distinguished, except by aid of an opera glass or a telescope; and there is nothing even remotely immodest in the pose or execution of the figure.

A closer inspection in situ from the platform from which the work is carried

Strand Statues: 1908–1937

out confirmed the first impression that the statues are inoffensive from the point of view of public morality, and in no way justify the strictures passed upon them.

The Times, leading article:

STATUES, MORALS, AND THE PRESS

The Committee of the British Medical Association will, it is said, meet to-day to consider whether the statues on their new building in the Strand ought to be "modified". The very idea of such a thing would not have occurred to anyone had not an enterprising journalist, in search of sensational "copy", discovered them. In these exceedingly inoffensive works, raised some forty or fifty feet from the ground, where nobody would see them unless his attention was directed to them, we are confident that a personal inspection of the statues would convince the vast majority of our readers that the attack upon them is wholly unjustifiable. They are single symbolical figures, some of them draped, or partly draped, some of them nude. Two of the latter are on the Strand front, and others, as yet only partially visible, are on the west side of the building, where the scaffolding is not yet removed. In none of these is there the slightest suggestion of evil. No hint of passion or impurity. Their spirit and their treatment, to use the word employed by our well-qualified correspondents—Professor Holmes and Mr. Laurence Binyon, Mr. Charles Ricketts and Mr. Charles Shannon—is austere. Their offence is that they represent nude men. Well, it is difficult in these days to be surprised at anything; but we confess that we are surprised to find any portion of the London Press assuming the moral attitude of the Pope who ordered the Vatican Venus and some of her marble sisters to wear tin petticoats. We trust that this appeal to the Philistinism and hypocrisy of a portion of our middle class will be met by the British Medical Association with the contempt it deserves.

British Medical Journal, June 27th, 1908, leading article:

"AN OLD MAID WITH A SPY-GLASS"

In a famous passage Macaulay says there is no spectacle so ridiculous as the British Public in one of its periodical fits of morality. Once in six or seven years, he says, our virtue becomes outrageous. We cannot suffer the laws of religion and decency to be violated. We must make a stand against vice. *The Evening Standard and St. James's Gazette* seems to be trying to work up the public to one of these periodical paroxysms. For a week or more it has been holding up its hands in horror at certain statues with which the new buildings of the British Medical Association are decorated. It has interviewed all sorts and conditions of men, including the inevitable Father Bernard Vaughan, without some platitude from whom no public discussion is now complete. We cannot congratulate our esteemed contemporary on the success of its appearance in the part of Mrs. Grundy. The only effect of the efforts, which we will assume it is making merely in the cause of decency, is to excite wrong ideas as to matters absolutely harmless in themselves. Swift well said that "a nice man is a man of nasty ideas". In this sense *The Evening Standard and St. James's Gazette* has shown itself "Nice" to a degree that can only be called morbid. It complains of the nudity of certain statues. Now there is a

243

great difference between half-veiled nakedness and simple nudity. The short skirts of a ballet girl are more suggestive than the chaste nudity of a Greek statue. As for the Statues to which the attention of the National Vigilance Association has been called, we confess we can see absolutely no indecency in them. If there is any indecency it is in the mind of the spectator, not in the work itself. If this sort of prudery is carried to its logical conclusion, anyone visiting a gallery of pictures or sculpture will have to get first a certificate of virtue from his pastor. These places are as open to the public as the Strand, and there, as Byron says of the well-known edition of the classics prepared ad usum Delphini by scholars of the Society of which Father Bernard Vaughan is an ornament, anyone whose mind hankers after that sort of delectation is able to glut his desire without being denounced in the newspapers.

> *For there we have them all at one fell swoop*
> *Instead of being scattered through the pages,*
> *They stand forth marshalled in a handsome troop,*
> *To meet the ingenious youth of future ages,*
> *Till some less rigid editor shall stoop*
> *To call them back to their separate cages,*
> *Instead of standing staring altogether,*
> *Like garden gods—and not so decent either.*

Works of art which might excite the moral wrath of *The Evening Standard and St. James's Gazette* are found in many churches. In some letters of the late J. K. Huysman published in the *Figaro*, 23rd May, 1908, there is a complaint of an equally foolish act of prudery perpetrated by the priests of the Cathedral of Chartres. He says that among the wonderful pieces of sculpture to be found therein, there is one representing the Circumcision, and he says with natural indignation: Par Pudeur! Il (le clergé) a collé un morceau de papier sur le ventre de Jesus. That is Mrs. Grundy all over. She calls attention to what would otherwise have passed unregarded.

Of the thousands of people who go up and down the Strand every day, not half a dozen would have noticed the statues had not *The Evening Standard and St. James's Gazette* pointed the finger of outraged virtue at the details in them.

It is significant that its crusade has found little support from the rest of the press, and we welcome the powerful help of *The Times* which, in a leader, confesses its surprise "to find any portion of the London press assuming the moral attitude of the Pope who ordered the Vatican Venus and some of her marble sisters to wear tin petticoats". We think it right to note that the suggestion of *The Evening Standard* that one at least of the statues which are as yet unrevealed to the public eye is of a still more objectionable character is simply untrue. The statue representing Maternity, which we suppose to be the one meant, is in fact more draped than any of the others.

The other female figures may, for aught we know, be pre-Pheidian, as the Oxford Slade Professor of Fine Art says; for our part we should rather call them pre-Adamite. They suggest "the woman wailing for her demon lover" of the old legend, but there is nothing about them to lead any rightly constituted human being into temptation.

We leave the discussion of the statues from an artistic point of view to those competent to judge of such matters, but it is worthy of note that the artists who have so far spoken have expressed a favourable opinion of them. We have already referred to the letter of the Slade Professor of Art at Oxford. Other artists have expressed similar views in *The Times*.

We may mention further that letters warmly praising the statues, and strongly deprecating any interference with them, have been received from:

Mr. Sidney Colvin, Mr. Martin Conway, D. S. McColl, The Keeper of the National Gallery, C. J. Holmes, and others.

We are glad to be able to state that, after full consideration, the Buildings Committee has decided to recommend the Council to leave the statues as they are.

We venture to think that the whole outcry about them is nothing more than a journalistic scoop. The attitude of *The Evening Standard* reminds us of an old picture in *Punch* of an elderly virgin in seaside lodgings complaining of men bathing in front of her window. When it is pointed out to her that they are a mile or more off she says: "Yes, but then one can see with a spy-glass."

Letter to *The British Medical Journal*:

DEAR SIR,

The series represents symbolical figures of scientific study and research and a presentment of Life, its origin and growth. Apart from my desire to decorate a beautiful building, I wished to create noble and heroic forms to embody in sculpture the great primal facts of man and woman.

The first figure, starting on the Strand side, presents "Primal Energy", a symbolic male figure, with outstretched arm in a forceful gesture, as if passing its way through mists and vapours, it blows the breath of life into the atom. Next work "Matter", a figure of rude and primitive aspect, who folds in his arms a mass of rock in which is vaguely enfolded the form of a child. Thus form and life emerge from the inchoate and lifeless. "Hygeia", symbolic figure of the Goddess of Medicine and Health, holds the cup and serpent. "Chemical Research", a male figure examining a scroll; these two figures form the corner decoration of the building. On Agar Street comes "Mentality". "The Brain", a figure holding a winged skull, symbol of Thought. Next is the "Newborn", an old woman presents the newborn child in a cloak, "Youth", an aspiring figure with head and arms upraised, "Man", a figure of man in his energy and virility. To-day great words like virility have become so besmirched by coarse shame that it becomes a hazardous thing for an artist to use them in a description of his work. This figure looks towards a figure of "Maternity", a brooding mother holding a child in her arms. The figures that follow represent "Youth", "Joy in Life", youths and maidens reaching out and stretching hands towards each other: they represent "Young Life", puberty (puberty is another word that is banned). Throughout I have wished to give a presentation of figures joyous, energetic, and mystical. That the figures should have an ideal aspect, and be possessed of an inner life, is a requirement of sculpture, and also that they should adhere to the forms of Nature, the divine aspect of bodies.

It is very difficult for me to say in words much that I have wished to put into these figures: the bald description does not sound adequate: they themselves will suggest meanings I cannot express in words. I was interested in the article you wrote about the statues, for your paper, and your characterising them as pre-Adamite pleases me very much.

JACOB EPSTEIN.

245

Epstein: An Autobiography

Letters to *The British Medical Journal*, July 4th, 1908:

From a letter by Mr. Ambrose McEvoy:

These works are, I believe, considerably finer than the decorations on any public building in London. They constitute a great art possession for us. Surely it is ridiculous to suggest that there is anything in these austere masterpieces to which any sincere person could take objection.

The sensational press will write anything that will result in sales, and is it not a common experience of dwellers in towns that neighbours will object to anything —even to a door plate.

From a letter by Mr. Sidney Colvin, Director of the British Museum:

Conceived in a spirit of primitive severity and directness which ought to have saved them from objection even on the part of the most prurient of impropriety hunters and sensational journalists.

From a letter by Mr. Martin Conway (late Slade Professor of Art, University of Cambridge):

I venture to write and suggest that no hasty action be taken (at your Council meeting) on this matter, and that time be left for the very warm approval of serious lovers of Art in this country to be expressed, and your Committee to receive the influential public support which can be united and brought to bear in favour of the artist.

From a letter by Mr. D. S. McColl:

I may say that before the attack was made, I happened to pass the building and was greatly struck by the strong and reserved character of the work, its gravity and austerity in strong contrast with the meretricious and floundering stuff that has been too commonly associated with recent architecture.

I said to myself, "Here at last is sculpture", and inwardly congratulated your Society on the fine thing they had done in giving a young man of talent a chance to show his power.

From a letter by Mr. Alfred East, A.R.A.:

Ill-informed and absurd attack on these decorative figures.

From a letter by Mr. Charles Shannon:

Severe and monumental sculptures.

It would be deplorable if a scientific body should become influenced by the prurient squeamishness of an obscure pressman who has seen the chance of a sensational poster.

ANN, 1950

ROLAND, 1950

Strand Statues: 1908–1937

Letter to *The British Medical Journal*:

DEAR SIR,

I see that an evening paper has started a virulent attack on the sculpture on the façade of your new building, and as I understand the paper in question refuses to print any letters refuting their attacks, and as the other journals seem to think that an agitation of this sort and from this particular quarter answers itself, I venture to address you a few lines regarding the statues on your building.

The assumption by the Pearson newspaper that it alone is the voice of the public, and the arbiter of what is moral, is a grave danger, and were such an equivocal "voice of the public" followed, many things we cherish to-day would long ago have ceased to exist. Even such an ultra-respectable work as the Ajax statue in Hyde Park was in its time as virulently assailed by the same kind of thoughtless jejune criticism. The use of nude figures in architectural sculpture is a cause that has to re-win its battle within the present generation. An important point is this, that those who have approved of photographs of the statues are told that their opinion goes for nothing, as they have not seen the figures close at hand; of course such argument is nonsense, as the statues are to be seen from the street which must be some forty feet below.

However, I made a careful study of all the statues on the building to-day, and should like to say how sincere and beautiful they are as Art, and how essentially clean-minded in motive. If there is anything approaching a fault they can be said to have, it is possibly that they lean too much to the side of an archaic austerity—anything less calculated to give offence to decent-minded folk could not be imagined. If a sculptor's work is to be at the mercy of every anonymous critic, his art would indeed be carried on under intolerable conditions. Certainly every objection against those statues of yours could be urged with equal force against the Greek sculptures in the British Museum, round which every Sunday School teacher is presumed to guide her pupils. I venture to hope with some confidence that the British Medical Association will pause well before doing these thoughtful and distinguished works an irreparable injury. But experienced men of science who have before now had to deal with popular misunderstandings of this kind touching their profession, will know how to deal with these passing popular clamours—of that I feel confident.

MUIRHEAD BONE.

Letter to *The British Medical Journal*:

DEAR SIR,

I have read the newspaper attacks upon the statues of Mr. Epstein's, which add so much distinction and beauty to your already fine buildings in the Strand, with indignation and disgust. I cannot imagine who the people may be who are attempting to defame the austere and refined work of your sculptor. It would seem, however, that such attacks could have arisen out of but two causes, one the desire of journalists to earn a guinea or so, and the other out of some petty jealousy or other.

I have examined the statues carefully and I cannot discover the least hint of voluptuousness or immorality: on the contrary, I find them nothing but a sincere and noble interpretation of the deepest things of human life. Any objection to them on the grounds of morality is foolish—if nothing worse. I do not know how you or your committee are affected by these baseless attacks, and I am venturing to send this note, in my capacity of Hon. Secretary of a society deeply interested in all that makes for the elevation and beauty of our city life, to say how much all genuine lovers of what is noble and beautiful would deprecate any tampering with these statues, which are works of rare genius, at the dictation of nasty-minded journalists.

HOLBROOK JACKSON.

Letter to *The British Medical Journal*:

LANGLEY PARK,
MILL HILL,
LONDON, N.W.

DEAR SIR,

Would you allow me to congratulate the British Medical Association on the austere and noble statues decorating their fine new building in the Strand.

I have read with amazement and indignation the various shifty and offensive articles published by *The Evening Standard and St. James's Gazette*. No one with any knowledge of nude figures decorating modern Government buildings in England and abroad, or with any memory for the art of the past, could have written them.

It would be lamentable if a body of cultured men should feel themselves called upon to modify their plans under the impression that these statues are unsuited to their present site. The public patronage of the Arts is too rare for so notable an addition to our streets to be injured or defaced at the impertinent demand of a sensational paper.

CHARLES RICKETTS.

In a leading article in *The British Medical Journal*, July 4th, 1908, the Editor mentions the opposition writers in *The Evening Standard* as

a motley group prominent in which are Father Bernard Vaughan, Dr. Clifford, Mr. Walter Reynolds, and Mr. W. A. Coote, Secretary National Vigilance Association. It is edifying to see the Jesuit and the nonconformist leaders side-by-side on the same platform, but the same thing cannot be said of Mr. Reynolds whose intelligence in such matters is shown by his description of the figures as "gargoyles". This is ignorance, but when he says "that the statues, if left in their present condition, will most assuredly become a splendid draw to all the unchaste and libidinous curiosity seekers of London", he makes what we can characterise as an abominable suggestion. The painter who gained for himself the title of Il Bracciatore succeeded in making things that were harmless, suggestive. This is just what *The Evening Standard* is doing. If simple nudity is subversive of public morals, we shall have to mutilate the animals running about the streets. It might of course go further in its educational enterprise and point out that Cleopatra's Needle is a phallic emblem, and explain to young men and maidens the symbolism which has been attributed to the "vesica window".

After mentioning that the London County Council received Mr. Reynolds' questions against the Strand statues with derisive laughter, the Editor of *The British Medical Journal* goes on to say:

. . . as for our own council we are glad to be able to announce that the following resolution which was moved by Mr. Andrew Clark and seconded by the treasurer

Strand Statues: 1908–1937

was passed with only two dissentients. That having carefully considered the objections raised, and the many favourable expressions of opinion by eminent authorities on art as to the statuary on the new premises, the Council instructs the architects to proceed with the work. Here, then, ends this foolish business, for we cannot take seriously the threat of private proceedings of which *The Evening Standard and St. James's Gazette* of June 30th has made itself the mouthpiece.

Let the old maid close her spy-glass and devote herself to less questionable topics.

In *The British Medical Journal* leader, July 11th, entitled: "The Scribe and The Sculptor", the Editor says:

whatever the object of the Scribe may have been, the decision of the council reported in our last issue, has received the approval of nearly all the press of the country. *The Times, Saturday Review, Observer, The Architect, The World, Daily News, Pall Mall Gazette, The Graphic, The Nation, The Building News, Manchester Guardian, The Manchester Courier* to mention only a few. The editor of *Truth* happily scoffs at the whole thing in a letter from his "aunt", who expressed her horror of the nude in such terms that the writer says, "as soon as I got her letter I went to have a look at the statues myself, and she ought to be quite satisfied with one thing, the whole Strand opposite was packed with people, most of them girls and young men, all staring up at the statues. And I couldn't help thinking what a good thing it was, and how pleased the writer of the article must be, because hundreds of these young people would never have had any idea that the statues were indecent, or even troubled to look at them at all if they had not been told, while now they will always be looking out for indecent things, and thinking about them, and wondering why they are indecent, and whether it does them any good or not. At least it will have given them a new interest in life."

The Lancet congratulated the Council on their decision. . . .

We could quote more expressions of opinion if space allowed, but we may at least congratulate the sculptor on the testimonials to the value of his work which have been elicited by an injudicious scribe.

The last leader in *The British Medical Journal* ends with these words:

We are glad that a sculptor of genius awoke one morning to find himself famous, but we are sorry and not a little ashamed that he should owe the foundations of his fame to the hypocrisy with which other countries, not wholly without reason, reproach the British people.

Appendix Two

THE TOMB OF OSCAR WILDE: 1912

The Evening Standard and St. James's Gazette, June 3rd, 1912:

THE TOMB OF OSCAR WILDE

MR. J. EPSTEIN'S DIGNIFIED SCULPTURE

Seldom in this country are we permitted to see such a dignified piece of monumental sculpture as Mr. Jacob Epstein has carved for the tomb of Oscar Wilde. It is on view at the sculptor's studio, 72 Cheyne Walk, for a month before being erected in the cemetery of Père Lachaise, in Paris. The first thing that strikes one is Mr. Epstein's regard for his material and its purpose. From the earliest ages it has been the almost universal instinct of humanity to set up a stone over the dead, but modern sculptors are too apt to forget that every touch of the chisel, though justified by the craving for expression, is a destruction of the monumental character of the stone. Mr. Epstein has not forgotten this, and his work, though an expression of human emotion, recognises the rectangular solidity implied in the idea of a tomb. It is not executed but conceived in stone. The stone he has chosen for his purpose is known as "Hopton Wood". It is a limestone that is not quite marble and has the advantage over the latter of looking already weathered, so that it takes its place at once in natural surroundings without the effect of rawness.

The conception embodied in this great block of stone is that of a winged figure driven through space by an irresistible fate. The Greek rather than the Egyptian Sphinx might have been the suggestion—though the figure is male—and in this case the Sphinx has become its own victim. The figure drives forward to sheer volition without aid from the limbs or tremor of the wings. The arms are extended backward along the sides, the knees slightly bent, and the plumes of the wings are horizontal in strictly parallel lines. Upon first approach the impression is that of the indomitable thrust of breast and shoulder. The face, remotely suggesting that of the dead writer, is a little upturned and blind to external light, the inner driving power being symbolised by little figures of Intellectual Pride and Luxury above the head. Fame, with her trumpet, is carved upon the forehead.

The work, in very high relief rather than in the round, is as reserved in execution as it is monumental in conception. The muscular divisions are suggested by linear treatment rather than by aggressive modelling, and a vertical plane would enclose the carved surface of the monument. Thus there is nothing to destroy the effect of a rectangular block of stone that has felt itself into expression.

The Tomb of Oscar Wilde: 1912

The Pall Mall Gazette, June 6th, 1912:

OSCAR WILDE'S TOMB

The tomb—for it is a tomb and not a "Monumental Marble"—which Mr. Jacob Epstein has carved for the sepulchre of Oscar Wilde in the cemetery of Père Lachaise, is now completed. Timid visitors who know much or little about sculpture have been popping in and out of Mr. Epstein's studio in Cheyne Walk during the past week, and have been retiring again in ecstasy or bewilderment, according to their temperament or their preconceived ideas of mausoleums and tombstones. For undoubtedly Mr. Epstein's notions of mortuary memorials are unconventional and quite likely to shock people who associate Gothic art so closely with religious ceremonial that a Pagan or Archaic formula becomes an offence when applied to the commemoration of the dead.

A SCULPTOR IN REVOLT

For Mr. Epstein is not only a real sculptor—a carver, not a modeller—but he is also a Sculptor in Revolt, who is in deadly conflict with the ideas of current sculpture, and who believes that it is on the wrong tack altogether. And one would be bold in denying that he may be right. Imitation of Nature, either in bronze or marble, becomes mere futility and ape-work unless it be illuminated by a plastic idea, not only closely associated with and deriving all its beauty from the medium in which it is worked, but suggested by it. As the painter's idea lies, not in literary suggestion or imitation, but in the perfection of the paint, so the carver's idea must be born in the marble and spring directly from it. It is obvious that Mr. Epstein did not propose to be either a literary or a moral critic of Oscar Wilde. This brooding, winged figure, born long ago in primitive passions, complex and yet incomplete, is a child of the marble, and is not an enlarged copy, by some other hand, of a highly finished plaster model. It has been created in anguish under the driving obsession of an idea. The hand of the sculptor has groped in the block of marble impelled to the expression, without words or definitions, of the haunting tragedy of a great career. How you are to apply this figure to the facts of Oscar Wilde's life—to his work or his character—is not a question that arises. You might as well seek for the character of the departed hero in the Funeral March. This is only Mr. Epstein's commentary, serious and profound, unobscured by conventional formulas, and inspired by an acute necessity for utterance. "Go and see it at once", is my urgent advice to all who are interested in sculpture, and think of it, if you can, on a hill-top in Père Lachaise, dominating all those tawdry memorials of the easily-forgotten dead.

Comædia, October 9th, 1912,

OSCAR WILDE

PRISONER OF THE PRÉFECTURE DE LA SEINE

On the 30th November 1900, nearly twelve years ago, Oscar Wilde breathed his last in a modest house in the Quartier Latin. His spirit, which had so often taken wing into the world of dreams, was now to take wing into the dream from which there is no awakening, the dream without end.

He had the right to believe that he was for ever rid of all the petty annoyances he had suffered at the hands of the enemies of genius, those shallow and material-minded mischief-makers who had tried—and by what foul means—to strike down this great mind.

It became evident that Oscar Wilde was never to know true peace, even beyond the grave. He had not lain at rest more than a few years beneath the flower-decked tombstone at Bagneux when he was removed to be tossed under a slab of stone surrounded by chains at the cemetery of Père Lachaise.

He was about to break these chains at last and take wing—in a halo of glory—no longer into the infinite but into immortality, but Officialdom was on the watch ... the prisoner of Reading Gaol is to-day the prisoner of M. le Conservateur du Père Lachaise.

Because of a narrow-minded official, and of the obscene laughs and remarks of some gross-minded keepers and stone-masons—no doubt deliberate on their part to win the good graces of their superior—a work of art, created in a spirit full of respect and reverence, is being kept hidden like something foul and loathsome.

Hidden? Yes; but I happen to know that these self-same keepers, enticed by a good tip, lift a corner of the thick and heavy tarpaulin to expose to the gaze of the visitors the exact place so offensive to the sight of M. le Conservateur. . . . There must be something comical about it for the smiles broaden and the coarse jokes begin to fly.

It is by low tactics of this kind that M. le Conservateur hopes to achieve his object, worthy of a M. Bérenger, to wit the fig-leaf.

Musset has his willow-tree, and M. le Conservateur would like the creator of *Salomé* to have his fig-leaf. . . .

As far back as the 16th September last, when the monument was just being placed in position, the sculptor, Jacob Epstein, went up to inspect the work, when his notice was at once drawn to a huge mass of plaster—a good kilo of it—covering up a certain part of the statue. . . . No doubt on that particular day M. le Confervateur did not have his fig-leaf handy. Jacob Epstein, incensed—as well as he might be—had the plaster removed immediately and it was then that orders were given for the tarpaulin.

The joke has gone far enough . . . M. le Conservateur has proved himself a good official, submissive, respectful of the public mentality; he will get his reward. But we ask M. le Préfet de Police or M. le Préfet de la Seine to go and see the monument in person—to examine it in detail and impartially—and then to state frankly whether a fig-leaf or a stroke of the chisel would produce the more ridiculous effect.

If the Under-secretary of State for the Beaux-Arts would condescend to take the trouble, his decision could not but be in favour of the artist.

Does M. le Conservateur mean to say he has never seen a man in his nakedness? Let him go to the Luxembourg—the Museum as well as the Gardens—and his eyes will soon be edified. The postures in certain of the statues will perhaps appear more indecent and ridiculous to him than that in the monument of Oscar Wilde.

The monument was on public exhibition in London throughout the month of June. Thousands of people, artists and otherwise, went to see it, and no official objections of any kind were raised. In fact young artists of both sexes have been conducted to inspect it by their elders—on no occasion did it give rise to the slightest remark of an indecent nature.

The newspapers, one and all alike, whatever their party and creed, were united in their eulogies.

The Tomb of Oscar Wilde: 1912

The monument has won the approval of all that have seen it, including, of course, the executor under the will of Oscar Wilde and the donor, a much-respected Scotswoman.

It was reserved for France to be the scene of this new attempt on the liberty of Art.

The work of placing the monument in position will be completed in a few days, when the date of the unveiling will be fixed. Let us hope that on that occasion no obstacle will be allowed to prevent all artists from worthily and piously commemorating the glory of the great artist of Letters, Oscar Wilde.

What point is there in trying to check his glorious flight into immortality?

GEORGES BAZILE.

Comœdia, March 21st, 1913:

A PETITION BY ARTISTS FOR THE LIBERTY OF ART

A certain number of writers and artists, contributors to "L'Action d'Art", have just proposed that a great petition be drawn up by workers with the pen, brush and chisel as a protest against the outrage on the liberty of Art contained in the decision of the Préfet de la Seine and of his Comité d'Esthétique regarding the Oscar Wilde monument at Père Lachaise.

This protest cannot pass unnoticed. In France, the land of Liberty and of Art, where the voice of the public has so often been raised with success against the acts of the Philistines, it behoves us to renew the movement of 1896, "the epoch of flaming lists and signatures"—I am quoting Ernest Lajeunesse—"the time when M. Octave Mirbeau contemplated appointing the prisoner of Reading Gaol to a promising chair at the Academie Goncourt, after M. Maurice Barrès had refused a ticket for a ball to Lord Alfred Douglas. *Salomé* was being played, and it later went on tour with Georges Vanor. *The Portrait of Dorian Gray* was hastily translated and the *Revue Bleue* published the two admirable articles by Regnier and by Paul Adam."

To-day it is not from the clutches of English judges that Oscar Wilde has to be wrested but from the hypocrisy that is holding his "Geni" a prisoner.

Following my article of the 9th October last in *Comœdia* under the title "Oscar Wilde, prisoner of the Préfecture de la Seine", Jacob Epstein, the sculptor of the monument, wrote me the following letter, and my only reason for including those passages too flattering to myself, is that they convey a mission:

"DEAR GEORGES BAZILE,

Thank you for your article in *Comœdia*. I *must* sail at once for South Africa where I have to carve some figures of lions in granite for Pretoria in the Transvaal. I have signed a contract and promised to go where my work awaits me.

After having seen your courageous attack in *Comœdia*, I can leave this hemisphere with an easier mind.

I leave it to Frenchmen like yourself to defend my work and the repose of the great soul who rests beneath it.

You can do it better than I ever could. I find my expression in a different material.

My works must speak for me.

JACOB EPSTEIN."

Epstein: An Autobiography

"I leave it to Frenchmen like yourself to defend my work." It therefore devolves on us to rise up and protest again and again and to make our voices heard in the cause of justice.

Besides, the question is not confined to the banned monument. The affair of the Oscar Wilde monument is in fact only an incident. There is something else. There is an attack on the liberty of art. The personality of the author of *Salomé* is beside the point, the religion or the nationality of the sculptor likewise, and likewise any personal views on the æsthetic quality of the monument, etc. etc.

Here is the text of the protest drawn up by the associates of "L'Action d'Art":

"... With the monument to Oscar Wilde it is the very principle of liberty for Art that is threatened. For this principle Charles Baudelaire, Gustave Flaubert, Catulle Mendes, Jean Richepin, Paul Adam, Lucien Descaves, Charles-Henry Hirsch, Steinlen, Forain, Louis Legrand, Willette, Poulbot, Grandjean, Delannoy, etc., have not shrunk from the rigours of the law.

The interdictions of the Préfecture are a danger for art, and an attack on the dignity of men of sound mind. . . .

Thinkers, artists and writers owe it to themselves to protect their rights and, beyond their rights, their ideal of liberty. We therefore trust that all will be anxious to sign our petition that the monument of Oscar Wilde shall be respected."

The signatures are already numerous. Precious support is coming from all sides. The petition must be general. There must be no abstentions. All personal grudges, all private quarrels must be wiped out in the presence of this movement in favour of liberty for art. Signatures will be received at "L'Action d'Art", 47 rue de la Gaieté.

GEORGES BAZILE.

Comœdia, April 23rd, 1913:

THE TOMB OF OSCAR WILDE

Even though M. Banville d'Hostel, director of "L'Action d'Art", does not do me the honour of including me among "the most prominent writers, poets and artists"—as he puts it; and though, in the company of M. Archipenko, Lecornu, Belisario and the ubiquitous André Arnyvelde of the modified Hebrew patronymic, this shepherd of pastoral rhyme regards me as an intruder, I nevertheless note with satisfaction the condemnation that has found voice against, and is so richly deserved by, the Préfecture de la Seine, from the lowest of its Jacks-in-Office to the august personage of M. le Préfet himself, for its dull stupidity and sickening hypocrisy.

The reader knows the facts. A sculptor, Jacob Epstein, who in no wise pretends to be a rival to Denys Puech or Antonin Mercie, modelled a figure to honour the sad memory of Oscar Wilde, the beauty of which is not called in question. Is this work by M. Epstein worth a chip from the chisel of Pierre Puget or of Rodin? "Do you only play the violin like Paganini?" asks Ducantal.

On this point the art critics—infallible as everyone knows—will pass judgment as soon as they, and with them the public, are allowed to see this piece of sculpture. But that is exactly where all the trouble lies. The pontiffs of the Préfecture, together with their minions and Jacks-in-Office, are preventing this work from seeing the light of day, under the pretext that it shamelessly shows the human form, which should be kept from the public eye because of the untold tortures it would inflict on its sense of modesty. How insane! How cowardly! A threadbare argument that will not hold water. But it is good enough for practical purposes, still serving as a weapon to wield against those men of independent mind who will not conform to the opinions of the concierge, and against those emancipated artists who refuse to butter their work to the taste of officialdom and turn out "decorative" sculpture, so-called because it unquestionably aggravates the ugliness—so characteristic—of the blanc-mange buildings that lend this officialdom support.

Virtue is a good pretext. This manœuvre, which consists of feigning a ridiculous indignation at the sight of the nude body of a man or of a woman, is designed surreptitiously to bring into bad repute rivals, competitors, men of superior quality. The defence of morals, of "principles", is designed to sharpen a weapon that helps the spurious talents to ruin the genuine ones, to single out for honorary posts and orders so many yes-men who only work to the narrow letter of instructions and merely aim at satisfying the meddling ignorance of the bourgeois.

These standards of public morals are, in France (and even elsewhere) of recent importation; they date back no further than to the invasion of the middle classes and the triumph of the Third State. They properly belong to democratic stupidity.

The Vicomte Sosthene de la Rochfoucauld, celebrated for having, under the Restoration, introduced the bustle and placed obscene plasters on antique statues, scored a success of undying laughter. He was ridiculed for his mock piety and stupidity. For prudish, deceitful and servile to hypocrisy and false values as was the transitory world from which Balzac took his models, a piece of stupidity such as this could not but shock the good manners it still retained, and its patrician habit of looking things in the face and calling a spade a spade.

The far-fetched idea of "moralising" in the plastic arts could only have occurred to shopkeepers in a state of unsound mind and strung to the stilted tune of "la Vache à Colas" by the influence of protestantism in France. The sociologists who speak of the Jewish "Conquest" are glad to omit mention of this other conquest, the conquest of the Huguenots, that invasion of the sanctimonious hypocrites, so well calculated to reduce to complete flabbiness what the public newspapers describe as the national spirit. No, not even the imagination of the Jesuits could have run to such ridiculous nonsense. They confined themselves to the "expurgation" of Horace and to watering down the ancient poets. The volumes of "ad usum delphini" satisfied their vandalism. They would not have carried their meddling to the point of practising on the marbles of Versailles or of the Vatican the operation that added to the list of the heretics the author of *Philosophoumena*. The Republic, of course, only has smiles, favours and graciousness for those sycophants who demand in the name of public morals (of which they are the agents) the sequestration of a true work of art. And this, mind you, while parents take their offspring to the theatre, the cinema, and here, there and everywhere, even to the unclean café-concert, at hours when children should be in bed; while young urchins read the newspapers bristling with adulteries, rape, lascivious and violent scenes, vulgar debauchery and blood and thunder, with illustrations to boot; while footballers, boxers, sprinters, and other intellectuals display in full sight of the heiresses of the middle classes, out in the open Bois de Boulogne and on the track of the velodrome, all that Nature endowed them with. The modern young things have known for a long time that babies do not come out of the blue carried by storks. And if one considers the filthy talk that is carried on among themselves by the pupils of the P.P. as well as by those at the University, it will take some effort to understand the reason for all this display of fig-leaves. Is anyone being deceived? No one disputes the complete harmlessness of works of art, except the aged Berenger, whose senility, without any doubt, has to endure the obsessions of an anchorite in the desert, and who—dare I say so—indulges in exhibitionism by counter-action. One can even go so far as to say, without risking anything more than shocking people with red-tape intellects, that pornography itself is not the danger it is supposed to be. Show me a man, a young woman, anyone you like, really corrupted or perverted by indecent books or pictures. Those who might be tempted by these lying, ugly and stupid portrayals of voluptuousness, will fall a prey—make no mistake about it—to more immediate temptations, to more tangible realities which the street, the college, the boarding-school and the family itself is continually giving them glimpses of.

      ·   ·   ·   ·   ·

It seems reasonable to suppose that in prohibiting the monument of Oscar Wilde, the Pharisees of the Préfecture mean to inflict yet another slur on the memory of the poet. On both sides of the Channel there is not lacking, when genius is crucified, Scribes and Sadducees to add thorns to its crown.

It is sweet honey to the failures, to the lice of literature, to the scum of journalism it is sweet and refreshing, to insult one who, from so far on high, scorned them, when he in his turn succombs, a victim of the passions which made his voice ring clear and his art persuasive. It is so easy to speak in the name of principles and of morals! Yes, easier than to write a line of prose or a distich, easier, let us say, than to have talent.

Unhappy Oscar Wilde, so triumphant at Stéphane Mallarmé's, terrifying the young poets with his dandyism, his loves, his pre-Raphaelite cravats, and his sunflowers. An "æsthete", he brought with him a singular taste, an affectation in clothes in the manner of the primitive Lombards or Florentines. One will never know what Ruskin contributed to his compatriots by way of seraphic waistcoats and robes of a pomme verte or lemon colour.

Oscar Wilde delivered himself of his paradoxes in a voice that was calm and rhythmic. He posed with the easy insolence of a Brummel or of a Sheridan, he posed as Jean Lorain would have wished to pose. But Jean Lorrain was, in spite of d'Antéros, nothing more than a provincial.

Then came the horrible adventure, the collapse, the hard labour, the unleashing of the hyenas and the asses, the poet succumbing a victim of his own pride, a pride that was English, of an arrogance superior to destiny. He could have fled from the shameful vengeance of the Marquis of Queensberry but he preferred to defy his enemy, to face him out to the end. This greatness of soul should have touched the heart of the inquisitors. It could not turn aside the verdict of twelve Anglican grocers. The rest is well known, the prison, the return to Paris, the fall of this phantom wandering among the haunts of his defunct glory. We also know the ignominious behaviour of the contemptible cowards and hypocrites whom he had once helped and obliged and who, now, did not recognise him. Death, the consoler, did not tarry long. Wilde, it is said, brought it on, himself, and died poisoned by his own hands.

To crown his posthumous glory, it was only necessary that he should be persecuted, proscribed in effigy and sequestrated by bureaucratic hypocrisy, by the stupidity of Jacks-in-Office. Nevertheless, it is not unreasonable to suppose that the name, glorious as it may be, of the Préfet de la Seine, will be more forgotten than a Pharaoh of the twenty-fourth dynasty when humanity of the future, with tears of pity and transports of gratitude, recites that sublime plaint, *The Ballad of Reading Gaol*.
LAURENT TAILHADE.

Appendix Three

THE FIRST STATUE OF CHRIST: 1920

I reproduce an article by a well-known art critic, which is a master-
piece of the taradidles which pass for thought in Bloomsbury circles.
It is written in the well-known "Fry" manner and appeared in the
Outlook of 21st February, 1920.

Having read that a figure of Christ was included in the works by Mr. Jacob
Epstein at the Leicester Galleries, I went there, fearing the worst. In the result, I
was agreeably surprised. The figure is not sensational. It might be described as a
study of a religious enthusiast. The high, compact head, earnest eyes, and eloquent
mouth are true to type; and the attitude and gesture are those of eager persuasion.

After this it may seem ungrateful to say that the figure is all wrong. It is wrong
in a way that applies to a great deal of modern art, and, therefore, it lends itself to
consideration. At this time of day neither Mr. Epstein's nor any other artist's ideas
of the Redeemer are of the least interest to anybody. They are, in the true sense of
the word, impertinent. Above a certain level of importance, all historical figures
are true in proportion as they are traditional, and any attempt to "re-interpret"
them makes them relatively untrue. Humanity may be a poor thing, but it does
not make that sort of mistake. The folly of interpretation applies even to more
accurate knowledge of the facts than is contained in the tradition. The story of the
painter, who, in the interests of accuracy, introduced into a picture of "The last
Supper" a basket of Jerusalem artichokes in ignorance that "Jerusalem" is only a
corruption of "girasole" is a lesson for all time. I have not read Mr. George
Moore's *The Brook Kerith*, but I am sure that it is full of Jerusalem artichokes.

But, apart from the folly and impertinence of all such re-interpretations, Mr.
Epstein has made another mistake: an artistic mistake. Re-interpretation, or even
interpretation, of the subject is not the business of sculpture. Rodin set a very bad
example to sculptors with his "Balzac". He might have made either a portrait of
Balzac or a symbol of his genius. As it was he combined the two, and so queered
the pitch of sculpture. Nobody would have boggled at a much more extravagant
symbol of Balzac's genius if it had not looked like a portrait. He may not be able to
reason it out, but the ordinary person seldom makes a mistake in his instinctive
dislike of artistic misapplication.

The business of the sculptor is to interpret not the subject but the material; to
make the stone or bonze or whatever it may be more like the subject than anybody
has made it before by the nice recognition and skilful handling of its properties.

257

This applies to every kind of art. If I am writing about Julius Cæsar my opportunity as an artist is not to say new things about Cæsar but to make words more like him than anybody has made them before. In his heart of hearts, Mr. Epstein knows this perfectly well, and he can do it, as may be judged from his portrait busts in this exhibition. Each of them represents a slightly different and generally felicitous translation of a living person into bronze: and collectively they establish Mr. Epstein as a sculptor of the highest talent.

Charles Marriott.

In contrast to this, I give a very thoughtful article by John Middleton Murry:

The Nation, February 14th, 1920:

There is much, and there is room for much, controversy as to who is our best painter; but there is none on the question who is our best sculptor. News editors, newspaper readers, cognoscenti—all apparently, save that strange and unknown company which hands out the commissions for our public monuments—are in agreement that Epstein is—the real thing. The real thing, we say, because the common factor in this curious consensus of opinion is not so much an agreement on the merits of Epstein's sculpture as sculpture, as an acknowledgment that he makes upon all beholders an intense and definite impression.

Epstein, in short, has succeeded to the position of Rodin, in the sense that to the contemporary mind he is Sculpture. Gaudier-Brzeska, who might have passed him in the race, is dead. Eric Gill, who had his supporters for a season, is hardly more than a stone-carver of unusual probity but not unusual imaginative power. Epstein alone is becoming a European figure on his own merits, for we have to admit that Mestrovic owed his elevation largely to the accident of a European war.

Epstein, then, is Sculpture to the modern world. That is a very good thing for the world, for Epstein is an artist through and through, and for the world to be impressed by an artist, no matter how, is a good thing. I do not doubt that more people will go to the Leicester Galleries to see a new Christ than will go to see a new Epstein. But surely that is how it was in the brave days of old, in those impassioned epochs of art which we are always in danger of regarding as animated by the exclusiveness of a modern Fitzroy Street.

The point is that several hundreds (perhaps even thousands) of people who will go to see a Christ will come away with the shock of recognition that, although they had never imagined such a Man of Sorrows, this strange embodiment of a traditional figure has impressed them deeply. So they will discover, though not in these terms, what Art can do; and they may feel, however vaguely, that civilisation itself depends, not on wealth or victories, but on the possibility of achievements like Epstein's Christ.

We may leave aside æsthetic criticism of the figure while we consider, from this angle, what its creation has involved. It has involved precisely the activity on which all ideal civilisation depends, the examination of tradition. I observe that Epstein has allowed himself to say to an interviewer: "Chacun à son Christ." Unfortunately it is not true. Millions of people have somebody else's Christ, which is equivalent to no Christ at all; just as millions of people have somebody else's justice, or patriotism, or democracy, or Mr. Lloyd George. I believe it to be true that almost as few people make up their minds about Christ as about Einstein's theory. It is one of the things they leave to other people. All the important things are. Christ is as familiar and as unreal as liberty.

And yet if one is to make up one's mind about life, one must make it up about Christ.

I do not mean that we must decide whether or not he was the Son of God—that may come afterwards—but we must decide whether he was the world's greatest man. Was he a failure? What is the true meaning of "My God! my God! why hast Thou forsaken me?" Are they or are they not the most fearful, agonising words that were ever drawn from human lips, the break of the world's greatest heart, the shattering of the sublimest and most human faith ever conceived by the spirit of man? And if they are, is it better to be broken thus on the wheel of reality? Such questions are urgent to the life of man, of which Christ is a supreme exemplar. Epstein's "Christ" is there to remind the world that it is always the artist who faces them. That is worth remembering.

Epstein's "Christ" is a man, austere, ascetic, emaciated, having no form or comeliness. He is a man of sorrows and acquainted with grief. There is pain, bodily agony, not merely in the gesture with which he points to the torn flesh of his outspread hand, but in the poise of his proud unseeing head. If he has risen from the dead, he rose as a man, by virtue of a tense and concentrated effort of the human will. Not by bodily strength. The weight and massiveness of this man are not in his limbs, not even in those large outspread hands and arms which are chiefly the symbol of his physical agony, but in the sharply cut, almost disdainful head. The head shows—or shows to me—that this Christ has suffered as a man and triumphed as a man. It has the gesture of assertion, not of surrender. I will not wait to argue with those who scent a paradox and demur that the man could not have risen from the dead. They have to learn that an artist uses symbols with mastery; he is their sovereign, not their slave. What Epstein had to express was the nature of the man who knew every second of his agony and disillusion. The man of reality swoons under the pain, gives up the ghost; but art can envisage a man who remains fully a man under suffering intolerable. This is a Christ-Prometheus.

This, at least, is my own reading of the figure, which gives me a standard by which to criticise it, though indeed there is little criticism to make. Yet it may appear that Epstein's emphasis is, in regard to the suffering, excessively physical. It is hyper-criticism, I know, when I consider the manner in which he has avoided all the melodrama of pain. But there is a suggestion of the stylite martyr, the gaunt and fanatical hermit, about the figure which, to some of us who are willing to risk being dismissed as sentimentalists, is less than adequate to the man of spiritual agony. Is there any chance of insulting a nation if we say that it is, after all, a Jewish Christ, and not the Christ of the Western World? "Why hast Thou forsaken me?" never came from this man's lips. He plumbed the depths of bodily pain, but not of spiritual disillusion.

And here we may find a sufficient clue to our reaction to the rest of the remarkable works which are being shown at the Leicester Galleries.

There has been no such masterly realistic sculpture in England, in Europe even, for years. All that a consummate apprehension of the physical object, and a superb skill in rendering it, can do, Epstein has done in these portrait busts. The modelling is extraordinary. To sit to Epstein is to assure oneself of a physical immortality. So much is certain. Yet one feels that the unique "Portrait of a Lady" in which the insistence upon the formal element is such that it has something of the air of a caricature, may have a more lasting excellence. Not because it is more formal and turns the mind to Chinese works whose force the years have not weakened, but because the more amazing triumphs of his pure realism may lack some final excellence of their own, the impress of a sensitiveness that is not solely physical.

Epstein is able to catch the equipoise of correspondence between the physical and the spiritual in his models at moments. The calm beauty of "Nan (No. 3)" is evidence of that. But the moments seem to come seldom. Of the rest of the busts one may say with complete conviction that their models were like that, but not that they were that. Take the human being at his most physical and Epstein will give a rendering before which criticism is merely vocal admiration. There are four studies of a baby which are the very culmination of the modeller's art in finding plastic equivalents for textures. But the human being who has begun to inhabit his body as a sojourner, identical with it only for fleeting seconds, seems loth to deliver himself up to Epstein's keeping. And indeed the soul would be none too safe in his hands, which are those of a ruthless craftsman, an artist of impassioned and dominating, yet somehow constrained and limited conceptions.

It is for this reason that we return to ask whether, although it is good for the world that Epstein should be Sculpture for it, it is good for Epstein? Here is an artist who, in addition to a technical mastery unequalled in our age, has a powerful and original genius, a genius which by its own limitations seems superbly fitted for the constraint and mastery of stone. Should he be side-tracked into portraiture by the necessity of having to fill a rôle? Here is a man of whom it could safely be said that were he given a Pyramid to decorate, his work would have congruity and significance. Let him then carve our monuments, and leave to others the task of immortalising the houris of the hour. Others have time to wait for conjunctures of soul and body; Epstein has not. The service of a new Ozymandias calls him urgently.

JOHN MIDDLETON MURRY.

For this article Mr. Murry, I remember, was severely taken to task by the *Nation's* art critic, and admonished not to enter a field sacred to himself. "If the intelligentsia are to speak on art let them do so with one voice and not divide their allegiance and so create confusion."

The Sunday Times, February 8th, 1920:

JACOB EPSTEIN

Nothing is more pleasurable for a critic than to find his judgment confirmed by time. After long years of neglect, of unintelligent and abusive depreciation, of misdirection and misunderstanding, the art of Jacob Epstein has become recognised and respected. Through all the sordid controversy over his work for the British Medical Association and the Wilde Monument in Paris, I reiterated, often to deaf ears, my conviction of the genius of the sculptor, and the belief in him, from which I have never wavered, has been amply justified by his continued production of masterpieces, works which during the last few years have gained the acceptance of all whose opinion counts.

The exhibition of Epstein's recent sculpture, which opened yesterday at the Leicester Galleries, is a splendid manifestation of his powers, revealing both his

First Statue of Christ: 1920

sculptural technique as a modeller and the inventive imagination which hall-marks his conceptions.

Of his portrait busts it is difficult to single out one for praise above the others, but if there is one more impressive than the rest, it is his new bust of "Lilian Shelley" (5), a model with whom he has excelled before. The bust shows the arms of the sitter, and there is a new note in the grace of the bent arms and exquisitely moulded hands, while the treatment of the head has a positive majesty.

It is a noble work, which will certainly count among the greatest and most beautiful of all Epstein's heads. If I refer first to these busts it is not because I am blind to the importance of his statue of Christ, but because I feel that the heads are beyond controversy, and since there may still be argument about the full-length figure. I would ask those not yet fully familiar with the sculptor's work to approach the statues by the busts.

The reason why I expect acrimonious discussion about the Christ is because Epstein, being an original creative artist, has not presented us with the conventional rendering. He has conceived a young Christ, not emaciated as that of Mestrovic, but gaunt, ascetic, with a slight suggestion of the Mongolian in type, and—now for it—with a dimly perceptible beard. It is amazing how a little thing like this upsets some people. "But he's got no beard". This was the first comment I overheard in the exhibition, and I'll wager it has been and will be repeated many times. Those who thus protest do not pause to think that all beards have to be grown, and that if the artist chooses to select an age when the growth is incomplete, that is entirely his affair, and is neither incongruous nor irreligious.

Epstein's conception of Christ—a strong, stern, ascetic young Christ—is not an ordinary one. But Epstein himself is not an ordinary man—if he were, he would not be the great sculptor he is, It has always been his conception, not his execution, that has puzzled the public and stood in the way of wider recognition of his talent, and that is why I say again: study the busts to learn respect for the master crafts-man before you attempt to criticise the stature, the work of the creative artist.

FRANK RUTTER.

The Sunday Times, February 8th, 1920

EPSTEIN'S CHRIST

A NOVEL ASPECT

By *The Rev. Edward Shillito*

In his daring figure of the Christ, Mr. Epstein has broken with the tradition of Christian art. This is not the Christ as Leonardo painted Him: nor is it the Christ of Russian art. There are some resemblances in method between Mr. Epstein and M. Mestrovic, whose Strange Man from the Cross revealed the sorrowful and broken-hearted Saviour; but the difference between the two interpretations is profound. Mr. Epstein has made his Christ before all things powerful; He is revealed at the moment when He says to Thomas: "Behold my hands and my side." There is an assurance of triumph in His face, and almost a touch of scorn in the curve of His mouth, as though He had overcome and derided the vain world which had crucified Him. Power is in every line; the flat crown of the head; the shoulders; the defiant chin; the intellectual brows; the immense hands and feet; by all such means the artist shows that for him Christ is not the gentle and passive

261

being of Christian art, but the fierce and even violent leader of men. There is an absence of charm; clearly there is no beauty that man should desire Him; He looks stern and austere, and yet terrible in His intensity of passion.

Such interpretations are new in art; are they new in the Gospel?

It must be admitted at once that this Christ would never make sense of the Gospel as a whole. No one could picture this Man taking children in His arms and sharing in feasts with publicans and sinners; the Christ of the Gospel was sharply distinguished from John the Baptist, the austere prophet. This Christ would have come like John, "neither eats nor drinks". This Christ would never have smiled or wept. Men would have feared Him and obeyed Him, and even died for Him; they would scarcely have loved Him.

Yet there is another figure in the Gospel, and the value of this great work lies in the insight which has led the artist to interpret this other strand in the story This may have been the Christ of whom men said: "Elijah is returned." This may have been the Christ who strode ahead of His disciples towards the city, and they were afraid of Him. This Christ might have cleansed the Temple and cursed the fig-tree. It is as though the artist has personified this aspect of the historical Christ.

It has surprised students of the Gospel that this has not been done by artists before now; the dramatic possibilities are great, and yet have remained unexpressed.

Because Mr. Epstein has dared to break new ground, his art is to be welcomed even by those who do not find in his interpretation, any more than in Leonardo's, the whole Christ. They will find a justice done at least to the power and mastery of the Saviour, who marched upon Jerusalem and took command, and held it in His grasp even after they had crucified Him.

YOUTH ADVANCING, 1951

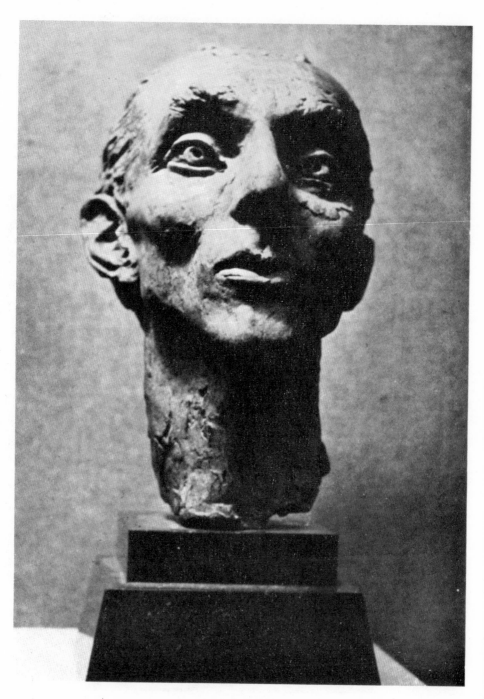

MARK JOFFE, 1952

Appendix Four

"RIMA": W. H. HUDSON MEMORIAL: 1925

COPY OF MEMORANDUM SENT TO HIS MAJESTY'S
FIRST COMMISSIONER OF WORKS

29th November, 1925.

To:
THE RT. HON. VISCOUNT PEEL, G.C.B.,
    H.M. First Commissioner of Works

MY LORD,

HUDSON MEMORIAL, HYDE PARK

As (A), a Member of the Hudson Memorial Committee, and as (B), one of the Trustees appointed to govern the modern side of the National Gallery, and as (C), a professional artist of some thirty years' standing, I beg respectfully to submit for your Lordship's consideration the following memorandum of points arising out of the controversy over Mr. Epstein's sculptured Panel which forms part of the W. H. Hudson Memorial in the Bird Sanctuary, Hyde Park.

(A) (i) It is in your Lordship's knowledge that the Memorial was erected by our Committee on due authority granted by His Majesty as Royal Ranger of his Parks, at the request of H.M.O.W., and on the favourable report of the Advisory Committee which assisted your Lordship's predecessor in arriving at a decision. The Minute Book of our Committee held February 21st, 1924, states that our Chairman, Mr. Cunninghame Graham, reported that he had received a letter from the Secretary of His Majesty's Office of Works, informing him that the Memorial had been accepted by His Majesty and H.M.O.W.

This permission was granted for our Memorial as it stands to-day, and in accordance with the usual practice, was taken by our Committee to cover any slight modification which the practical carrying out of the work rendered necessary, or such as were the results of requests on the part of H.M.O.W. In the professional opinion of our official architects, expressed in the course of their letter to *The Morning Post*, November 27th, 1925, "We think that unusual care was taken that all parties concerned should be quite satisfied as to the exact nature of the Memorial, of which Mr. Epstein's Rima Relief formed the most important feature."

Our Committee deposited for the consideration of H.M.O.W.:

(1) The customary architects' plans and elevations of the Memorial.
(2) A large plaster model to the scale of 1 inch–1 foot, made under the

263

sculptor's direction and showing clearly the Rima Relief Panel and the Bird Baths.

(3) A correct perspective drawing of the whole Memorial as it actually has been carried out, also clearly showing Mr. Epstein's Panel as the central feature of the scheme.

I submit that the only alternative open to our Committee must be deemed fantastic and entirely novel, viz., to get our sculptor to complete his carved Panel in stone and on some carriage capable of bearing the immense weight, perambulate your Lordship's Office for authority and afterwards the inhabited globe for subscriptions; for even then the landscape setting would be missing and the fact that the public cannot approach the Panel closer than a distance of seventy feet from the eye, be misunderstood, as it is misunderstood even to-day, by those who judge, not the Memorial itself but, "close-up" newspaper photographs.

In a word we followed scrupulously the best procedure in these matters, and I venture to assert to your Lordship that few Memorials of any kind have more closely resembled the pictures and models submitted on their behalf to a First Commissioner for his information and decision than did ours.

(ii) Turning now to the allegation that the Memorial does not carry out the wishes of its Subscribers, this is, I submit, a pure assumption which is easily disposed of by the following facts and figures:

It is true that the first Public Appeal by our Committee (issued very soon after the Meeting of Mr. Hudson's friends and admirers convened by Mr. Cunninghame Graham on November 28th, 1922, at which our Committee was nominated) does not mention the Rima Panel by Mr. Epstein, but only that the Meeting "desired a representation in stone or marble which should bear a medallion of him and also serve as a drinking and bathing place for birds; such Memorial to be erected if possible in conjunction with a Bird Sanctuary in one of the Royal Parks of London," and a certain amount of money was received as a result of this Appeal. Subsequently, Mr. Epstein the sculptor, was approached to give his advice to the Committee and submitted his first model for their consideration. This showed a Relief of Mr. Hudson with Bird Baths underneath. Mr. Epstein did not consider a Medallion suitable for the site which H.M.O.W. told us they were now prepared to grant as the Hudson Memorial Bird Sanctuary (if we could produce a scheme meeting with H.M.O.W. approval), because it was evident that the Bird Baths must be placed at some distance within the enclosure to which the public could have no access, and a Medallion would consequently not be seen.

This sketch model was submitted to H.M.O.W., but the Committee were informed at once that no representation of an individual could be allowed in the Royal Parks and only some sort of decorative Relief would be permitted. Hence *any* representation, by Medallion or otherwise, of Mr. Hudson was now ruled out.

After deliberation our Committee evolved in consultation with Mr. Epstein another scheme with "Rima" from Hudson's *Green Mansions* as the subject, and he was formally commissioned by a letter from our Hon. Secretary, dated February 15th, 1923, to undertake a Relief Panel of "Rima", and the commission was formally accepted by him in a letter to the Committee dated Feby. 18th, 1923. In these letters exchanged, the sculptor undertook that he would "Be prepared to endeavour to satisfy H.M.O.W. with regard to the design." This commission was given to the artist after a visit to his studio to see a model of the Rima Panel, to which visit all members of the Committee were invited.

Accordingly, Mr. Epstein completed his model which was submitted together with a careful perspective drawing and plans by our architect to H.M.O.W. and its Advisory Committee on June 22nd, 1923. Our Committee were informed in due course by H.M.O.W. that their scheme had been rejected as unsuitable.

Notwithstanding this disappointment our sculptor and architects undertook to prepare a new design and after consultation with our Committee this was finally evolved and submitted to H.M.O.W. It was accepted by your Lordship's predecessor at a Meeting with his advisors in February, 1924, before which Meeting I was called as the representative of the Hudson Memorial Committee prepared to furnish any information about our scheme which might be necessary. The exhibits which were before this Meeting have been already described.

On receiving official notification from H.M.O.W. that our Memorial had been accepted for erection in Hyde Park (February, 1924), our Committee prepared a new and wider appeal for funds to carry out the project which had now received official sanction and which they could now confidently assure intending subscribers would actually be erected. Up to the date of this new Appeal we had received £680, of which sum the Committee themselves had contributed £167. As none of our Committee have resigned, their contributions may fairly be deducted from the first sum given, leaving £513 as contributions received before our scheme included Mr. Epstein's Rima Panel, though in the case of many of these contributors to our funds in this first category we actually know that they consider the final scheme as erected a great improvement on our first and necessarily tentative ideas.

Be that as it may, we actually received £1,150 new money as a result of our new Appeal, which contained a clear description of the Panel, Mr. Epstein's name as our sculptor, and (what is more important) a good reproduction of the same careful perspective drawing showing clearly the Panel as the central portion of the scheme which had been produced at H.M.O.W. when the matter was up for your predecessor's approval.

There seems no doubt that the promise of this Panel by a well-known, and, in the opinion of many, distinguished sculptor, induced many people to subscribe who would not otherwise have been interested in our Memorial. This perspective picture also accompanied our Appeal for funds in *The Times, The Manchester Guardian* and elsewhere in March, 1924. *Country Life* kindly opened a special fund for our scheme on March 22nd, 1924, and received money for us by an Appeal in which the same picture was again given great prominence. For the information of our subscribers and to aid our funds we were now anxious to exhibit Mr. Epstein's large model of the Panel, together with plans of our whole scheme. As, however, the leading sculptors in the Royal Academy were believed to be out of sympathy with Mr. Epstein's work, and we had little grounds for supposing his model would be accepted for exhibition if offered there, and as the Royal Academy is the only exhibition in London which exhibits sculpture, we were glad to take the opportunity of showing the model at the public exhibition of the Architect Club in

Grosvenor House in the spring of 1924—an Exhibition widely commented upon in the Press and where our model met with friendly criticism.

As the figures given above will show, we are a Committee with only modest financial resources and were anxious to keep subscribers' money on the Memorial itself. Hence we could not keep in touch with our 850 subscribers in all parts of the globe. It was financially impossible and, I submit, unreasonable, to expect us to do this. We looked to the official opening to satisfy everyone their money had been well spent, as they clearly understood from the pictures and descriptions in these Public Appeals exactly what we desired to do. We did our best to secure publicity for our scheme, fully understanding that it was that scheme alone which we were authorised by H.M.O.W. to erect in Hyde Park.

As those who sent us their subscriptions before the final form of the Memorial was evolved and widely reproduced, have in but a few cases expressed dissatisfaction to the Committee, it is a pure assumption that many of them object to the finished Memorial. In any case, apart from the Committee they number 259 subscribers out of a total number of 850, and they contributed £513 out of a total of £1,830 received. From their 850 subscribers the Committee have only received four letters of complaint.

Doubtless some subscribers in addition to the above four are disappointed with the finished Memorial, but of what Memorial can that not be said? And against it may be set off the enhanced pleasure of other subscribers who tell us they did not expect anything so good, together with the receipt of a number of subscriptions since the Memorial was unveiled by the Prime Minister.

It is clearly impossible to assemble our subscribers from all parts of the globe. This course, for instance, has never been suggested even in the case of the Cavell Monument, with which wide dissatisfaction has been publicly expressed.

The attitude of some unruly members of the London public (a public to whom we consider we have made a present of a notable and dignified work after considerable financial costs to ourselves and anxious labours) should not be allowed to outweigh the claim we respectfully make for your Lordship's protection to save our Memorial from violence and disrespect. A public work duly authorised being, in our respectful submission, like a peaceful citizen who relies confidently upon the protection of the Law.

(B) Again, as one of the Trustees of the National Gallery, British Art, appointed by H. M. Treasury and whose duty it clearly is to reflect carefully on the permanent interests of art in our country, other considerations arise in my mind.

(i) If the question of retaining or removing the sculptured Panel (forming the central feature of the Memorial and without which it would be artistically of little moment) be referred to the Fine Art Commission because this controversy has arisen, and not withstanding the correct official title on which it was erected; then clearly *all* public monuments can be so referred and the labours of the Commission enter at once a truly formidable field of retrospective deliberation. I submit to your Lordship that the overwhelming responsibility of this gigantic task should not be lightly thrust on the Commission by any Government of the day. For it is obvious that if a mere manifesto by thirteen members of the public supported by a newspaper can set a reference to the Commission in motion, any other thirteen persons supported by another newspaper must be granted, in common fairness, equal rights.

This cannot be to the public interest, as the chopping and changing of our public statuary would be endless and degenerate at last into mere expressions of reprisals. Moreover, the Commission would inevitably, I imagine, find itself as divided as any other body on the merits of past work and could not hope to speak with an authoritative voice; and your Lordship, I submit, is the best judge if the question is simply one of determining whether or no the work was erected with proper official permission.

(ii) It is true that a valuable principle may emerge from the present controversy, namely, that no Memorial, however good its title, should be considered irremovable, and there I reach agreement with the objectors to the Hudson Memorial. How such a revision of existing public monuments can best be set in motion where the objections raised (as in this case) are those of artistic merit, is a difficult problem which might well engage the attention of the Commission; but there will be general agreement, I think, to this proposition: That it is unreasonable to destroy any such works a few months after unveiling, when no general agreement on their merits can be possible, and when the subscribers who have paid for the work have not yet had the opportunity of viewing it, and moreover, in an age when artistic ideals are so sharply at variance as in our own time.

That the permanent public interest might suffer by authorities yielding to hasty action, and mistaking a momentary feeling for a reasoned verdict, the contemporary account of the stoning of Michael Angelo's "David" by the Florentine public on that statue being first unveiled in the square at Florence and the account of the strong guard that was required to defend it night and day, is one pertinent footnote; and the brutal attack by Charles Dickens in *Household Words* on the very picture by Sir John Millais (then aged twenty) for which we, of the Tate Board, had no difficulty in raising the £10,000 required for its purchase for the National Gallery, is another.

(iii) And it cannot be in the public interest to humiliate a well-known and experienced sculptor who has done his best with a public commission, in case the unfortunate precedent is established that no sculpture of a bold or unconventional kind can ever hope to secure official permission for its erection or official support afterwards—a depressing conclusion which would be fatal to the true interests of English sculpture, an art in which we lag behind other nations and hence require every stimulus that is possible.

(iv) In conclusion, from this aspect a broad and tolerant comprehension of the many opposed styles of contemporary art seems called for on the part of the authorities. Legitimate artistic discussion and disagreement is one thing, but for the authorities to intervene at the bidding of one small group of disputants and their newspaper and destroy work which at the moment was unpopular, would, I submit to your Lordship with confidence, be disastrous and short-sighted.

(C) (i) Glancing now hastily (for I fear to weary your Lordship) at the third aspect of the matter I am competent to discuss (viz., from the standpoint of a professional artist), I think it is forgotten by the objectors to the Hudson Memorial, that removal, however carefully carried out, of the Rima Panel is tantamount to its destruction.

Not only is it a deep stone and a real part of the wall and not a mere face to it, but it is peculiar in having to be effective to the eye at a long distance, as it is set far back in the Sanctuary to which the public have no access. Hence small niceties of workmanship were judged by the sculptor to be out of place and a work bold and generally effective, even if rough, was thought desirable. The work would consequently be useless if detached from its position. As well expect that one of the large Apostles by Bernini from the top of the western façade of St. Peter's would prove a desirable ornament in the gallery. A familiar example of similar work is the figure of Nelson in Trafalgar Square—all these works having been designed with the exaggerations of form their sculptors' experience decided was necessary for the peculiar positions they were destined to occupy.

(ii) Another consideration is this—wasting of the Portland Stone exposed to the open air in London.

Mr. Epstein had observed that in the small Portland Stone fountain (by Bruce Joy) not far from the Hudson Memorial and representing a nude girl arising out of the basin of the fountain, the wasting of the stone on small and neatly finished shapes has eaten the modelling of the face and figure completely away and produced a most unpleasant effect. He therefore came to the conclusion that stone carvings exposed to London air must become completely obliterated and sink into shapeless stone in a comparatively short space of time. In order therefore to allow for this inevitable wastage (especially disastrous in the case of bas-relief, as that work has no outline beyond the square of its slab), and as his material is not marble or bronze or granite, but relatively soft stone, he considered it his duty to his clients and his own reputation to provide no small forms which such wastage could immediately seize upon, but rather to keep the effect as large and weighty as possible.

As the Relief is a work entirely carved by his own hands (and an interesting example of this modern movement to get back to real carving by the artist himself, and not the mere mechanical reproduction of clay originals) he has been able to leave the stone when he has defined the principal masses and given figure and birds that sense of movement and energy which is the imaginative spirit of the work. Consequently to many eyes the work in its present state may be said to look "raw" and unnecessarily heavy, but I am convinced that Mr. Epstein's instinct in the matter has been right and that no other course was open to an artist hewing a work in rough stone for a London climate, and a work, be it remembered, meant to be seen a long distance off.

It is highly probable, for careful attention was given by architect and sculptor to the known weathering of Portland stone in a south-eastern aspect, that in a few years this "rawness" will no longer exist and that "the margin of safety" allowed by the sculptor for weathering will have completely justified itself and a mellow weathering will have lent chiaroscuro to the whole Memorial stone.

The uninstructed public cannot, of course, be expected to understand these matters at present, but will doubtless come to see that the sculptor's work was informed by a real and far-sighted knowledge of the conditions of his craft. If the above is considered it will be apparent on this ground alone how unspeakable is the cruelty which would destroy an artist's work but a few months old and so frustrate all hope of our seeing its maturity.

(iii) And it should be weighed here, I think, that the claim of the younger unacademic artist to represent contemporary artistic thought, as well as older and typically academic artists, is not altogether an unreasonable one.

However that may be, to my mind there is a rough nobility and energy in the Panel which is impressive and agrees well with the austerity of the whole architectural and garden setting. Better than a pretty and polished thing it gives a feeling of power and remoteness which to my mind (and I knew the man) is very well in keeping with that strange figure, who was of English descent but born of American parents in a wild part of the Argentine and there reared; who saw England for the first time when in his twenty-ninth year, and lived amongst us an unnaturalised alien till his sixtieth, yet who taught us more than any other modern writer wherein lies the true savour and beauty of our own land.

I have the honour to be,

Your Lordship's obedient Servant,

MUIRHEAD BONE.

Appendix Five

THE UNDERGROUND HEADQUARTERS'
BUILDING: 1929

The discussion that followed the exposing of the groups was as usual carried on with vehemence. Sir Reginald Blomfield took up the cudgels against what he called "The Cult of Ugliness" and sent the following letter to *The Manchester Guardian*:

"THE CULT OF UGLINESS"

By *Sir Reginald Blomfield*, Past President of the Institute of
British Architects

The sculpture by Mr. Epstein and his colleagues in the new building of the Underground Railway at St. James's Park has raised in an unusually acute form the question what one is to think of it all. Is this new manner serious art or is it just bluff? It is regarded with enthusiastic admiration by some and with loathing not less whole-hearted by others. That it is something quite new in the art of civilised countries is obvious; indeed, its advocates openly condemn modern sculpture from Pheidias down to the present day, and its exponents repudiate what has hitherto been regarded as the normal anatomy of the human figure. Yet it is entitled to a hearing, and as in his sympathetic article (*Manchester Guardian* July 20) your correspondent "J. B." has stated very ably the case for the new manner I venture to offer one or two considerations on the other side. I doubt if everyone will accept his statement that "Rima" no longer arouses the angry feelings that she did at her first appearance in Hyde Park, and, though it is difficult to assess the effect of fashion and connoisseurship in forming permanent opinion, it is, I think, begging the question to assume that it is only a matter of time before the new manner comes into its own and that the fashionable opinion of the moment will be the verdict of posterity.

At the St. James's Park station the new manner is in full blast with varying degrees of blatance; for Mr. Epstein was not the only sculptor there. In regard to his two groups, I admit the impressiveness of the group of "Night" with all its sinister suggestiveness. As to his group of "Day" I keep silence, yea, even from good words or any other words, because our judgments of contemporary art must to some extent be tentative and experimental. Mr. Epstein's ability is undeniable. He is not perhaps on the level of any artists we have produced since the middle

270

years of the Eighteenth Century, as a Mr. Sitwell had the temerity to say under the auspices of the B.B.C., forgetting all about Alfred Stevens, but Mr. Epstein showed what he could do many years ago in the remarkable figures of the well-known building in the Strand. The promise of those halcyon days seems to have faded away, and Mr. Epstein seems to me to have imprisoned his considerable natural powers within the iron cage of formula—of a simplification which has degenerated into distortion and an expressionism which has ended in the grotesque.

For one reason or another, the cult of ugliness seems to have taken the place of the search for beauty which from time immemorial has been the aim of artists. In so far as this is a breakaway from insipidity and convention it has the sympathy of thoughtful people; but there is another and very much graver side to the question —so far this has only shown itself in isolated cases in England—and it turns on the fundamental issue—Is there or is there not an absolute beauty? Because, if there is not, one thing is as good as another, and this appears to be the view of some people judging by the subjects they choose and the manner in which they present them. I think a stand should be made in these things—as liberal as possible, yet a definite stand. Bestiality still lurks below the surface of our civilisation, but why grope about for it in the mud, why parade it in the open, why not leave it to wallow in its own primeval slime?

The Manchester Guardian article:

EPSTEIN'S ART

HIS LAST TWO SCULPTURES

By *James Bone*

Storms of criticism, rising at times into terms of honest, full-blooded abuse that are rarely heard in art controversy in England, although common enough, indeed usual, in France at the appearance of any new expression in art, have greeted the appearance of the two sculpture groups by Mr. Epstein over the portals of the new Building of the Underground Railway at St. James's Park Station, Westminster. At the same time a number of artists, architects, and critics, whose opinions are worthy of respect, have expressed their admiration for these works. The position to-day, indeed, is like that which followed the unveiling of Mr. Epstein's Hudson Memorial relief in Hyde Park a couple of years ago, and also that of his statues on the British Medical Association Building in the Strand some twenty years ago. No party would raise an outcry now about the Strand figures, and if they did, people would now probably be only surprised, while even Rima in her grove in Hyde Park has ceased to arouse angry feelings, and has become, indeed, one of the sights that the modern Londoner likes to take his visitors to see after the cloying candy of the Peter Pan statue. The figures on Underground House, however, are now on trial, and as the Scots say "tholing their assize". That they are extremely distasteful on first sight to a considerable number of people of culture and taste is undeniable, much as Rodin's Balzac was to the Parisians of that time. Mr. Epstein has at any rate succeeded in making people look at and even think about architectural sculpture, and one cannot easily remember any other architectural sculpture in London that has done that. Whether we like it or not, Mr. Epstein in whatever he does commands our attention and makes us think about the nature of sculpture. And his work, however he may shock the complacency of a country that is as poor in sculpture as it is rich in poetry, and has very little to show the stirring of new ideas in art that are moving over Europe, has to be taken seriously, for no one acquainted with the subject will deny that he is a skilled and gifted artist, and that his portrait busts, at least, are among the outstanding works of this age. If he chooses to express himself in the arbitrary forms of sculpture he uses, we cannot say it is because he has not the skill to represent a man as closely as a Madame Tussaud figure does. The groups at Underground House must be accepted as his conception of architectural sculpture, however naughty it is of him to think so. He really must know something about his job.

"NIGHT"

"Night", which was the first of the two groups to be free of scaffolding, did not quite rouse the old hostility, although most people frankly did not like it. The subject is a mother figure of a heavy Eastern type with a male figure lying on her lap, whom she is stilling to sleep with a gesture of a mighty hand. The shapes are simplified to their bare essentials and carved with a hard square expressiveness without regard to anything but the sculptural idea. The horizontal line of the recumbent figure repeats with a curved variation the line of the stone course over the doorway: the leg of the male figure, curved at the knee, with its drooping foot is echoed on the other side by the shoulder and hand of the female figure. The rhythm of the design runs through all its parts, which fall into three main planes receding towards the top. It is an elemental conception of night, ponderable and remote, making strange calls to our consciousness.

"DAY"

"Day" is harder to accept. A large father figure with a fierce face, flat and hard and round like the sun at noon, holds and presents a male child standing between his knees, while the child stretches up his arms towards the neck of his father, his face turning upwards in a gesture of reluctance to face his task. The main pattern of the group is made of the two pairs of arms, the small ones within the larger, and the four legs forming the base. It is one of the most inventive Mr. Epstein has evolved; again the sculptor has sought to express his idea in the starkest, most simplified forms, with a severe squareness of effect. His task was to produce an architectural decoration by carving a projecting part of the actual stone of the building, and this he has done with an appropriate imagination and evocative power adequate for the emphasis of the portal on the face of this sheer, tower-like building with its regiments of windows.

But there are points about this group that are difficult to get over, particularly the modelling of the upper part of the child's body, where the chest seems to have been carved away, and the treatment of the arm; while the squareness of the legs changes to a rounded treatment of the body as though the sculptor had two minds about his technique. But the powers to imagine and deliver his idea, with its uncanny fire, are tremendously there. Learned men tell us that there is nothing Assyrian or African about his art and no resemblance to Archaic rock-carving! In short they deny the art pedigree that many writers would force upon him. But if Epstein has taken his studies of these works so deeply into the body of his art that they cannot be identified it only increases the suspicion that there is something new as well as something alien to our habits of thought in his sculpture. Before we reject it with abuse we might perhaps take a little time to get used to it. We can't be quite sure right off that he is not saying new things to us that we have to tune our ears to hear.

> *Change is the pulse of life on earth;*
> *The artist dies but art lives on:*
> *New rhapsodies are ripe for birth*
> *When every rhapsodist seems gone*
> *So, to my day's extremity*
> *May I, in patience infinite*
> *Attend the beauty that must be,*
> *And, though it slay me, welcome it.*

Yes, but do we know that Epstein is bringing new beauty to our generation. Well, it seems to the present writer to be here "burning bright", although to many it is still "in the forests of the night".

The Evening Standard, July 1st, 1929, article by R. H. Wilenski:

Epstein's "Day" and "Night" are the grandest stone carvings in London. To say this is grossly to under-praise them.

It is like saying that the Great Pyramid is a grander headstone than any to be found in England, or that "Tristan and Isolde" is a grander love song than "I can't help lovin' dat man".

The groups may not be a suitable decoration for the headquarters of a railway that exists because Londoners to-day scurry like rats underground to seek their daily bread. It may not please those who are flocking to see the picture of "Salomé" of which a glimpse is vouchsafed with much trumpetings every other week.

"Day" from the standpoint of such art lovers is lamentably lacking in bowdlerized sex appeal. It cannot be apprehended by the man who has left his deeper self at home, while he transacts business or enjoys himself. It cannot be apprehended by a vain woman or a self-satisfied modeller in clay. But it can be apprehended by every man and woman who can grasp the ideas of the words Time and Form in the abstract. Because the spirit that created these grand carvings is a spirit of all time, and the brain that carved them is a brain that can invent symbolic form.

Such spirits and such brains are rare. They are the brains and spirits of the great artists.

"Night" and "Day" are certainly the best things that Epstein has yet done.

Appendix Six

"GENESIS": 1931

I will quote a few only of the criticisms of this statue so long worked and brooded over by me.

Here is an extract from *The Daily Express* of February 7th, 1931:

EPSTEIN'S BAD JOKE IN STONE

MONGOLIAN MORON THAT IS OBSCENE

O you white foulness! He called you "Genesis"! O yes, he has a genius for titles, this man who cracks bad jokes with a chisel. He called you "Genesis".

The place was the Leicester Galleries in Leicester Square. I have told you the title of the statue, the man who did it was Jacob Epstein. He was holding there an exhibition of his work. He was also exhibiting this thing called "Genesis".

Over "D.D." I occasionally write light accounts of things and people in the newspapers. Yesterday I was sent to the Galleries, to be humorous, maybe slightly witty. About this statue I cannot.

This thing, fashioned from white marble, shows a Mongolian type of woman. One gigantic hand, with square fingers, rests across the stomach. It has no legs, the body merging into a chunk of roughly chipped marble. The face is the face of a Moron, with the vapid horrible stare of the idiot! The thick lips pout with beastly complacence under the stone blob which I presume is the nose.

Artistically the thing is absurd. Anatomically, it is purely comic. It is a bad joke of expectant motherhood.

The Daily Mail article:

MR. EPSTEIN'S LATEST—AND HIS WORST

The latest contribution of Mr. Epstein to art is a large statue in marble called "Genesis"—he is good at titles—which will be on view at the Leicester Galleries, London, next week.

The photograph we publish affords clear proof that the sculptor in his ideas of beauty grows every year more peculiar.

It is possible to make out a case for the stone images of his which have excited so much wrath and derision—quite unjustly, think many broad-minded critics—but it is difficult to imagine what defence can be offered for this simian-like creature whose face suggests, if anything, the missing link.

"Genesis": 1931

The rest of the statue is in keeping with the brutish face. Apart from the extreme ugliness of the figure, the conception is harsh and unsympathetic to the theme, doing violence to the cultured observer's sense of the fitness of things.

HE DOESN'T ARGUE

I have been among the warmest admirers of Mr. Epstein; this time I have warned him that he has flagrantly invited trouble. But he is as unrepentant and as self-satisfied as ever.

"What need was there," I said to him more in sorrow than anger, "to give the lady such an ugly face?" "Ugly!" was his astonished reply. "*You* say ugly, but *I* don't agree with you. It is not ugly to me. I pursue only my own ideas, not anybody else's."

The mischief is that you cannot argue with Epstein. He is a law unto himself. Like most artists and sculptors, he has no gift for self-criticism. The last thing on earth he knows is whether his work is good or bad. As a rule he is prepared to believe that his last performance is the best.

"Genesis" will be a great draw, but it will be a draw for the very opposite reason that a sculptor of Mr. Epstein's quality should desire.

His next exercise in stone should be Einstein's "Relativity"—a subject on which he could be positively paralysing, and as only eight people in the world understand "Relativity", he would be safe against criticism.

The Daily Telegraph, February 7th, 1931 :

A STATUE UNFIT TO SHOW

JACOB EPSTEIN'S "GENESIS"

COARSE AND REPELLENT

By *R. R. Tatlock*

The central feature of the exhibition at the Leicester Galleries, to be opened privately to-day and to the general public on Monday, is the immense statue in marble entitled "Genesis" by Jacob Epstein.

The widespread criticism of this artist's "Night" and "Day" on the building of the Underground Railway by St. James's Park will be recalled. The new work eclipses these so far as oddity of design and peculiarity of psychological conception are concerned. It portrays a pregnant woman.

Both in ancient and in modern art, fecundity has been represented many times with the delicacy and reverence proper to the theme. The ideas and emotions associated in the thoughts of normal healthy-minded artists and art lovers with this subject have again and again been expressed by artists. But this sort of thing is in an altogether different category.

HEAVY AND INARTISTIC

As an art critic, I am bound to consider as best I can a work of art purely from the æsthetic standpoint. But there are times when this habit of detachment breaks down; and this, so far as I am concerned, is one of those occasions.

275

Regarded purely and simply as a work of art, the statue appears to me to be uncouth. I mean by that I do not very much like the effect of the relationship of the forms. The ensemble is, or appears to me to be, far too heavy—so much so, indeed, that one's impression is of something uncouth and inartistic.

The statue, as a work of art, lacks altogether that finesse and elegance and that lyrical quality invariably present in a first-rate creation. The object has not a note of music and not a line of poetry in it, and in this respect is in a sharp contrast with some of the portrait busts in bronze, by the same artist, which surround it.

VISION OF HOLINESS

But it is not unfair to an artist if the observer, whether he be an art critic or not, should take exception, if he is so minded, to anything like gratuitous coarseness. That "Genesis" is coarse few will doubt.

Epstein goes out of his way to impress us, not with his sense of beauty (a sense which he certainly possesses), but with what is ugly, and does not hesitate to thrust upon us a vision of maternity, usually treated as a thing almost sacred, that can only repel and cannot conceivably delight or entertain.

For our delectation he presents us with the figure of a woman with a face like an ape's, with breasts like pumpkins, with hands twice as large and gross as those of a navvy, with hair like a ship's hawser. There are other details of the figure which one simply does not care to discuss.

With these remarks I am content to leave the question except to add the suggestion that the proprietors of the gallery would be well advised to remove the statue from the collection as being unsuitable for public exhibition.

As against these passionate diatribes, I reproduce two articles, one by R. H. Wilenski in *The Observer*, February 8th, 1931, and the other by the Belgian critic, Sander Pierron, in *Neptune*, February, 26th, 1931:

Mr. Jacob Epstein is one of the few contemporary artists who can still provide us with a shock. He has been before the public for more than twenty years, but he still gives us the unexpected. In other words, his creative fount is not exhausted. He can still enlarge his own experience and ours also unless we are of those who think that our experience is already sufficient.

In this new exhibition at the Leicester Galleries the shock is provided by the marble carving entitled "Genesis". Colossal in size, staring white in colour, this mass of marble shocks us in the first place because it calls up a rush of emotive ideas with which the object before us is instantly associated. The moment we have glanced at this statue the mind registers: "Naked woman . . . half human face . . . last stage of pregnancy . . ."; and then we can either turn away and seek elsewhere for something pretty to look at—or stay and begin to contemplate an object fashioned with hammer and chisel and a rare man's mind and spirit.

To begin with, it is important to realise that the images associated with the words "Naked woman . . . half human face . . . last stage of pregnancy . . ." are not irrelevancies in the contemplation of this work. Mr. Epstein's statue is called "Genesis", and it is in fact the embodiment of a Genesis idea. Mr. Frank Dobson's statue, acquired last year for the National Gallery, Millbank, was called "Truth";

but it was only called "Truth" because it had to be called something to attract the subscriptions which made its acquisition by the nation possible; it might as appropriately have been called "Duty" or "Diana" or "Sophonisba", because Mr. Dobson was not thinking of sculpture as a means for the expression of an idea that could be paralleled by any word or title; he was thinking of sculpture as an activity divorced from all other activities and existing on its own resources as the expression of man's interest in and response to plastic form as such. But Mr. Epstein's statue could not be entitled "Duty" or "Diana" or "Sophonisba". The word "Genesis" here helps us to comprehension and sanctions the retention of the first incoming associated ideas.

To appreciate this statue, therefore, we can, and must, retain our initial emotive ideas and reconsider them in the light of the experience provided by the statue. That the work enforces such reconsideration is a sign, of course, of its unusual merit. It is not often that an artist can drive us to re-examine our deep-seated attitudes to the solemn facts of life, birth and death. If an explorer were to discover Mr. Epstein's "Genesis" to-morrow in an African jungle, he would stand before it in respectful wonder. "Here", he would say, "is primitive man's image of the act of destiny unconnected with the sexual act. Here is a pathetic being, a mind uninstructed, hardly awakened, a lean body swollen to produce another. Here is the first Mother." But when the same man discovers it instead at the Leicester Galleries he is more likely to mutter the one word "disgusting". . . .

The truth is that we cannot begin to appreciate this "Genesis" until we have forgotten our habitual environment, until the Leicester Galleries and our rival theories of sculpture, our civilisation of steel, speed and comfort, the Prime Minister and "Miss 1931" have all faded from our minds. As sheer sculpture, in the modern sense, this carving, in my judgment, is a failure; the forms are not homogeneous, the plastic language is diverse, the flow of the lines downward suggests a falling body rather than an organisation rising upward from the ground. But this carving must not be considered as sheer sculpture. It must be considered as "Genesis", and, thus considered, the divergencies of the forms, the contrasts of lightnesses and weight, and the downward-forward movement of the lines contribute to a significance which is undeniably primeval and profound.

No other sculptor in England to-day could have produced this "Genesis", because no other is mentally so removed from everyday life as to be able to arrive at this primeval conception, and to rest upon it as sufficient. And no other modeller could have produced the portrait bronzes that constitute the remainder of this exhibition, not only because Mr. Epstein is far and away the most skilful and powerful modeller in this country—perhaps in Europe—but also because no other sculptor, now that the Romantic Movement is spent, regards the difference between one young woman's head and another's as a matter of such absorbing interest. To Mr. Epstein every form in each of these girls' heads, every deviation from the average, has psychological significance, and by recording these characteristics with his devastating skill and dynamic energy, he has fashioned bronzes which are aspects of life itself.

From the standpoint of the purist amateur of sculpture, these bronzes violate all canons; they suggest colour, and qualities such as sensuality, intelligence, stupidity, breeding and under-breeding, which from classical standards are no concern of the sculptor's art. But even the purist must bow down before Romantic art of this compelling intensity, before "Esther"—olive-skinned, dark-eyed, warm with the unconscious sensuality of adolescence—and before "Isobel Powys", with the faun's ears, aquamarine eyes, nervous mouth and intelligent brow. And no one, I imagine, who has once seen Mr. Epstein's presentment of Lord Rothermere is ever likely to forget it.

R. H. WILENSKI.

Neptune, February 26th, 1931:

THE EPSTEIN SCANDAL

Let there be no confusion of the issue. We are not here concerned with Einstein but with Epstein. We are not concerned with the illustrious German physicist but with an English sculptor. Yet we are in the domain of relativity, but of æsthetic relativity.

We can assure you that we are not alluding to a financial matter or to a matter of morals. The scandal about which we want to speak is purely and exclusively of an artistic order, and at the present time it is causing much ink to flow in the newspapers and reviews on the other side of the Channel.

And what is all this scandal about?

The reader must understand that an English sculptor, Jacob Epstein by name, has taken it into his head to endow his country with a monumental form of sculpture founded on new principles of æsthetics, and has substituted expressionism for realism. Passing from theory to practice, he has produced a series of works which are nothing less than so many acts of heresy in a country where the most advanced sculptors have by no means emancipated themselves from conventional rules. Reflect, if you will, that England, among her distinguished masters, has never had others than her John Flaxmans, her Sir Joseph Edgar Boehme, her Lord Leightons, her Alphonse Legros, her Alfred Stevens, her John Macallan Swans, her George Frederick Watts, her Alfred Gilberts, superb passéistes, creators of forms elegant, forceful and harmonious, it is true, but all closely related to the forms modelled by the traditional masters of the past, a phalanx of masters not in tune with their own times.

Now Jacob Epstein has felt the urge to free the sculpture of his country from the depths of secular traditions and to subject it to the victorious laws of æsthetic evolution. And this, despite the fact that he has received an academic training and does not in any way discard the canons of an almost academic construction, although as an impressionist he runs to a passionate colourful composition, for example when modelling a bust—for if in his portrait busts he attempts to lay bare the mind of his subjects, he does not consider it necessary, when delineating their essential features, to have recourse to the deformities so dear to the surrealists.

This æsthetic evolution, in its positive manifestations, unites across the centuries the primitive principles of the great sculpture of Egypt, Central America, Southern Asia and ancient Greece. It is a sculpture designed to serve architecture, a sculpture which, based on the expression of the mass, is at the same time impregnated with the ideal; that is to say, it speaks to us equally by its spirit and by its form; a sculpture, in short, supremely symbolic, adding to the language of the lines of the building, of which, to a certain degree, it is the soul; or, if it is considered apart, as an isolated object, sheds round about it a lustre of innate meaning, by virtue of its decorative quality.

Can one imagine greater audacity in a country where conservatism, through the ages has placed a curb on the daring of its rare, progressive spirits who must always have had the feeling of moving in chains? And what a hue and cry is being

A Corner of the Studio, 1947
(Showing the incomplete "Lazarus" and "Ecce Homo")

A Corner of the Sitting-room at Hyde Park Gate, 1948

raised in London, at this moment, about certain works by Epstein exhibited at the Leicester Galleries! It is a new war of the ancients against the moderns, and, in that vast and conservative city where heated conflicts about æsthetic questions are scarcely common, it is assuming epic proportions.

The great daily newspapers of England are full of unheard-of diatribes against this accursed sculptor, who, as an enemy of all puritanism, has the temerity to strike out in quest of a nonconformist ideal. He is accused of disowning his ancestors, he is charged with infamy. It is no longer criticism, it is prejudice, it is attack, it is sometimes even slander, slander trimmed with threats. For certain journalists go so far as to demand the removal from this *salon*, resounding with the din of their outcry, such part of the exhibit as, so there hypercritics pretend, is an offence to good taste and consummate in its ugliness. The public provides a chorus to these would-be extinguishers of the flames of genius, and few and far between are those who, recognising the metamorphism of art, form up at the side of the master, and at the risk of falling foul of the blows dealt out, bravely defend his virile and transforming philosophy.

Intellectual circles on the other side of the Channel are in a ferment. Revolt is not yet an actual fact, although in the exhibition rooms revolt is already in evidence. But a scandal it is. Or rather it is the acute climax of a scandal begun some two years ago. At that time there were unveiled on the building of the St. James's Park Station of the Underground, two enormous stone groups by Epstein, which let loose a furious campaign of protest. The removal from the Leicester Galleries of the marble statue representing "Genesis" is being demanded. These two groups are still in place, although repeated attempts were made to damage them, to degrade them and to destroy them because they upset conventional standards. Nevertheless, there they still are. A day will come, no doubt, when it will be discovered that in them reside the æsthetic aspirations of a disturbed epoch .trying to find its bearings. Then, in their turn, these pieces, subversive at the present time, will have become classic.

These two gigantic groups, hewn with a passionate and mysterious brutality, and reminiscent of the earliest works of Chaldea and ancient Greece, conjure up "Day" and "Night". If we are far from Michelangelo who, in the Florentine mausoleums of the Medicis, treated these subjects with divine splendour, we are nevertheless on a plane of monumentalism identical with that on which Buonarroti set his enchanting creations. "Day" shows a nude, bearded man, seated, holding with both hands, between his knees, a child clasping his neck. In "Night", a sort of free transposition of the "Pietà", we see a woman, also seated, but draped, holding on her knees the inert, extended body of a nude youth, her right hand supporting his head and her left hand held low down over his face in a vain gesture of protection. These two groups are worked in sharp planes, on which the light and shade play, to form clear-cut antitheses, and these, in giving bold definition to the planes, impart to these decorative compositions an architectural value.

No detail; a heavy silhouette, well-balanced, in which the great, antique law of frontality survives. Gestures, as if geometrically conceived and synthesised in the expression of life and of death that dominates in each group; the gravity of the faces, graven into rude features, the thought which, without dominating the form, heightens it with deep spiritual accent.

Convention is absent in these works which, rising above all sense of time, unite the pure plastic of the primitives with the plastic, stripped of inessentials, of the artists of to-morrow. They are among the most beautiful and healthy wild flowers of the extremist art of our time, the paths of which are broadening out more and more on to the future, thanks to the stubborn will of those fighters who, freed from superstitions like Jacob Epstein, do not care two hoots for the insults with which their enemies would like to overwhelm them.

The majority of English critics, who would hold back the hands of the clock, deny all talent to this futurist. They have said that Epstein's productions are absolutely negligible, considered as works of art; that they are quite insignificant from an æsthetic viewpoint, coarse in design, and repulsive in conception; that their author has but a poor regard for formal beauty; that the symbolism he claims to have put into his groups is obscure; that they are the product of an intellect not fired with any imagination.

This, then, is some of the abuse that at the time was showered on Jacob Epstein, who was also censured for cherishing alleged ambitions to decorate London with sculptures that no one likes or understands. To determine the real value of the master, it is necessary to strike out in a direction opposite to that along which this systematic abuse and prejudice are directed. For it is certain that, with Epstein, there is being opened up for English sculpture an energetic movement for the en-franchisement of rules newly evolved and in harmony with Continental innova-tions. But Epstein, even though he has not rallied young artists to his standard, is strong enough to make his personal participation effectual.

Of late the Press had stopped abusing this man, for whom these attacks act as a stimulant, when all of a sudden he committed the same crime over again. And what is this crime? It is that he is showing at his exhibition an enormous figure hewn out of marble and representing "Genesis". And how has the artist conceived it in the form of a female of apparently monstrous proportions whose countenance, marked with a fierce animalism, conjures up the woman of paleolithic times. The upper part of the body, with its firm breasts and shoulders solidly set, is normal in its magnificent bulk. But from the waist downwards, the body broadens out in formidable curves, to make the lower part of the trunk and the thighs of colossal size. The left hand, turned up and of usual size, is placed on her abdomen, while the right hand, which is enormous, rests, open, on her groin. One has the feeling that these two hands, each so different from the other, want to restrain the pal-pitations in her entrails, the mysterious echoes of which, penetrating to the under-standing of this "Mother of Humanity", impress on her bestial and thoughtful features, the full consciousness of the destiny she carries in her flanks, infinite as the universe. An awesome image in white marble, the disproportions in which, as Diderot would say, are justified because they are called for by the imperious necessity of the symbol striven after. In this piece of sculpture, the disproportions and deformities are the essential qualities, since it is they that express the supreme idea to which Epstein has been obedient. That enormous right hand is on a scale with the lower part of the abdomen, of which it feels the heat of the child enclosed within. That small left hand is on a scale with the bosom below which its fingers lie folded, and the roundness of which will soon be swelled to fullness by the event to come. Everything about this figure, so full of clarity and mystery, is expressive; it is the realisation of a conception which has taken long to ripen, a realisation born of deep, emotional reflection. And this woman, the synthesis of the genera-tions, this mother of all mothers, who carries within her the first child whose cries will soon be heard—the first cries of man on earth—is of an immense chastity, in her flesh made fruitful by the divine touch.

How is it possible for critics, shocked and indignant with this work, which will mark a date in the history of art, to say that this figure, which holds such a universal emotion, must be considered as an acceptance of the Darwin Theory, "for it is more in keeping with the occupants of the monkey-house than with the Eves chiselled by academic sculptors". A journalist ironically says: "The majority of people will be hurt in their ideas of pleasure by the type here selected for the pregnant woman." Another critic, after pointing out that in ancient and modern art fecundity has habitually been depicted with the delicacy and the respect appropriate to this theme, says that "Genesis" is a coarse work, in which the relative arrangement of form is such as only to produce an effect of heaviness in a weird and unæsthetic object". In the case of another, "it lacks refinement and grace and that lyrical quality always present in a creation worthy of the name. In this piece of marble, not a note of music, not a trace of poetry; the eloquent spirit of melody inherent in every masterpiece is here altogether absent". In a word, Epstein does not seek to impress by beauty but by ugliness. And yet another, more lively than all the rest, finishes up by demanding the removal from the Leicester Galleries, as a thing whose public exhibition is a disgrace; "the figure of a woman with the face of a chimpanzee, breasts like pumpkins, hands twice as large and heavy as those of a navvy, hair like a ship's cable, and displaying other extravagances it is not worth the trouble of discussing".

Jacob Epstein is keeping his own counsel. He, too, is not going to the trouble of discussing anything. He does not treat all this foul trash with contempt for the simple reason that he ignores it. He has the fierce and inflexible will of those men of primitive times to whom his "Genesis" takes us back. Is it not true that he is related, across the millenniums, to those sculptors in ivory who chiselled that famous and astonishing figure of fecundity, called the Venus of Brassempuy, whose body, so small in size yet grandiose æsthetically, displays the same "fatal" deformities as the lofty marble figure by Jacob Epstein? This primitive artist has been guided solely by instinct. The sculptor of "Genesis" is guided uniquely by reason. But both of them, in their care for pure form, have expressed the most profound human symbol, that of our carnal origin, in matter which they have quickened with the throb of eternal life. The cave-dwellers would have taken no offence at this work so fraught with meaning. There would have been no scandal among the Pyrenean tribes. All of which proves that modern man often has the short-sightedness of an individual who has failed to completely develop.

SANDER PIERRON.

Appendix Seven

"BEHOLD THE MAN!": 1935

The Sunday Pictorial, article:

"A STATUE THAT SHOULD BE HIDDEN"

Having seen for myself Jacob Epstein's new statue, "Behold the Man!" I can appreciate, and indeed, heartily sympathise with the feelings of those people whose sensibilities are offended by this grievous monstrosity in marble, weighing seven tons.

The sculptor must be of a singularly optimistic nature to have hoped to avoid a public outcry. If testimony were needed to the widespread resentment which the ugly work has aroused, it is to be found in the correspondence pouring in on our sister paper, *The Daily Mirror*, in approval of its decision not to reproduce a photograph of the statue, as well as in the question to be asked in the House of Commons to-morrow.

During my long journalistic career I have had much to say about Epstein's "creations", both by way of praise and of blame, but quite frankly, I do not remember an occasion when I have been more moved to condemnation than the present.

Prepared beforehand to admire, I came away from a study of the grotesque symbol saddened and disappointed, wondering why a gifted artist, who can fashion clay and bronze into such admirable portraits, need go so lamentably wrong.

And when I say this I have in mind, too, that much-criticised Epstein production which, for reasons known only to him, was labelled "Genesis", and those graceless figures which are such an uninviting feature of the London Underground headquarters.

As regards his latest "sensation"—one hesitates to use such an overworked term, but it is the only one applicable—beyond the wreath of thorns, there is nothing outwardly visible to suggest Jesus; and with equal appropriateness it could be labelled "Confucius". Who will not recall the famous artist who, out of sheer mischief, insisted on describing his pictures by the first suggestion that came into his head irrespective of the fitness of the definition?

Alternatively, if, every time he perpetrates an atrocity, we are to take Epstein seriously, then, judging his capacity to represent sacred themes from the ugly effigy which he has now given us, it is our duty to warn him that he is out of his element and, for the future, would be well advised to seek subjects more congenial to his talent. Obviously, the sweet personality and benign atmosphere of Christ elude his heavy imagination.

History scarcely knows an example of a long-lived artist or sculptor who, at some period or other of his existence, did not produce work below his genius. The most charitable remark to make about Epstein's statue is to describe it as the product of one of his off-colour days. They are not his best friends who persuade him otherwise, for if ever a figure sinned lamentably against taste, it is this latest performance, so sadly, nay, so absurdly, misnamed.

It is difficult to understand by what mental process a sculptor of Epstein's experience reconciles his carving of a primitive man—suggestive, if of anything at all, of an Egyptian or Assyrian sculpture long buried in the sand—with humanity's traditional idea of the Gentle Shepherd, comely and somewhat tall, who walked in Judea nearly 2000 years ago.

I say at once that, in this grotesque symbol, I fail to find any recognisable relationship to "Gentle Jesus, meek and mild", or taking the records into account, to any known Nazarene type. We are far away from Christ, the Healer, Who preached loving kindness, and we are many worlds apart from the beautiful and spiritualised representations, bequeathed to us by the great painters of old, to whom, as in prophetic vision, was revealed the likeness of Christ.

I will go further. In Epstein's sullen and sombre effigy, I discern as little historical reality, as spiritual or religious significance. On me the statue makes the same impression as the totem poles of the Red Indians—both intellectually and emotionally I am repelled.

Personally, I have yet to see any sense in paintings, or carvings, which are liable to be interpreted as direct challenges to religious conceptions, sanctified by Faith and tradition.

People grow up with a lovely idea of Christ in their minds, an idea which, if allowed to influence all their actions in life, would render this a much finer and much more tolerable civilisation. What purpose is served by confronting them with a harshly treated symbol, palpably divorced from the familiar attributes of Jesus, whose face shone with pity towards all men?

Mr. Epstein should think, not only of the so-called intellectuals who, to flatter him, may profess to see, in his monumental abstractions, merits denied to ordinary eyes, but also of the generality of people who, not being constituted on the same lines, cannot view his assaults on traditional conceptions with cold, cynical or amused detachment. He should think of the feelings of the average child who, seeing in some paper a reproduction of this effigy, may be affrighted to learn that it is a well-known sculptor's 1935 version of Jesus.

If Mr. Epstein replies that he does not work for children, then I make bold to ask: Wherein is he more greatly privileged than those inspired masters whose glorious paintings of Christ enrich the National Gallery, just a few hundred yards from where his own oppressive marble stands on exhibition? So far from being upset, no schoolboy or schoolgirl can stroll through the Italian section of the Gallery without his or her idea of Christ being ennobled.

Admirers of Epstein describe his ideal in stone as simplicity, coupled with strength. But in "Behold the Man!" there is not strength, but crudeness and even a suspicion of coarseness. Rodin, on the other hand, generally managed in his work to be strong and impressive, without forfeiting a sense of rugged beauty.

We must not expect from Epstein the grace and beauty of those magnificently gifted Greeks who 200 years before the Christian era, with a thousand lovely fancies in marble and bronze, made civilisation their debtors. But, in default of adding to our store of beautiful conceptions, he should not cause us to lose any.

If he cannot give us a stone portrait of Christ before which the religious-minded can bow their heads in reverence and thanksgiving, let him not affront us with a figure that does violence to treasured ideas. Or, at least, if he is impelled to desert his true work, the small bronze head, for these prodigies in stone, let him have them shown in private, for the benefit of the few whose sensibilities are proof against shock.

Otherwise, which would be regrettably unjust, Mr. Epstein is in danger of having it said that he deliberately provokes these public outcries. For my part, I have never suspected him of relishing the unpleasant advertisement to which certain of his works inevitably give rise. But has he ever thought how much higher his reputation would stand if it were not marred by these controversial statues, produced as though in desperation, at regular intervals?

Like most artists and sculptors, Mr. Epstein is not the best judge of his own work, which explains why he continues to inflict upon us these painful atrocities. I am prepared to hear that, in his mind, he had formed a less inappropriate conception of Christ than his statue expresses. If this were indeed the case, then he has been unfortunate with his medium; and doubly unfortunate not to have been told so before its exhibition was arranged.

My own opinion is that Epstein's inspiration does not lend itself to this kind of subject. He despises conventional beauty, and has little consideration for ideals which do not appeal to his grey artistic conscience. Certainly, to have produced his deplorably inept statue he must have been armed with the feeblest knowledge of the picture of Jesus which lives in the hearts of most Christians.

There is, surely, enough ugliness in the world without one of our leading sculptors, at the sacrifice of much time and painful effort, being betrayed into supplementing its mass. For his monstrous creation, Epstein, on æsthetic grounds alone, deserves to be reproved. But lack of beauty would not, in itself, earn for the statue such widespread and almost wholly adverse, criticism. Mainly the indictment bases itself on the insult, none the less real for being unintentional, proffered to average religious susceptibilities.

No higher courage could be shown than for the sculptor, convinced, we hope, by now that he has committed a grave blunder, to withdraw his offensive statue from exhibition. Sinking his pride and obstinacy, will Mr. Epstein be big enough and bold enough to rise to the occasion? That is the question to which many people this week-end will be anxiously awaiting an answer.

The gentleman who wrote the foregoing was, I remember, an editor, who published a weekly account by a certain Rev. Vale Owen of a "Journey into Heaven", which for sheer silliness outdid any of the Marble Arch spiritualists I had listened to on first coming to London. I remember meeting him and remonstrating with him for this attempt to gull the newspaper reader, and he responded by saying gleefully: "But don't they fall for it. They positively eat it up." That the public did not positively eat up my message was natural and evidently caused him to write the solemn warnings and threats which he so liberally handed out.

The Daily Telegraph article:

The exhibition of recent sculpture by Jacob Epstein which opens on Friday at the Leicester Galleries, is certain to rouse controversy. The sport of playing policeman to this artist has become an annual event for the more obstinate detractors of his work, and possibly they would be disappointed if he gave them no occasion for it.

Sometimes he has provided it in plenty, but such is not the case this year.

The chief feature of the show, a figure of Christ entitled "Behold the Man!" offers fascinating opportunity for discussion from the point of view of æsthetics. Offence at it on other grounds suggests unreasonable haste in judgment, when it is not suspiciously artificial.

In any case, the qualities of the figure are so essentially sculpturesque that it must be seen in order to be praised or condemned. No adequate conception can be formed from photographic reproduction.

In Subiaco marble, weighing six tons and standing eleven feet high, it represents Christ crowned with thorns and bound hands. It follows closely, in its finished structure, the elongated cubic block from which it was carved.

Even in the gallery it is not viewed at best advantage. The head is over-size in proportion to the rest of the body—as is proper for seeing it from below, on a tall pedestal or raised above the ground as a part of a building. In the confines of a room it is unduly dwarfed.

But through all the mass there is a diffused energy inherent in its form and ordered by a discipline of pattern. This force of impulse radiates within the strictly-bound shape. There is no violence of gesture, no sensational disturbance of the calm, straight pose. The effect is compelling and impressive.

The only strangeness in the work lies in the elimination of all but the barest detail and the broad lines on which the features of the face are indicated. But seen outside the limit of four walls, and at a greater height, the economy of detail would be a benefit. Also, closer facial likeness would be wasted, and the rudimentary, formal features would stand out more visibly.

It may always be debated whether definite likeness is helpful in religious art, whether distraction from a greater purpose is not caused by realistic representation. Epstein's figure is nearly akin to the earliest Romanesque Church sculpture, which with rough primitive shapes yet triumphantly conveyed its idea. This symbolism has survived in peasant art and another relationship may be found in Breton religious sculpture. Faith was never stronger than when the Romanesque sculptors worked, and it was always ardent in the Breton carvers' hearts. There is something of the spirit of these craftsmen in "Behold the Man!".

The most unwilling critics concede Epstein's power as a modeller. The portrait bronzes at the exhibition display his accustomed skill. They all are marked with the print of the sitter's character, swiftly grasped, and all are splendidly alive. The subjects include Lord Beaverbrook, Bernard Shaw, Hugh Walpole, Tiger King ("Man of Aran"), and many women's heads, alert with grace and vitality.

T. W. E.

Appendix Eight

Also in the same vein as the article by Charles Marriott (*The Times*, October 27th, 1933) is the critic in *The New English Weekly*, Hugh Gordon Porteous, whose gospel of "prevention is better than cure" gives the show away for these really sterile minds. Contraceptives may be all very well for those who can "conceive," but in the case of our highbrow critics I do not think the necessity exists.

The New English Weekly, October 28th, 1937:

Everyone just now is trooping to the Leicester Galleries to see Mr. Epstein's new recumbent colossus. It is a serious piece of sculpture, very well worth seeing. It should not have been shown, however, in a small gallery. One has the sensation of viewing an elephant in its cage, or an engine in its shed. These things require to be seen in a more appropriate and spacious habitat. Or it is as if a new symphony had to endure its *première* in a summer-house.

In the circumstances, it is not an easy work to review. It is a vast block of alabaster, hewn into an agreeable, forceful, though not I think wholly satisfactory, system of shapes. Where the plastic quality ends and the rather gloomy streak of naturalism begins it is difficult to say, but certain it is that the two exist side by side, somewhat uncomfortably. It is interesting to compare with other works by Mr. Epstein, in the same class, such as "Behold the Man!" and "Night" and "Day". It lacks some of the dramatic power of those works; it gains in dignity and simplicity. Shorn of the kind of non-plastic excrescences that spoiled, sculpturally, those works, the new piece nevertheless fails to make use of the plastic possibilities of what remains. One has only to compare it (and that the comparison is possible is a tribute to it) with a piece of early Chinese or Egyptian statuary to feel that it lacks the placidity of the one and the dynamism of the other. It is, in fact, as usual, a compromise; and those who feel uneasy about its form, together with those who are repelled by its inhuman bleakness, will have to fall back, as usual, to speculating on the meaning of the title: "Consummatum Est". The sensationalism implicit in its bulk, no less than in its symbolical "content", is intimidating.

Once more many of us will turn with relief to the contemplation of Mr. Epstein's miraculous portrait-busts. Here the attack is direct: there is no compromise, no fumbling, but the complete mastery of a highly personal gift. Whether the busts are "good sculpture" or not is beside the point. Each is a triumph of successful interpretation. They set out to do something useful—to seize and fix the psyche of a contemporary personage—and they achieve that end. The big monoliths set out to do something more ambitious and perhaps less worth while. It is sad, but the new Christ doesn't quite come off, and there it is. At least, I am one of a number of admirers of Epstein's genius who feel that way about it; and I cannot see that any useful purpose is served by pretending that better sculpture is not accessible, even if there isn't very much of it about.

One of the disadvantages of attempting anything on the gigantic scale is that, if it doesn't quite "come off", there is a natural temptation to pass it off, even upon oneself, as if it had. It must be extremely galling for a man who has spent months or years of hard labour in hacking a cliff into the semblance of a figure, or in painting an acre of canvas, or in writing a million-word book to find at the end of it all the thing has failed. Even to recognise the fact to oneself would take a good deal more honesty and courage than common men possess. And it is only the rare artist who has the nerve to destroy, in such cases. On the analogy of "prevention is better than cure", the colossal in art should perhaps be avoided always. The urge "to do something big" is a constant spur to genius. It is, however, a pity that it should so often take the unfortunate form of something merely *physically* big.

Appendix Nine

"ADAM": 1939

Picture Post, June 24th, 1939:

EPSTEIN'S ADAM

MORE THAN THE USUAL STORM HAS GREETED EPSTEIN'S MASSIVE
SCULPTURE OF THE FIRST MAN OF ALL

Epstein's name is better known to the man-in-the-street than that of any other British sculptor. Yet you will rarely find examples of his carvings on public buildings, whilst the works of other sculptors, with less technical ability, and with not a tenth of his artistic power, appear regularly on our new buildings and at international exhibitions as representing the best in British sculpture.

Why are Epstein's larger carvings so spurned and neglected by officialdom? It cannot be that he is unknown. Nor can it be that his work is not appreciated, for he has been commissioned to do in bronze the heads of more celebrities than any sculptor in Britain. Conrad, Einstein, the Emperor of Abyssinia, Ramsay Mac-Donald, J. B. Priestley are only a few of them.

Are his carvings, then, not suitable for public buildings? You would think that the architects of the buildings would be the best judges of that. And yet there are buildings in London, where there are blocks of bare stone, left uncarved, because the architects have refused to allow anyone but Epstein to touch them, whilst the responsible bodies of laymen have refused to have his work. This is a sad state of affairs. The reason, however, is simple. Like many significant works of art in the past, Epstein's sculpture is so powerful and stimulating that it is bound to lead to violent reactions. Before his work can be appreciated or understood, the mind of the spectator must be clean and free from prejudice. It is so easy to hate something we do not understand. It is so easy to abuse something we are afraid of. But when a thing is so powerful that we are even afraid of trying to understand it, our only hope is to persecute it out of existence.

It is not true to say, as some people are so apt to say, that Epstein is purposely seeking this form of publicity. After all, he sculpts not only because he cannot help himself, but, like the carpenter and the plumber, to earn his bread and butter. It is typical of Epstein's deep sense of duty and service to the community that, when I remarked to him the other day that more of his work should be acquired for the general public after he has put so much work and concentration into it, he replied: "It's not the work; it's the time." For he feels he has still so much to give to the

288

world, if only the loud-mouthed section of the public would give up their attacks on him, and allow his work to appear on those buildings which are already awaiting his chisel to complete them.

Epstein is now 59 years of age, and has spent most of his life in New York and London. For something like forty years he has devoted himself to sculpture. He has no hard and fast rules of work. When he is on the job, he knows what he wants to do and works hard on it. But he has no fixed hours. Yet his output in sheer physical labour is terrific. He does not know what it is to compromise. And, unlike the advanced artist, whose friends say that he has now become an R.A. and died happily ever after, Epstein has no such ambition.

In conception and in size, the "Adam", carved in alabaster, is the most important work in his exhibition, which is now being held at the Leicester Galleries. To understand this work, and to feel its tremendous power, it is essential to stand before it, and let it sink in. All that the critic can do is to offer a few hints about the grammar that Epstein has used to express his sculptural conception.

A little knowledge of this grammar may make it more easy to master the prejudices which will arise in a number of people's minds.

Every original conception in art must create also its own unique technique. It is only the third-rate artist who goes to his work with a preconceived formula, asserts it on his subject, and consistently repeats what his patrons have learnt to expect of him.

To understand this "Adam", too, one must know the meaning of the words naturalism and realism as used in relation to art. Naturalism in sculpture is a slick kind of reporting of the shapes and forms into stone. Each form and shape will be practically similar to that of the subject, although little differences will be introduced here and there for the sake of emphasis. In other words, the naturalistic sculptor will report his subject like a good reporter. Any trained sculptor can do this, but if he knows his job he will not call it art. He knows that it is merely acting as a sort of recording camera. Naturalism in sculpture is a recording in stone of shapes and forms observed by the artist.

Realism in sculpture, on the other hand, is closely bound up with realisation. First, there is the conception of the idea. The idea must be conceived in terms of the particular medium. If it is to be carried out in wood, its forms and volumes must be seen in the artist's mind as forms and volumes natural to wood; if clay, then the particular nature of clay, and if stone, the nature of the stone must not be violated. That is the first essential, but it is not the whole story.

Then comes the realisation of the conception in its particular medium. The wood or stone now has to be carved in such a way that none of its own nature is sacrificed. The finished work must look as if it grew, almost of its own accord, out of the wood or stone. But, even if this is realised quite adequately, it still does not mean that a work of art, as distinct from a piece of craftsmanship, has been produced. It may be just a dead bit of stone or wood, with a few interesting forms thrown in, yet still inert.

It only becomes a work of art when it lives in its own right; when the artist, by some almost magical power, inbues it with life. It must have such a perfect sense of unity that, if one form is altered, every other must be changed in order to capture the new unity.

This "Adam" is a great work of art, because it has all of these properties. It is conceived in stone, its nature has not been violated by the chisel, and the forms and volumes are so magically related, one to the other, that there is an upward surge and flow which brings it to life—a kind of pulsating stone.

The forms are stone forms. They have a kind of everlasting life. They will not go the way of all flesh. It is partly this feeling of permanence, combined with this surging sculptural movement, which makes the "Adam" so powerful. And yet there is no suggestion of violent naturalistic movement. Any movement there is is suggested purely by this genus of related volumes and forms, rather than by arms flung out in action. The movement takes place in the very stone itself, and not in space. Epstein does not distort forms for the sake of some abstract principle of design. He re-creates the forms to bring them to life.

He has too great a respect for his block of stone to distort it in order to make it look like flesh. He has that kind of humility which respects innate differences of nature; an artist, not a dictator.

I wonder if it was the overwhelming power of the "Adam" which accounted for the following incident when I was at the gallery the other day.

A charming old lady came forward into the room, and, with a supercilious air, raised her lorgnette to look at the sculpture. In another moment the lorgnette seemed to be swept clean out of her hand and with it went all the haughtiness and supercilious gesture. She hurried away. I thought she looked too charming to blame Epstein or abuse him, but there was no doubt that she had been deeply horrified.

Should any of the readers of this article have this kind of mishap, it might be better for them to pick up their spectacles, think about some of the points I have brought forward and have yet another look, remembering at the same time that a man who has given forty years of his life to the intensive study of a subject, as Epstein has done, probably knows a great deal about it; as much, at least, as the plumber who has served his apprenticeship does in his particular craft.

It is surprising the amount of respect we have for the plumber when he is on his job, and yet every Tom, Dick or Harry accepts it as his right to tell the artist how he should or should not do his job.

If the "Adam" still overwhelms you, go and see it again and again. It is worth it. But, in the meantime, turn to the bronze heads and the drawings in the exhibition. With complete mastery of his craft Epstein models his heads so that the full play of light will bring out the metallic quality of the bronze. You will then see how cleverly he adapts himself to each new medium.

He has been criticised for painting the lips and eyebrows of Tiyi, one of his exhibited works. I asked him about this, and he pointed out that there is nothing very original or revolutionary in painting parts of sculpture.

The Greeks always painted their marbles, and the Italian sculptors did so too, until just before the time of Donatello. But this is typical of the petty criticism which surrounds the name of Epstein.

WILLIAM McCANCE.

INDEX

Index

Index

Index

The Modern Jewish Experience

An Arno Press Collection

Asch, Sholem. **Kiddush Ha-Shem:** An Epic of 1648. 1926

Benjamin, I[srael ben] J[oseph]. **Three Years in America:** 1859-1862. 1956. Two vols. in one.

Berman, Hannah. **Melutovna.** 1913

Besant, Walter. **The Rebel Queen.** 1893

Blaustein, David. **Memoirs of David Blaustein.** 1913

Brandes, George. **Reminiscences of My Childhood and Youth.** 1906

Brinig, Myron. **Singermann.** 1929

Cahan, A[braham]. **The White Terror and the Red.** 1905

Chotzinoff, Samuel. **A Lost Paradise.** 1955

Cohen, Morris Raphael. **A Dreamer's Journey.** 1949

Cowen, Philip. **Memories of an American Jew.** 1932

Cooper, Samuel W. **Think and Thank.** 1890

Davitt, Michael. **Within the Pale.** 1903

Dembitz, Lewis N. **Jewish Services in Synagogue and Home.** 1898

Epstein, Jacob. **Epstein:** An Autobiography. 1955

Ferber, Edna. **Fanny Herself.** 1917

Fineman, Irving. **Hear, Ye Sons.** 1933

Fishberg, Maurice. **The Jews:** A Study of Race and Environment. 1911

Fleg, Edmond. **Why I Am a Jew.** 1945

Franzos, Karl Emil. **The Jews of Barnow.** 1883

Gamoran, Emanuel. **Changing Conceptions in Jewish Education.** 1924

Glass, Montagu. **Potash and Perlmutter.** 1909

Goldmark, Josephine. **Pilgrims of '48.** 1930

Grossman, Leonid Petrovich. **Confession of a Jew.** 1924

Gratz, Rebecca. **Letters of Rebecca Gratz.** 1929

Kelly, Myra. **Little Aliens.** 1910

Klein, A. M. **Poems.** 1944

Kober, Arthur. **Having Wonderful Time.** 1937

Kohut, Rebekah. **My Portion** (An Autobiography). 1925

Leroy-Beaulieu, Anatole. **Israel Among the Nations.** 1904

Levin, Shmarya. **Childhood in Exile.** 1929

Levin, Shmarya. **Youth in Revolt.** 1930

Levin, Shmarya. **The Arena.** 1932

Levy, Esther. **Jewish Cookery Book on Principles of Economy Adapted for Jewish Housekeepers.** 1871

Levy, Harriet Lane. **920 O'Farrell Street.** 1947

Lewisohn, Ludwig. **Mid-Channel.** 1929

Lewisohn, Ludwig. **The Island Within.** 1928

Markens, Isaac. **The Hebrews in America.** 1888

Martens, Frederick H. **Leo Ornstein.** 1918

Meade, Robert Douthat. **Judah P. Benjamin.** 1943

Mendoza, Daniel. **The Memoirs of the Life of Daniel Mendoza.** 1951

Meredith, George. **The Tragic Comedians.** 1922

Nichols, Anne. **Abie's Irish Rose.** 1927

Nordau, Max. **The Conventional Lies of Our Civilization.** 1895

Nyburg, Sidney L. **The Chosen People.** 1917

Pinski, David. **Three Plays.** 1918

Roth, Cecil. **A History of the Marranos.** 1932

Roth, Cecil. **A Life of Menasseh Ben Israel.** 1934

Rubinow, I[saac] M. **Economic Conditions of the Jews in Russia.** 1907

Sabsovich, Katherine. **Adventures in Idealism.** 1922

Sachs, A[braham] S. **Worlds That Passed.** 1928

Seide, Michael. **The Common Thread.** 1944

Steiner, Edward A. **From Alien to Citizen.** 1914

Untermeyer, Louis. **Roast Leviathan.** 1923

Weinstein, Gregory. **The Ardent Eighties.** 1928

Yezierska, Anzia. **Hungry Hearts.** 1920

Yiddish Tales. 1912

Zangwill, Israel. **The Melting-Pot.** 1932

Zunser, Eliakum. **Selected Songs of Eliakum Zunser.** 1928